Silent Steel

The Mysterious Death of the Nuclear Attack Sub USS *Scorpion*

Stephen Johnson

WILEY

John Wiley & Sons, Inc.

This book is printed on acid-free paper. ∞

Copyright © 2006 by Stephen Paul Johnson. All rights reserved

Published by John Wiley & Sons, Inc., Hoboken, New Jersey
Published simultaneously in Canada

Illustration Credits: page 3: Courtesy of Vernon and Sybil Stone; pages 6, 12, 25, 45, 131, 137, 145, 168, 172, 176, 179, 209, 210, 212, 217, 220, 222, 223, 225: U.S. Navy; pages 23, 101: Courtesy of Mary Broderson; page 38: Author's collection; page 56: Courtesy of Mike Newman; page 61: Courtesy of Dorothy Watson Reese; page 79: Photograph © William Gill; page 86: Courtesy of Allan Hartley; page 88: Courtesy of Erich Livingston; page 152: Photo © Stephen Johnson; page 158: U.S. Navy: Courtesy of Frederick Bowers; page 202: Photo © Houston Chronicle; photographed by Steve Ueckert

For general information about our other products and services, please contact our Customer Care Department within the United States at (800) 762-2974, outside the United States at (317) 572-3993 or fax (317) 572-4002.

Wiley also publishes its books in a variety of electronic formats. Some content that appears in print may not be available in electronic books. For more information about Wiley products, visit our web site at www.wiley.com.

Library of Congress Cataloging-in-Publication Data:

Johnson, Stephen P. (Stephen Paul), date.
    Silent Steel: the mysterious death of the nuclear attack sub USS Scorpion / Stephen Paul Johnson.
        p. cm.
    Includes bibliographical references.
    ISBN-13 978-0-471-26737-9 (cloth)
    ISBN-10 0-471-26737-6 (cloth)
    1. Scorpion (Submarine) 2. Nuclear submarines—United States—Safety measures.
    I. Title.

    VA65.S394J64 2005
    359.9'3834—dc22
                                                                    2005003233

Printed in the United States of America

10 9 8 7 6 5 4 3 2

To the men of the Scorpion, and to their families

And to Wendy

When a shipmate dies, straightway we sew him up, and overboard he goes; our world-frigate rushes by, and never more do we behold him again; though, sooner or later, the everlasting under-tow sweeps him toward our own destination.

—Herman Melville, *White Jacket*

Contents

Preface

About 450 miles southwest of the Azores, in darkness 2 miles beneath the Atlantic, are the shattered remains of the nuclear-powered attack submarine USS *Scorpion*. The debris field in which the submarine now rests is not only a sacred memorial to ninety-nine men but also the epicenter of an enduring nautical controversy.

On May 27, 1968, those awaiting the boat's ninety-nine men gathered in a driving rain at Naval Station Norfolk to welcome the *Scorpion*. Lashing rain and destructive winds arrived, but the *Scorpion* did not. No distress signal had been sent, and its last message, six days before, indicated that all was well. No one knew where or when it had been lost. Unknown to all, the *Scorpion* had plunged to its doom five days earlier. After the largest search in navy history failed to locate the submarine, disbelieving and grief-stricken family members were then left to confront bitter reality.

To the astonishment of all, Chief of Naval Operations Thomas H. Moorer revealed five months after the disaster that the *Scorpion*'s fate was no longer a total mystery. As a result of an unprecedented deep-ocean search that overcame incredible technical challenges, the navy's civilian scientists found and photographed the *Scorpion*'s wreckage.

Unfortunately, the remnants of the *Scorpion* did not provide unambiguous evidence of how it sank. If anything, the shocking condition of its wreckage only served to stoke additional disagreement and speculation among the navy's investigators.

Navy scientists and undersea warfare experts, knowledgeable about submarines in general and the *Scorpion* in particular, have, over time, formulated reasonable scenarios that might explain how the submarine met its end. Fiction writers, journalists, and others have darkly hinted that the Soviet Navy, if not the mythic Bermuda Triangle, were to blame. Self-destruction with one of its own torpedoes, a dramatic and shocking event, was officially considered, and this scenario remains a flash point of controversy.

It is also not unreasonable to suspect a lack of safety improvements whose installation was delayed due to problems plaguing submarine maintenance during the 1960s. Ironically, many of these maintenance problems—kept remarkably quiet during the period—were unintended results of a program to make submarine operations safer after the 1963 loss of the USS *Thresher*, the first American nuclear-powered submarine to be lost.

The aura of mystery surrounding what happened to the *Scorpion* has been abetted by the navy's hesitancy in divulging information about its investigations. When pressed by the media, contradictory information has been released piecemeal.

In *Silent Steel* I have tried to clear away much of the confusion surrounding this disaster by providing the fullest possible story about the *Scorpion*'s final eighteen months. I have also attempted to place a human face on the *Scorpion* disaster, which has been consistently characterized as the loss of nothing more than a complex machine, rather than a catastrophe that ended the lives of ninety-nine dedicated men.

For me, this effort began when I answered the phone.

In 1987 I was contacted by former submariner Daniel Rogers, who first told me about the *Scorpion* disaster, an event about which I was unaware. If this tragedy had eluded my recollection, it had certainly been seared into the memories of those such as Rogers, who served aboard the submarine, knew those who died, and remained deeply affected by the event. The enormity of this tragedy, compared with the dearth of information regarding its cause, prompted me to learn what I could about this seemingly forgotten naval disaster.

With the passage of years, officers, sailors, and scientists who had long ago retired decided that enough time had passed for them to speak openly about their roles as onetime crew members on the *Scorpion* or their involvement in the investigations the navy conducted into the disaster. Many others graciously agreed to speak frankly about the submarine force of the 1960s, providing an unvarnished view of this unique and complex military subculture and the difficult issues it faced. I interviewed hundreds of sailors, officers, and civilians at every level of the submarine force, including former *Scorpion* executive officer Admiral Carl A. H. Trost, who later served as the chief of naval operations.

Perhaps the most extraordinary coincidence to befall my research occurred when I telephoned the wrong home in Florida looking for the relatives of a deceased *Scorpion* sailor. The man insisted that I speak to his brother-in-law Vice Admiral Joe Williams, the former commander of the Submarine Force, U.S. Atlantic Fleet, and commander of Norfolk Naval Shipyard during the 1970s. Williams became one of the hundreds of people to whom I am indebted for their time and their knowledge.

To all those who contributed their recollections I extend my deepest appreciation, particularly to those who overcame their wariness about talking to a complete stranger to reveal the hazardous and complex world they once inhabited.

Some of the most selfless and generous contributors to the effort to tell this story are the family members of the *Scorpion*'s crew. It is for them and the ninety-nine men still on patrol that I have written this book.

1

Returning to Duty

As the summer of 1967 drew to a close, the USS *Scorpion* was beginning to stretch and yawn. It had been sidelined for nearly eight months of refueling and repairs at Norfolk Naval Shipyard in Portsmouth, Virginia.

Although expected to be in the shipyard from February 1 to June 16, 1967, problems replacing the nuclear fuel, malfunctions, and unanticipated repairs delayed its release until October 10, just seven days before its new skipper, Cmdr. Frank Slattery, assumed command.

The need for refueling had been the chief impetus for bringing the *Scorpion* into the shipyard for dry-docking. Between the completion of its first refueling in April 1964 and reporting to Norfolk Naval Shipyard on February 1, 1967, for its second, the submarine had operated for thirty-one months. In the meantime, said its sailors, the boat was "ridden hard and put up wet." During a reactor core replacement a section of the pressure hull known as a "patch" is cut through the hull aft of the tall fairwater, incorrectly known as the "conning tower," to access the reactor containment vessel. Shipyard workers perform the actual fuel replacement under the watchful eyes of inspectors from Vice Admiral Hyman Rickover's Naval Reactors Branch.

Despite the miraculous energy output of the reactor's nuclear core, the fuel assemblies of the early 1960s barely lasted thirty-six months. Because the *Scorpion* had conducted vigorous operations since its 1964 refueling, its core was seriously depleted after only twenty-four months. By early 1966, a sharp reduction in the *Scorpion*'s operational schedule was necessary to prevent its nuclear fuel from flickering out by November 1966, a full two months before its reactor was to be replenished in February 1967.

The *Scorpion* had done much during the first half of 1966 while under the command of its fourth commanding officer, Cmdr. James R. Lewis. During one wintertime mission along the Soviet Union's northern coastline, the submarine entered an inland sea—most probably the White Sea—where it was said to have videotaped the test launch of a Soviet missile. When discovered, the *Scorpion* had to make a dash for open water. Some later swore the submarine had to outrun a torpedo launched by a pursuing Soviet destroyer.

By the end of the summer, the *Scorpion's* nuclear core was on the verge of sputtering its last neutron collision. With its limited number of fast attack submarines stretched from the Barents Sea to the South Atlantic— and in spite of various naval commands expecting the *Scorpion's* participation in a variety of exercises—Submarine Force, U.S. Atlantic Fleet (SUBLANT) was forced to reduce the *Scorpion's* time at sea.

The amount of available energy in a fuel core is measured in "effective full power hours," and it was determined that the *Scorpion* could operate until its February 1967 refueling only if its energy consumption was slashed 37 percent. This prompted the decision to exclude the *Scorpion* from not only scheduled antisubmarine warfare exercises in July but also from an Operational Test and Evaluation Force exercise in August.

Refueling nuclear reactors was a procedure for which the Norfolk Naval Shipyard was poorly prepared. It had performed only one such refueling, on the *Skate*, and that effort had been fraught with problems. Although the *Scorpion* entered Norfolk Naval Shipyard on February 1, 1967, technicians did not begin the refueling process until March 21. Machinist Mate Second Class David Stone, a sailor with nuclear propulsion training, found himself in the middle of the activity as a coordinator between the ship's watches and the shipyard personnel installing the nuclear core. Stone noted the apparent lack of expertise among the shipyard workers doing the refueling. In a letter written to his parents on March 25, 1967, he explained the scene:

> Most of the yardbirds . . . don't even know what they're doing and a few—physicists, etc.—direct the work so I get treated like a big wheel since everyone wears anti-C [contamination] clothing. Because I am on speaking terms with the shipyard commander, and the *Scorpion* CO, they think I'm some sort of nuclear inspector. We all laugh about it because in a few hours we'll be sweeping down the decks or carrying out the trash.

Scorpion machinist's mate David Stone, standing as if at bat, noted a lack of expertise among Norfolk Naval Shipyard workers installing nuclear fuel during 1967.

The nuclear core would not be fully installed in the *Scorpion* until April 9. When an attempt was made to operate the *Scorpion*'s S5W reactor on July 5, 1967, problems with a steam generator indicator forced the reactor operators to lower the neutron-absorbing control rods and edge the reactor back from criticality. Less exotic components provided problems as well. A pair of the boat's high-pressure air compressors—necessary for refilling the main ballast tank blow system's storage flasks—suffered malfunctions. Even more troublesome was the discovery that two of the main feed pumps that provided cooling water to the steam boilers had suffered damage during installation. A recurring problem with the AN/BRA-19 flexible communications antenna—which was habitually cut and gouged during extension and retraction—also required repeated repair and adjustment.

Sea Trials

Once the *Scorpion*'s propulsion system was readied and its reactor tested, the *Scorpion* had to be judged capable of resuming submerged operations. There would be tests and inspections of both submarine and crew.

The effort would involve a series of inspections to evaluate the submarine's mechanical condition and its crew's training. These examinations began with a two-part inspection known as Phase I and Phase II training certifications, supervised by Cmdr. James P. Shelton, the commanding officer of Submarine Division 62, and Cmdr. Robert L. Kelsey, skipper of the *Scorpion*'s sister ship the *Shark*.

The Phase I Crew Certification inspection was conducted on September 18 and focused on the *Scorpion*'s personnel records to determine the crew's level of expertise. Shelton and Kelsey confirmed how many crew members were qualified submariners, the level of training in their primary job skill, and if the proper number of men had qualified as watchstanders in crucial tasks such as ballast control panel operator and helmsman.

Phase II was the Training and Readiness Inspection. During this process, key watchstanders were quizzed to ascertain their familiarity with their jobs. Among those grilled by Kelsey were an officer of the deck, a ballast control panel operator, a chief petty officer, and a planesman. Kelsey was impressed with the competency of the crew. Shelton was equally pleased with the submarine's state of readiness and granted the *Scorpion* permission to begin a "fast cruise" while tied fast to the pier. This simulated cruise would last twenty-four hours, during which the *Scorpion*'s crew would do everything but move and submerge.

The performance of the crew rather than the condition of the submarine is the focus of a fast cruise. For safety, it was crucial that SUBLANT ensure that months in the shipyard had not dulled the ability of the *Scorpion*'s crew to competently operate their boat. The *Scorpion*'s crew performed well.

"My general feeling was that she was in a very high state of training," said Kelsey of his observations during the fast cruise. "I was completely satisfied with her readiness to conduct sea trials with no reservations whatsoever."

Successfully negotiating this hurdle meant the *Scorpion* could return to submerged operations for postshipyard sea trials where the *Scorpion*'s condition would be assessed. On October 2, the *Scorpion* cast off and made her way from the pier at Norfolk Naval Shipyard, past Hampton Roads, and into the Atlantic. Aboard to observe three days of sea trials was Capt. Wallace A. Greene, who had replaced Shelton as commander of SUBDIV 62 on September 29.

After clearing the shallows east of Chesapeake Bay, the *Scorpion's* crew opened the hydraulically operated vent valves to allow water to rush into the perennially open bottoms of the ballast tanks. Once submerged, Lewis would operate every system on the boat while also pushing the submarine to its depth and speed limits, testing not only its potent propulsion system but also its hydraulically operated control surfaces—the stern and fairwater planes and its massive rudder.

Lewis would eventually order "flank speed" to take advantage of the boat's freshly refueled nuclear reactor and the 15,000 horsepower it provided. The seven highly skewed blades of its propeller—each looking like a scimitar—bit into the seawater, generating small, noisy bubbles in a process called cavitation. During submerged exercises or when operating near Soviet warships, this problem would be avoided by diving to deeper depths, where the bubbles would be compressed by hydrostatic pressure, or by simply reducing the revolutions per minute. During sea trials, however, silence wasn't always the goal; pushing the submarine to its limits was.

As the *Scorpion's* submerged speed increased, the crew could sense the forces of acceleration, something they had not experienced for more than seven months. Running fast and deep was thrilling and set the submariners apart from the skimmers, those sailors who operated the navy's surface ships.

Despite the exhilaration of dashing submerged along the Atlantic seaboard, sea trials for a submarine following a long period of inactivity demanded great vigilance by the crew. Submariners are by nature wary of problems within their shrunken world. They are intensely mindful of any malfunction, be it telltale smoke from a motor-generator or the heart-stopping taste of salt from an invisible, high-pressure leak. Sailors on sea trials focus a nearly hypnotic attention on such things as the pressure hull, seawater shutoff valves, and even the air they breathe. All knew the sad history of submarines lost during sea trials, including the *Squalus* in 1939 and the nuclear-powered *Thresher* just four years before, in 1963. Each man was fully aware that a minor flaw or mistake could end their lives.

The things that could go wrong individually or as part of a cascading series of events triggered by a malfunction were nearly incalculable.

The smooth, hydrodynamic form of the *Scorpion*'s teardrop-shaped hull is dramatically apparent as the boat nears completion at Electric Boat Shipyard in 1959.

While a submarine's crew could be thoroughly trained to operate its systems safely, a seemingly minor malfunction of a component could trigger a larger problem, which could lead to the loss of the submarine. This harsh reality led many submariners to believe that there was, at best, a two-strike rule for undersea boats.

Crew members were especially mindful of pipe joint connections and flexible hoses that carried seawater at ambient hydrostatic pressure into the submarine. The navy endured its greatest loss of life when the fast attack boat *Thresher* was lost during a postoverhaul test dive. Though conclusive evidence was never acquired, the navy believed the *Thresher*'s loss was most likely due to a faulty piping joint that sprayed the submarine's electrical equipment, triggering an automatic shutdown of its S5W reactor. Without the ability to drive to the surface, and unable to impulse water from its ballast tanks against the sea pressure, the *Thresher* drifted helplessly below its crush depth, killing 129 men.

One area of intense scrutiny during the *Scorpion*'s postavailability sea trials was the propulsion shaft seal. This component prevented water from entering the *Scorpion* around the 16-inch-diameter propulsion shaft where it exited the pressure hull. As the submarine descended deeper into the Atlantic, it was not long before the engine room watch reported water entering the seal at an unacceptably high rate. The seal—which had been replaced while in the shipyard—was not meant to provide absolute watertight performance, but it wasn't supposed to leak more than 3 1/4 quarts per minute. At the acceptable rate, the leakage provided the intended benefit of cooling the seal where it surrounded the spinning shaft and was quickly pumped overboard.

As concerned sailors and officers watched, the new seal was allowing more than eight times this rate of leakage as 7 gallons a minute entered the boat. However, a leakage problem following seal work was not unheard of, and a simple solution was to reverse the rotation of the propeller shaft to seat the seal. This was done, and the excessive leakage stopped almost immediately. When measured again, the leakage was well within limits, at an acceptable 2 1/5 pints per minute. This defect, however, would reappear weeks later.

With his men seeking and correcting problems, Lewis pressed on, ordering higher speeds until the *Scorpion* was pushing its way through the water as fast as an auto cruising a boulevard. This was a significant speed for a submerged ship only 50 feet shorter than a football field. Although their top underwater speed remains secret, *Skipjack* class boats could travel in excess of 30 knots, with some sailors claiming the boats could achieve a 40-knot submerged speed.

Curiously, the *Scorpion* fell 2 knots shy of its established top speed. In addition, hydroacoustic recordings would subsequently reveal that the *Scorpion*'s cavitation signature—sounds produced by its turning propeller—were excessive. The *Scorpion* was now slower and noisier than it had been prior to its refueling and refit work. Considering the immense speed of which the *Scorpion* was capable, the loss of 2 knots might seem inconsequential, but to submariners who knew they might need to outrun an enemy torpedo, they could mean the difference between life and death. The noisier propeller was itself a cause for concern, since silence was essential to stealth—a submarine's primary military advantage.

While there is no official record of the *Scorpion* performing a test-depth dive during sea trials, this was a standard procedure following an extended maintenance period. The *Scorpion*'s original "maximum authorized operating depth," or test depth of 700 feet, provided a 50 percent safety margin, since the boat's estimated collapse depth was about 1,050 feet—or more likely 1,400 feet.

The *Scorpion*'s operating depth during ordinary operations was decreased to 500 feet in 1964 because the submarine lacked safety systems required after the shocking 1963 loss of the attack submarine *Thresher* with all aboard during its own test depth dive. Such dives determined the worthiness of not only the pressure hull but also the fittings and packing boxes through which the propeller shaft, seawater piping, and hydraulic rams penetrated the boat's hull. A test depth dive would also determine if the hydraulic fittings exposed to sea pressure were resistant to seawater infiltration as the various hydraulic mechanisms were systematically operated at various depths.

Although the crew and the shipyard expect some problems to arise during postrepair sea trials, the *Scorpion*'s performance appeared refreshingly free of malfunctions. Except for the reduction in speed and the shaft seal leakage, the sea trials had gone remarkably well and were concluded on October 4, 1967. The near-flawless performance of the *Scorpion* was a great relief to all. Memos written during the period reveal that officers of SUBLANT, the *Scorpion*, and the Norfolk Naval Shipyard were extremely pleased.

Finished with the sea trials, Lewis prepared to surface by ordering a check for sonar returns followed by cautiously rising close enough to the surface to perform a careful sweep of the surrounding sea by periscope and radar. Only then did the boat's ballast control panel operator release air from the *Scorpion*'s high-pressure air flasks to displace seawater from its six main ballast tanks. The boat rose to the surface with a slight up angle and broached. As water streamed off its black hull, the bridge watchstanders clambered to the top of the fairwater, and the *Scorpion* steamed triumphantly into Hampton Roads.

The *Scorpion* was so sound and so free of defects that it was returned directly to its berth at the Destroyer & Submarine Piers at Naval Station Norfolk rather than churning dejectedly back to the shipyard for more work. The only flaw—the puzzling reduction in top speed—was not a shortcoming the shipyard was responsible for, meaning the *Scorpion* had no claim for additional work under warranty. This problem would have to be addressed by "forces afloat," the industrial resources of the submarine tender *Orion*.

Cmdr. Harold L. Young, SUBLANT's material officer for nuclear-powered attack submarines, was nearly ecstatic over the *Scorpion*'s performance during the sea trials and said so eight months later, during the Court of Inquiry investigation of the *Scorpion*'s loss. Comparing the *Scor-*

pion's sea trials with twenty-five others he previously observed, Young told the court, "I put that [Scorpion sea trial] in the top five and that includes new construction trials." In a word, Young described the Scorpion's condition as "excellent."

Capt. Charles N. Mitchell, SUBLANT's deputy chief of staff, also believed the sea trials had gone smoothly and related Lewis's own high praise for the shipyard's work. Lewis, he said, was "thoroughly pleased" and "highly enthusiastic [about] the condition of the ship and the way it operated. The sea trials went beautifully."

The Scorpion's executive officer at the time, Lt. Cmdr. Robert Roy Fountain, also spoke glowingly of the sea trials during his own inquiry testimony, though he gave much of the credit to the professionalism of the crew. "It was my opinion that at the time that we proceeded on sea trials, that Scorpion was unusually well trained and had an unusually experienced crew. The sea trials themselves, I felt, bore this out. I considered them very successful."

Fountain—viewed by some sailors as a martinet in his role as the overseer of crew training—might have surprised his former subordinates with his generous assessment of their abilities. While Fountain's stern demeanor led some to believe he was perpetually displeased with their progress, the executive officer actually believed his men were as capable as those aboard any other submarine, if not more so.

Despite the overall success of the sea trials, the loss of speed remained a concern, and the most likely suspect was the propeller. Upon its return to Norfolk, Lewis requested and received an inspection of the Scorpion's propeller by divers from the Orion. The inspection dives were made, but no defects were found. The Scorpion was officially released by Norfolk Naval Shipyard on October 6, marking the official end of its maintenance period. The submarine returned to sea to conduct four days of individual ship exercises beginning on October 9. Lewis's time as the skipper of the submarine was nearing its end, and his final days aboard were spent ensuring that he turned over a capable crew and a fully functioning submarine to his successor.

The New Captain

The newly refueled Scorpion that was now recertified for submerged operations was given over to Cmdr. Francis Atwood Slattery on October 17, 1967. Slattery was inheriting a submarine that had operated at sea for only six days during the previous eight months. It would be up to him and his officers to oversee the *Scorpion*'s return to full-fledged operations, an effort that began immediately.

Slattery was from West Paris, Maine, a small inland hamlet on the picturesque Little Androscroggin River. Unlike many who entered the U.S. Naval Academy, his family had no tradition of naval service. Though far from affluent, his parents were pillars of their small community; his father was an employee of a clothespin factory, and his mother was a teacher.

Those who knew Slattery don't recall him talking much about the navy, but the youth's ticket out of West Paris was an appointment to the U.S. Naval Academy, a high honor in the patriotism-laced days following World War II. Once at the Naval Academy, Slattery spoke little of his desire to enter the submarine force. While his academy roommates don't recall Slattery studying, he graduated a respectable 66th among 586 midshipmen in the class of 1954.

Slattery spent a year aboard a destroyer before transferring to the submarine force and his first submarine, the diesel-powered cruise missile boat *Tunny*. This was followed by nuclear power training and a stint as a nuclear power instructor. More sea duty followed when he was transferred to the nuclear-powered *Nautilus*. During his five years on the *Nautilus* he handled close to every position and ended his tour as executive officer. Following a one-year assignment to the Naval War College, a normal stop for an officer on the fast track to promotion and plum assignments, Slattery was ordered to take command of the *Scorpion*.

Along the way he earned a reputation as a down-to-earth officer with a lightning-fast wit of unlimited aridity and an appreciation of irony. When he was thrown overboard to celebrate completion of his qualification as a submariner, a fellow officer aboard the *Tunny* guffawed as Slattery was helped from the icy water. Sopping and shivering, Slattery silenced the braying officer by announcing, "What are you laughing about? I'm wearing your shoes." Slattery is also remembered by former *Tunny* crew members for slamming the bow of the submarine into the pier at Pearl Harbor's Naval Submarine Base while trying to fishtail the boat into its berth at high speed, a common practice among junior officers. Before his captain could complain, Slattery exclaimed to his fuming superior, "Do you see what a man can do when he puts his mind to it?" This quip gave him high marks among the enlisted submariners.

While Slattery said little about his aspirations to be a naval officer, and even less about entering the submarine force during his youth, the sea had been on his mind. As editor of the West Paris High School yearbook—coincidentally titled the *Nautilus*—Slattery would pen an ironic vignette for the 1950 edition. The story was titled "Undersea Drama" and seemed to foretell Slattery's future:

> The soft, oozy mud settled smoothly around his ankles as he plodded slowly across the ocean floor in his heavy lead shoes. Green water was surrounding him on all sides. It was hot and stuffy inside that rubber suit and he could feel his heart beating methodically and hear blood pound against his temples as the terrible pressure seemed to suppress him. That horrible push that was ever present on every square inch of his body trying to squeeze him like an accordion.
>
> He was alone, the only living human in that vast wilderness of water. Deep down inside him he knew he wanted to turn back. He wanted to step back into the comparative safety of the platform that had brought him to this infernal place where the weight of the whole ocean was upon him, but he could not turn back now. His life, his fortune—yes his whole future depended on this trip into the depths.
>
> His thoughts turned to his immediate dangers: That lifeline didn't look too good—"My God! What was that?" A drop of water on his shoulder—his hair stood on end at the thought, he froze in his tracks. Then he saw it, a small trickle of water coming in through a crack in the helmet. He emitted a scream which turned quickly to a gurgle as the helmet gave way leaving him enveloped by that slimy, green liquid.
>
> With the weight of the ocean upon him he bent forward and sank out of sight beneath the mud.

Precisely eighteen years later, when the *Scorpion* slammed into the seafloor after a two-mile free fall, it would land in soft, enveloping ooze. Now in command of a submarine, Slattery was indeed a man whose "whole future depended on this trip into the depths."

Naval Submarine Base New London

The day after Slattery took command, the *Scorpion* departed Norfolk for three days of submerged operations while traveling to Connecticut's Naval Submarine Base New London—known as NLON—for crew refresher training, or REFTRA. The crew would practice firefighting and damage control as well as submarine escape techniques using the 100-foot water-filled tower that rose above the base.

The *Scorpion*'s fifth and final commanding officer was Cmdr. Francis Atwood Slattery, a Mainer who took command of the boat on October 17, 1967.

Although drills had been carried out while the *Scorpion* was in the shipyard, there was no substitute for actually operating the submarine. It would be up to Slattery, like other new arrivals on the boat, to heed those most familiar with the submarine. The intense crew training and drills conducted by Lewis and Fountain had paid dividends by producing a crew practiced in the choreography of handling the *Scorpion*. Despite his own experience as a submarine officer, Slattery needed to gain the feel of the *Scorpion* and to learn her unique handling characteristics.

In his effort to understand the engineering history and the subtleties of his new boat, Slattery was in luck.

Helping smooth his transition to command would be the continued presence of Lt. Cmdr. Fountain, the *Scorpion*'s XO. Fountain was the most experienced line officer in the navy regarding the *Scorpion*, having spent two lengthy tours on the boat. After Slattery assumed command, Fountain remained aboard the *Scorpion* for another fourteen weeks until his own replacement arrived.

A 1955 graduate of the U.S. Naval Academy, Fountain initially served on the *Scorpion* for twenty-seven months between 1961 and 1963. During that time he held nearly every job on the submarine except the position of engineer officer, a demanding task for which he was also qualified. In early 1966, after serving as an engineer officer aboard the ballistic missile submarine *Calhoun*, Fountain requested and received a transfer back to the *Scorpion* as executive officer.

The trip to New London was mostly uneventful until October 20, the day of its arrival, when crew members in the engine room noticed smoke. Word was immediately passed that a fire was detected. As men reached for their emergency air breathing (EAB) masks it was soon learned the culprit was the no. 2 air conditioning unit, and the source of the smoke was quickly extinguished. The emergency was more drill than hazard, although next to uncontrollable flooding, the danger posed by a serious fire inside the enclosed space of a submarine was a sailor's greatest fear.

Although overwhelming heat and flame will drive even the bravest submariner from a compartment, a fire's true agent of death is the production of toxic gases, including carbon monoxide, that invariably kill fire victims before they are "burned to death." A fire on a submerged submarine will quickly poison the enclosed environment, making immediate action to extinguish the blaze and ventilate the boat essential. Sailors who fail to don their air-hose-attached EABs or their portable oxygen breathing apparatus, the OBA, would be quickly rendered unconscious.

Fires were nothing new to submarines in general, or the *Scorpion* in particular.

During a "northern run" in 1962, while operating close to the heavily patrolled coastal waters of the Soviet Union at the height of the Cuban Missile Crisis, the *Scorpion's* operations compartment began filling with acrid smoke. The alarm was sounded, and the crew pulled on their EAB masks connected to the submarine's fresh air manifold system. With Cmdr. Robert Young (Yogi) Kaufman in command, the executive officer—future chief of naval operations Carl Trost—led the firefighting efforts. When the doors of a storage locker were wrenched open, it was seen that rolls of toilet tissue had been ignited by an overheated electrical connection. Seawater fire hoses made short work of the blaze, leaving much of the toilet paper in a soggy state.

Kaufman still had to complete his mission with a vital part of his ship's stores now waterlogged and unusable. "We had to take that wet toilet paper out of the locker and put it all over the boat to dry it out," recalled Kaufman with a laugh. Despite its comedic aspects, Kaufman knew the fire could have triggered a secondary and perhaps fatal problem.

As the *Scorpion* departed New London to practice firefighting techniques during submerged operations, a leak was discovered in the stop bolt housing inside the no. 6 torpedo tube. The stop bolt was a device akin to a deadbolt that was raised to position a torpedo in the torpedo tube. Although the leak did not threaten the boat, it allowed unwanted seawater to fill the tube. Because the component's housing could only be reached through the bow's free-flood space outside the pressure hull, the *Scorpion* was placed in dry dock at New London.

Since the *Scorpion* was going to be out of the water, and the undiagnosed propeller problem was considered a suspect in the *Scorpion*'s loss of speed, the propeller shop at New London was to inspect it and repair any damage.

Upon returning to New London on October 28, the *Scorpion* was carefully positioned at the rear of the partially submerged floating dry dock *West Milton*. Once centered on the blocks, the water in the *West Milton*'s ballast tanks was displaced by high-pressure air until the *Scorpion* rose from the water.

Over the ensuing three days, workers clambered inside the slimy space within the bow's superstructure to make repairs on the stop bolt housing. When workers inspected the seven-bladed propeller they found a single, insignificant gouge in the face of one of the blades. At 4 inches long and $1/16$ inch deep, the scar was just large enough to stretch across a man's open palm. The workers also found and removed torpedo guidance wire wrapped tightly around the submarine's shaft. Neither the gouge nor the fouled wire was associated with the loss of speed.

The relatively thin guidance wire was a common entanglement for submarines. Miles of the wire unreeled from two types of torpedoes used during the late 1960s, the Mk-37 Mod (modification) 1 torpedo and the Mk-45 nuclear torpedo. Wire guidance enabled the submarine to direct the weapons to a distant target using sonar. Unfortunately, the wire had a propensity for entangling propellers, stern planes, and rudders. Fountain had once seen so much guidance wire bunched in the stern of a submarine that it interfered with the movement of the boat's stern planes.

Oddly enough, at the time the wire was removed from the *Scorpion*'s propeller shaft, the submarine had not launched torpedoes, though it was scheduled for weapons firing tests at the navy's Atlantic Fleet Weapons Training Facility in the Caribbean on November 9. A logical explanation is that during its trip to New London, the *Scorpion* may have crossed paths with the wire somewhere off the Virginia Capes, where submarines often launched exercise torpedoes.

The propeller shop polished the propeller's seven blades and expertly sharpened the edges of each. It did not attempt to grind out the gouge, since this might cause more problems than it would solve on the carefully sculpted and balanced propeller. When the work was completed on October 30, the *West Milton* lowered itself into the Thames River to free the *Scorpion* like a robust fish released from the hand of a merciful fisherman.

The New Breed

The *Scorpion* was commissioned July 29, 1960, as one of six nuclear-powered attack submarines of the *Skipjack* class. Although an array of nuclear-powered submarines preceded the *Skipjacks*, these earlier SSNs (submarine service, nuclear) wore the bulky, shiplike superstructure familiar on older diesel boats.

The *Scorpion* and her sister ships were gracefully streamlined with sleek, rounded hulls referred to as the "teardrop hull" by engineers. This radical new hull form reduced hydrodynamic drag and cut flow noises to provide the dual benefits of increased speed and quiet operation. The *Skipjacks* were a revolutionary step forward in submarine design. The *Skipjacks* were the future, the sleek archetypes for the modern submarines that now prowl the world's oceans, designed for speed and maneuverability.

This slippery shape was coupled with the installation of the S5W pressured water reactor that provided 15,000 horsepower to give the 3,500-ton *Scorpion* an extraordinary amount of speed, the specifics of which remain secret. The bow control surfaces found on older boats were moved to either side of the *Skipjacks*' knifelike fairwater sail to reduce flow noises that might interfere with sonar transducers inside the smoothly curved nose of the boat. To reduce weight and increase speed, a single propulsion shaft and propeller completed the design, further distancing the *Skipjacks*' appearance from that of their predecessors with twin screws.

It's also notable that the *Skipjacks* were the first submarines to combine magnificently strong High Yield-80 steel in both the hull and framing rings. (What was originally developed as armor for aircraft carriers was previously only employed as the hull skin on the prototype submarine *Albacore*.) This improved structural material allowed the *Scorpion* to dive to 700 feet under ordinary circumstances—nearly twice the 400-foot depth that World War II–era submarines could reach. HY-80 contained the dual properties of hardness and ductility, with the latter attribute providing the ability to absorb explosive energy by bending rather than breaking.

The *Skipjacks* were, in their day, the hottest submarines at sea, and those who rode them were considered elite sailors within the already elite submarine force. The design was considered so successful that America's first ballistic missile submarine, the *George Washington*, was built using a hull initially begun in 1957 for the *Scorpion*, whose construction then began anew in 1958. By 1967, two more classes of attack submarines were operating, but the *Skipjacks* were still considered submarines of great ability.

2

Weapon System
Accuracy Trials

Though it had demonstrated its ability to conduct submerged operations, before the *Scorpion* could return to the world of secrecy-
shrouded missions or play hide-and-seek with Soviet warships, it would
have to prove itself as a weapon of war.

To do this, the ability of the submarine and its crew to successfully
launch torpedoes would be assessed during Weapon System Accuracy
Trials (WSAT) at the navy's system of ranges that stretched from Puerto
Rico to the nearby island of St. Croix. Known collectively as "Roosey
Roads," this system encompassed Naval Station Roosevelt Roads on
Puerto Rico's eastern coast and a series of open-ocean and island target
ranges stretching south and east.

In the beautiful waters near St. Croix in the U.S. Virgin Islands, the
navy had established a 450-square-mile underwater range monitored by
hydroacoustic sensors for tracking the accuracy of submarine-launched
torpedoes. The Underwater Tracking Range was the eventual destination
of every submarine of the U.S. Atlantic Fleet, where crews demonstrated
their proficiency at killing ships, their raison d'être.

On November 8 the *Scorpion* arrived at Roosevelt Roads, where it
loaded two dozen exercise torpedoes and four exercise mines. To do so,
the crew opened the forward escape trunk's upper and lower torpedo loading hatches, which were angled in opposition to each other. This configuration allowed torpedoes to pass diagonally into the torpedo room. With
the assistance of a winch and a skid, the crew sweated in the tropical heat
to guide the massive "recoverable exercise torpedoes" (REXTORPs) into
the *Scorpion* as if they were feeding bullets into a rifle magazine. The job

was painstaking, since some torpedoes weighed as much as 3,000 pounds. After each REXTORP was gingerly lowered tail first into the torpedo room, it was placed in a rack and tightly secured.

The Weapons

The REXTORPs included unarmed training versions of the Mk-37 anti-submarine torpedo; the Mk-14 antishipping torpedo; and the Mk-45 torpedo, also known as the "Astor." When fitted with their respective warheads, the three types of torpedoes were the standard weapons issued to the *Scorpion*. The Mk-45 was designed for the destruction of deeper-diving submarines than the Mk-37 could reach. A live Mk-45 was a devastating weapon. Fitted with a W-34 implosion-type fission warhead, its blast yield was equivalent to 10,000 tons of TNT. Its name "Astor" was a contraction of "antisubmarine torpedo."

Of the *Scorpion's* weapons, only the Mk-14 was not propelled by an electric battery. This workhorse torpedo was originally designed in the 1930s and used during World War II to sink 4 million tons of Japanese shipping. Its propulsion power came from the combustion of pure alcohol blended with compressed oxygen to drive a steam turbine engine. Its warhead contained 640 pounds of high explosives capable of damaging or sinking the largest ships.

Perhaps the most important weapon carried by the *Scorpion* was the Mk-37 torpedo, which was ordinarily powered by a high-performance primary battery packed with silver and zinc plates. (A primary battery is a one-time-use battery that does not require recharging.) REXTORP Mk-37s, however, were powered by a rechargeable battery known as a secondary battery.

Packed within the Mk-37's warhead were 330 pounds of HBX-3, the navy's standard torpedo explosive of the period. HBX-3 was relatively insensitive to accidental detonation due to shock and fire. It was a blend of the high explosives TNT and RDX that were mixed with powdered aluminum, calcium chloride, and wax, making it twice as potent as TNT alone. Heated into a slurry, HBX-3 was poured into molds and cast into warheads.

Though crude by present-day standards, the vacuum tube electronics of the Mk-37's acoustic guidance system were smart enough to adjust its travel pattern so it could doggedly pursue a moving target while discriminating against stationary objects such as the seafloor. A newer, wire-guided modification—the "Mod 1"—could be steered from the submarine as well. The Mk-37 was roughly half the size of the 20-foot Mk-14, and its small size, coupled with its electric propulsion, enabled the torpedo to swim silently from a torpedo tube, negating the need to noisily impulse the weapon with a slug of pressurized water. The Mk-45 could also swim clear of the tube under its own power.

The original Mk-37 initially used passive (listening-only) sonar for guidance and began pinging with active sonar once it closed within 700 yards of its target. When close to its prey, the Mk-37 Mod 1's target-seeking system transmitted an active acoustic signal for final target acquisition before slamming into its victim. At its maximum speed of 26 knots, the Mk-37 could travel nearly 6 miles, although its range could be doubled if its slower, 17-knot speed were utilized. The wire-guided version was limited to a speed of 15 knots while receiving commands from the wire unreeled in its wake.

Activation and initial guidance signals to the Mk-37 were transmitted from a fire control system by cable to a connection on the exterior of the torpedo tube breech door. This data then traveled through the Mk-37's own "A" cable, which plugged into a watertight connection on the inside of the breech door. When the torpedo received the signal to swim out, a cutter sliced through the "A" cable where it entered the Mk-37's aluminum casing.

The Mk-37 torpedo was equipped with a number of safety features, including an anticircular run switch designed to deactivate the torpedo should it suddenly turn back on the submarine that launched it. The weapon could also be programmed not to arm its warhead until it traveled a minimum of 300 yards and no farther than 9,500 yards from its launching submarine. Prior to launch, the weapon could also be instructed by the fire control system to not attack a target at the depth in which the launching submarine had positioned itself. The wire-guided version could be steered to the proximity of its intended target, further ensuring that the weapon would not kill its owner.

A safety feature common to most conventional torpedoes was the mechanism for detonating the warhead. In the Mk-37 this was a removable exploder device containing a small detonator that touched off a larger booster charge, a cylinder of highly explosive tetryl whose detonation generated a sufficient shock wave to set off the warhead. The exploder's purpose was to mechanically separate the detonator from the tetryl-filled booster, which was also shielded from the explosive warhead until the exploder was armed. The exploder mechanism of the Mk-37 would not arm until it reached a distance from the submarine specified by the torpedomen.

Torpedo Room

In many ways, the *Scorpion*'s torpedo room was similar to that of the navy's fleet submarines of World War II. At the forward end of the torpedo room, the *Scorpion*'s torpedo tube breech doors were set like large bronze buttons into the massively strong bulkhead that capped the pressure hull.

The remaining 20 feet of the bow forward of the bulkhead was merely a facade of streamlining that hid the torpedo tube barrels inside a free-flood area. The barrel muzzles extending into this free-flood area were sealed by watertight doors. After a torpedo was inserted and the breech door closed, the corresponding muzzle door was opened along with one of six bow shutters that swung inward. When closed, the curved outer shutters conformed to the eggshell smoothness of the bow.

The *Scorpion* was equipped to carry from twenty-four to twenty-eight torpedoes, depending on the makeup of the submarine's "weapons load," since the *Scorpion*'s three main torpedo weapons were of differing lengths. The number of torpedoes could also vary depending on the amount of space needed for food storage in the torpedo room.

Not only was the torpedo room a weapons magazine and the repository of its six torpedo tubes, it was also a bunkroom for half a dozen enlisted sailors who slept alongside the weapons. With space for stowage and living areas sacrificed to keep the *Scorpion* as sleek as possible, the original berthing on the *Scorpion* was limited. During its first three years of operations, *Scorpion* sailors sometimes endured "hot bunking," in which one sailor crawled into a bunk still warm from the previous occupant.

This problem was alleviated somewhat in 1962 when *Scorpion* Torpedoman's Mate Robert McClain spotted an unguarded pile of destroyer bunks near Naval Station Norfolk's Destroyer & Submarine Piers. He immediately organized a raiding party that soon discovered the destroyer bunks were too wide for the *Scorpion*'s 25-inch hatches. "We just cut them down the middle and reassembled them inside," chuckled McClain. "This gave us six more bunks mounted on the torpedo skids."

In the fall of 1967 the *Scorpion* torpedo room was under the command of weapons officer Lt. John Patrick Burke and his senior enlisted man, Torpedoman First Class James M. Peercy. Burke, a 1963 graduate of the Naval Academy, served on the diesel-electric boat *Tench* before being assigned to the *Scorpion* in September 1966. Peercy was a career enlisted man originally assigned to the boat's precommissioning crew during its construction in the late 1950s. As a "first class," Peercy was the lead torpedoman and the bedrock of the torpedo gang.

Fountain, who had served as weapons officer on the *Scorpion*, paid particularly close attention to the operation of the torpedo room and expected the torpedo gang to be well trained despite their enforced inactivity in the shipyard. Skills were perishable, and not having torpedoes aboard or the chance to launch them did not mean the torpedo gang would be allowed to languish. While in the shipyard, each torpedoman was expected to prepare and deliver a lecture on an aspect of torpedo room procedures twice weekly.

At the time of the Weapon System Accuracy Trials, the torpedo gang consisted of nine enlisted men. First among these was Peercy, followed by Second Class Torpedomen Donald Karmasek, Eugene Jaskiewicz, David Tennant, and David Huckelberry. The third class torpedomen were Robert Violetti, Steven Miksad, and Robert Domanski. The least experienced torpedoman was Torpedoman's Mate Seaman John Driscoll Sweeney Jr. Of these, Peercy, Jaskiewicz, Tennant, and Domanski would be transferred from the *Scorpion* before it was lost. Torpedoman's Mate Third Class Joseph Miller arrived in November 1967, followed by the December arrival of Torpedoman's Mate First Class Donald Yarbrough, who would replace Peercy.

Sweeney's family had a tragic history of naval service. Sweeney's mother, Frances O'Neill Crane, was the widow of a U.S. Navy lieutenant, Leonard Oscar Crane, a 1931 Naval Academy graduate and aviator who perished with five crew members when his PBY-1 patrol aircraft crashed in the stormy waters off Oahu's Kaena Point on March 30, 1938. Frances Crane later married John Driscoll Sweeney, another Naval Academy graduate who commanded destroyers during World War II. John Driscoll Sweeney Jr., the first child of Frances and John Sweeney, was born April 27, 1945. The elder Sweeney would eventually attain the rank of rear admiral.

Sweeney's lack of familiarity with the *Scorpion* was revealed during a 1967 damage control drill in Norfolk, when Jaskiewicz was ordered to remain in unbroken contact with the operations compartment with Sweeney at his side in the torpedo room. When Jaskiewicz was instructed to order Sweeney to close a hard-to-find valve, the more experienced torpedoman recognized Sweeney's bewilderment and closed the valve himself.

Jaskiewicz, a qualified submariner with twenty months on the *Scorpion*, knew the boat completely. "What was I going to do, send Sweeney down there to look for a valve among a hundred others during a flooding drill?" growled Jaskiewicz, who was chastised by his superiors for his decision.

When the plainspoken Jaskiewicz earnestly recounted this incident to the *Scorpion*'s Court of Inquiry, the board members broke into a spontaneous laugh. Jaskiewicz, grief-stricken over losing dozens of friends, was outraged. "I started cussing at them and told them they ought to be ashamed of themselves for laughing," said Jaskiewicz bitterly.

With the loading and securing of the REXTORPs completed, the *Scorpion* departed Roosevelt Roads for Frederiksted, St. Croix, to begin its weapon trials on November 9, 1967. During its ten-day deployment to the Underwater Tracking Range, the *Scorpion* conducted firings of twenty-four exercise torpedoes with decidedly mixed results.

The complex process of aiming and launching torpedoes was prone to problems, and the *Scorpion* had its share. The weapons, the complicated torpedo tubes, and the *Scorpion*'s Mk-113 fire control system all had to function perfectly to obtain good results.

During several attempts to impulse Mk-14s with water slugs, the torpedo gang experienced problems with low water pressure but quickly made repairs. As soon as one malfunction was resolved, another cropped up. One of the Mk-37 REXTORPs began to flood through the propeller shaft seal and sank after being launched. A Mk-14 exercise torpedo was lost as well. Another launch was tainted when a Mk-45 REXTORP that should have been allowed to swim out silently under its own propulsion was loudly belched from its tube with water pressure, an error by the torpedomen. The electronics of one Mk-45 REXTORP later failed to function.

To make up for these problems it was decided that the *Scorpion* would load two more Mk-45s and a Mk-37 at Roosevelt Roads and return to the Underwater Tracking Range. Launching these torpedoes successfully would ensure that the submarine's fire control systems were working properly and provide additional training for the crew. All three weapons were launched without incident.

The *Scorpion* approaches the Frederiksted Pier at St. Croix, U.S. Virgin Islands, in November 1967 during a break in its Weapon System Accuracy Trials.

With the WSAT successfully completed, the *Scorpion* departed the Roosevelt Roads naval complex on November 19 and conducted "individual ship exercises"—training conducted at the discretion of the skipper—during its return to Norfolk.

Hot Run

On December 4, the boat departed Naval Station Norfolk for the nearby Virginia Capes to launch more Mk-37 exercise torpedoes. A potentially hazardous torpedo malfunction would occur during the launching of the weapons. It was a fairly minor event, but one that would later cast a long shadow over speculation as to what killed the submarine nearly six months later.

On December 5, the *Scorpion* had a pair of Mk-37 REXTORPs loaded in the tubes. During the firing exercises one of the Mk-37s refused to accept electronic instructions, prompting the torpedomen to assume that there was a short in the firing transmission circuit. The unresponsive weapon was left alone inside its flooded tube.

Another loaded Mk-37 readily accepted its operating instructions and was launched. Before the torpedomen could turn their attention back to the dud Mk-37, they heard the unmistakable sound of its motor running inside the torpedo tube. The weapon had activated and was now a potentially dangerous "hot run" torpedo. Even though the weapon lacked an explosive warhead, the weapon's battery was generating a high volume of heat as well as a substantial quantity of explosive hydrogen from the electrochemical process of generating electricity. Still, the seawater surrounding the torpedo would cool its casing, and if any gases escaped, they would simply bubble into the seawater.

The procedures for this type of emergency were explicit: if not done so already, flood the torpedo tube to cool the weapon, and report the situation to the control room. Had the weapon been armed, procedures called for the submarine to execute a turn of at least 180 degrees to activate the anticircular run switch to sterilize or deactivate the warhead. After the torpedo's battery exhausted itself, the weapon was to be extracted from the torpedo tube for examination and repair.

What took place in the *Scorpion* torpedo room that day was far less calm and precise. The scene was one of chaos as the torpedomen, caught flatfooted by the hot-running torpedo, attempted to determine the best course of action.

Domanski told the Court of Inquiry: "At this time Peercy and myself were in the torpedo room [with] the rest of the weapons department and torpedo handlers and Peercy tried to get hold of [the] control [room] on the phone. Between me and him we got so excited, I guess, we didn't know what was going on. Peercy thought it was going to get too hot inside the tube, so he just turned the stop [bolt] and let it go out the tube."

Peercy would later admit to the Court of Inquiry that he released the torpedo without gaining proper permission from the control room. He had assumed the buoyant Mk-37 exercise torpedo would swim away from the submarine and float to the surface for recovery. Instead, the torpedo sank and was lost. Peercy would later say he was surprised by the malfunction, since he had never before experienced a Mk-37 hot run. He and his torpedo gang immediately conducted tests on the torpedo tubes and the fire control system but were unable to locate the problem.

The battery-powered Mk-37 acoustic homing torpedo could chase enemy submarines and was a vital submarine vs. submarine weapon from the 1950s to the 1970s.

One hazard spotted early in the life of the Mk-37 was its relatively rare but worrisome ability to be activated unexpectedly while stored or loaded in a torpedo tube. This malfunction prematurely released the stored electrolyte into the potent silver-zinc battery that powered the weapon. The worst situation was the inadvertent activation of a warhead-equipped Mk-37 "warshot" torpedo fitted with the exploder containing the detonator and booster charges for touching off its 330-pound warhead. While safety mechanisms on the torpedo would probably prevent the exploder from detonating the warhead during a hot run, procedures for deactivating the Mk-37 were frequently practiced.

To protect the Mk-37 propellers from damage and to keep them from spinning if they were inadvertently activated while being stored, Mk-37s had a propeller lock clamped over the weapon's in-line twin propellers. Torpedomen who experienced hot runs on Mk-37s outside the torpedo tube recalled the eerie sound of the propellers clacking against the lock like an angry animal eager to escape. This was soon followed by silence, since this resistance would trip a breaker and disconnect the power going to the propeller motor, although the battery would continue generating electricity.

A percentage of Mk-37 hot runs were initiated by torpedomen testing the fire control system without first disconnecting the "A" cable that could carry an activation signal to a loaded torpedo. Some hot runs were attributed to faulty test cables used when connecting the torpedoes to a diagnostic set for checking the torpedo's electronics. Other hot runs were blamed on lazy torpedomen who—in violation of regulations—connected additional cables to allow weapons to be tested in their storage racks, accidentally introducing the activation signal. The causes of other hot runs seemed to defy explanation, such as the December 5, 1968, incident that mystified Peercy aboard the *Scorpion*.

Although only a few torpedomen ever dealt with a hot-running Mk-37, it happened often enough to prompt the Bureau of Ordnance to issue a directive that only the latest version of the testing cables used for Mk-37s be kept and that no submarine have more than one such cable. There is some doubt as to how closely this order was followed. Peercy admitted to the Court of Inquiry during the summer of 1968 that the *Scorpion* had a spare test cable when he left her in December 1967, although its firing voltage pin had been sheared off and it was chained to the bulkhead. Peercy's testimony cast doubt on the effectiveness of the safety instructions regarding the testing cables when he told the court he had never been instructed to discard the spare cable.

Considering the *Scorpion*'s experience during the December 1967 torpedo launching exercise, the court gave serious consideration to whether another Mk-37 hot run had been improperly released and returned to destroy the *Scorpion* at the time of its loss six months later in the mid-Atlantic. Although this speculation influenced the Court of Inquiry board, the condition of the *Scorpion*'s wreckage later seemed to argue strongly against this hypothesis.

Vibration

A seemingly indecipherable problem had emerged while the *Scorpion* was in the Caribbean. As the submarine accelerated toward Frederiksted on November 15, the boat experienced vibration so severe it worried some sailors and led to efforts over several months to resolve the mysterious problem.

The vibration began as the *Scorpion* accelerated to 24 knots and subsided at higher speeds. To some, the oscillation felt as if the *Scorpion* was corkscrewing through the water. Wallace A. Greene, the Submarine Division 62 commander who was aboard observing the *Scorpion*'s operations, later admitted to being puzzled by the submarine's behavior.

It was also a surprise to one enlisted man. "It was really something," said Electrician's Mate Second Class Dan Rogers. "I never experienced anything like it. Nobody screamed or anything but as you passed the other guys in the passageway you just gave each other that look submariners give each other when something wasn't right."

Although worrisome, the vibration did not materialize at speeds on either side of 24 knots. Soon after the boat docked at Frederiksted Pier, navy divers were ordered into the water to ascertain the nature of this latest problem. They found nothing wrong with the propeller or the stern control surfaces that had been inspected two weeks earlier, in New London.

The *Scorpion* encountered more bad luck while gliding into Frederiksted Harbor on the surface on November 17. While approaching the pier, the submarine struck a submerged warping cable securing a work barge. The cable made a sickening sound as it dragged across the *Scorpion*'s hull and sheared off an external sonar transducer. The incident caused no harm to the barge, and the *Scorpion*'s damage was easily repaired.

The *Scorpion*'s problems during the Caribbean voyage were not over. On November 19, as the submarine was accelerating to near 24 knots, the unusual vibration again rumbled noticeably through the *Scorpion*. The problem reminded some members of the crew of a near-calamity on December 5, 1961, when the *Scorpion*'s sister ship *Scamp* was nearly lost during submerged operations 40 miles west of San Francisco.

Sailors serving on the *Scamp* said the submarine was engaged in "emergency backing" procedures while traveling at 300 feet of depth. This frequently practiced maneuver is used to counteract a stern plane failure that forces the submarine into an uncontrolled and potentially lethal dive.

After being thrown into reverse, the *Scamp* backed up violently, pulling the submarine stern-first toward the surface as planned. All went well until the *Scamp* suddenly lost propulsion. This momentarily confused the crew, since the reactor was producing steam and the propulsion shaft was still spinning. The heart-stopping realization was that the 16-inch main propulsion shaft had snapped outside the pressure hull and was carried away by the spinning propeller. Had the shaft failed a few feet farther forward, it would have left a 16-inch hole open to the sea that could push $2\frac{1}{4}$ tons of water into the engine room in a minute. In the face of uncontrolled flooding and a lack of propulsion, recovery would have been impossible.

Submarine propulsion shafts were built with great precision and required extraordinary skill to manufacture. The 16-inch-diameter shafts were bored out, machined to precise tolerances, and perfectly balanced. They were then flame-hardened and cooled to temper and strengthen them. Before being installed on the *Skipjack* class submarines, the interiors of the hollow shafts were tamped with Wausau quartz sand to dampen noise-making vibration.

The shattering of the *Scamp*'s propulsion shaft stunned the submarine force, awakened to the possibility that its other submarines might possess this dangerous flaw as well. Built in 1958, the shaft had endured just three years of service at the time of its failure, a remarkably short period, since many shafts lasted the life of a ship, which could be thirty years or more.

One curious aspect of the shaft was that it had been slightly altered to accept strain gauge instrumentation by the navy's David Taylor Model Basin, although a thorough analysis found these modifications blameless. The navy eventually determined that the contractor that did the final machining on the shaft inadvertently machined a notch into the shaft's steel, creating a weak spot. When placed under stresses during the emergency back maneuver, the notch precipitated a catastrophic crack that severed the shaft.

These findings prompted the navy to inspect the shafts of all its fast attack submarines, and the *Scorpion* received a new main propulsion shaft from a different manufacturer. Inspected and fully certified, this shaft remained with the *Scorpion* until the time of its loss. Subtracting time the eight-year-old *Scorpion* spent in maintenance, the new shaft had experienced just over three and a half years of operational use by the time of the submarine's loss in 1968.

Mindful of the hazards posed by a potentially flawed propulsion shaft or propeller, Slattery and his immediate superior, Capt. Jared E. Clarke III, commander of Submarine Squadron 6, continued to push for a definitive diagnosis of the *Scorpion*'s vibration problem. Another underwater inspection of the *Scorpion*'s propeller and stern was requested. On December 1, 1967—for the fourth time in two months—the *Scorpion*'s propeller shaft and stern were again scrutinized.

Orion divers pulled on their scuba masks and plunged into the water at Norfolk's Pier 22. The divers removed a section of the propeller rope guard and installed an instrument to measure shaft "runout"—a lack of straightness that might cause the shaft to bump against its stern tube bearing. The divers rotated the shaft two full revolutions and saw no indication of crookedness. An inspection of the stern control surfaces also failed to uncover any problems.

The findings of these diagnostic efforts were communicated by the *Orion*'s skipper, Capt. J. C. Bellah, in a letter hand-delivered December 5 to Clarke at SUBRON 6. Clarke was a gracious and conscientious officer from Houston, Texas, who had assumed command of Submarine Squadron 6 on September 30, 1967. The 1941 graduate of the Naval Academy was a veteran of World War II submarine operations and was keenly interested in the vibration problem reported by Slattery.

On the same day he received Bellah's December 5 letter stating that the propeller and shaft appeared to be in good order, Clarke drafted his own two-page message to SUBLANT detailing the *Scorpion*'s baffling vibration problem, which he described as so severe it was akin to "a washing machine with an unbalanced load." His review of the *Scorpion*'s maintenance history revealed that the submarine's propeller shaft was removed during its recent shipyard maintenance period to allow installation of a fresh stern tube seal. (This was the seal that had leaked during sea trials.)

With an eye toward the *Scorpion*'s upcoming schedule, and with the engineers on the *Orion* stumped, Clarke suggested to SUBLANT that additional technical help be provided by the Naval Ship Systems Command (NAVSHIPS). Clarke hoped additional expertise would "determine the cause of the excessive vibration and recommend a course of corrective action in order that timely repairs may be made to enable *Scorpion* to meet her commitments."

In what appears to be partly a result of Clarke's request to understand the vibration issue, two reels of audiotape containing the sound signature of the *Scorpion* under way were sent to the Acoustical Research Development Division's Engineering and Repair Department at Naval Submarine Base New London for analysis. The division was commonly referred to as the "Acoustic Lab," and was the epicenter of navy activity for studying submarine acoustic signatures. The lab also studied how to reduce noises caused by water flowing over submarine surfaces and ways of silencing machinery. One of its senior researchers was Robert York Chapman, who analyzed the *Scorpion*'s tapes and later reported the results to Slattery and SUBLANT.

Chapman found that the acoustic signature of the *Scorpion* did not disclose any abnormal noise levels associated with either the submarine's propulsion shaft or its stern bearing. This finding partially substantiated the observations of personnel at New London as well as those of navy divers from the *Orion* and at St. Croix. Chapman believed the *Scorpion*'s acoustical signature indicated its propeller had a defect other than the gouge found earlier in New London. Chapman's analysis indicated the *Scorpion*'s propeller had a "slight outer perimeter disfiguration of one blade or the existence of a small nick."

A well-meaning but superfluous suggestion by Chapman was that the *Scorpion* be given an inspection of its blade by divers, indicating he did not realize the submarine's propeller had been inspected four times during the previous five months. Chapman warned against allowing the hand-grinding of the blades, which might worsen the problem. He informed SUBLANT, "it is recommended the propeller be changed at first opportunity."

Chapman's recommendation that the *Scorpion* be provided a new propeller arrived too late to be considered. The letter bearing Chapman's analysis was not mailed until February 12, 1968, just three days before the *Scorpion* departed for the Mediterranean and duty with the Sixth Fleet.

Like its shaft, the *Scorpion*'s propeller was also relatively new. The submarine was initially fitted with a five-bladed propeller with traditionally wide, rounded blades that provided tremendous speed but generated an unacceptable amount of noise. During 1965 the *Scorpion* acquired a seven-bladed screw with narrower, highly curved blades that assured quieter operation. This "improvement" also reduced the submarine's top speed, a most unwelcome trade-off in the eyes of the crew, who might have to outrun Soviet warships or torpedoes.

An odd event involving this propeller occurred at the time of the *Scorpion*'s 1967 refueling. During efforts to replace the submarine's stern tube seal, the propeller was removed from the propulsion shaft, which was then withdrawn from the *Scorpion*. After the seal was replaced and the shaft reinserted, it was discovered that the propeller would not fit over the shaft from which it had been removed. Puzzled shipyard personnel made measurements that showed the shaft had the correct diameter, so the internal diameter of the propeller's hub was ground. After this modification, the propeller was finally forced onto the shaft.

The investigation of the elusive vibration continued. Chief Warrant Officer William Wild Jr. came aboard the *Scorpion* from the *Orion* in early December 1967 to diagnose the vibration problem. Heading for open water, the *Scorpion* submerged and commenced a series of maneuvers as Wild and Slattery prowled the *Scorpion*'s engine room. Slattery told Wild of a "grunt" that would "come and go" in the aftmost section of the *Scorpion*. As the submarine maneuvered and operated its control surfaces, Wild could hear the phantom noise emanate from various places in the engine room.

Wild told the Court of Inquiry, "The sound seemed to transmit a little bit. If you listened to it over behind the hydraulic pump, then it would move a little bit into the overhead. It was not a sharp, loud, banging noise."

Wild was surprised at being unable to feel any vibration associated with the mysterious sounds. To confirm this, he resorted to a mechanic's trick of using a long screwdriver like a monaural stethoscope. Crawling throughout the engine room, Wild held the screwdriver's plastic handle to his ear like a nineteenth-century physician while pressing its blade tip against machinery and the hull. With Slattery at his side, Wild listened— or more precisely felt—the machinery vibrations through the bones of his skull. The baffled warrant officer was unable to pinpoint the source of the noise.

"Captain Slattery did kind of feel that possibly there was air binding in the [hydraulic] system and to my knowledge this is what he was satisfied with," the mystified Wild would later testify. "I couldn't say what it was." Unlike Slattery—who suspected the hydraulic system—Wild did not believe the bumping sounds could be correlated to the movement of the hydraulically operated rudder or stern planes.

To please Slattery, Wild vented the hydraulic system twice to bleed off air that might make the system spongy and cause the control surfaces to flutter. For his part, Wild remained baffled by the problem and was unsure if his efforts resolved the eliminated phantom sounds or the vibration.

Sonarman Bill Elrod later testified that the rudder was indeed dithering back and forth, causing the problem, but agreed that the malfunction was eventually corrected. Whether due to Wild's efforts or not, at some point between late December 1967 and mid-January 1968 the vibration problem appears to have been resolved, since no other official mention is made of the issue.

One problem rectified by fall 1967 was the return of the missing two knots of speed. A memo written by Clarke revealed that the fine-tuning of the propeller at New London had recaptured the *Scorpion*'s original speed capability, even if it had not completely eliminated its excessive noise.

The *Scorpion* was another step closer to its return to full operational duty. When commanded to deploy on its first extended mission in twelve months, the news would arrive abruptly, catching the submarine and its crew by surprise. The *Scorpion* would be a last-minute replacement for another fast-attack submarine that narrowly escaped destruction in an undersea collision, the details of which were hidden from the public for decades.

3

Into the Breach

B y early 1968, the fast-attack submarine *Seawolf* was once again conducting missions for Submarine Force, U.S. Atlantic Fleet, having returned to Naval Submarine Base New London after a twenty-seven-month overhaul.

Although it had been sorely needed by SUBLANT during its time at the Portsmouth Naval Shipyard in New Hampshire, the *Seawolf's* overhaul enhanced the safety and capabilities of the boat. It had received Submarine Safety Program modifications—mandated after the scandalous 1963 loss of the *Thresher*—which included an emergency main ballast tank blow system.

Electric Rabbit

The *Seawolf's* first mission would have it serving as an intruding Soviet boat during a secret analysis of American hunter-killer submarine capabilities during January and February 1968. Upon completion of these exercises, the *Seawolf* would prepare for a three-month deployment to the Mediterranean to fulfill SUBLANT's long-standing obligation to provide a nuclear-powered attack submarine to the Sixth Fleet.

On January 22, 1968, the *Seawolf* began performing its role as an "electric rabbit" roughly two hundred miles north of Cape Cod, in the Gulf of Maine. The *Seawolf's* pursuer was the advanced, nuclear-powered hunter-killer submarine *Sturgeon*. Not yet a year old, the *Sturgeon* was the lead ship of the first new class of attack submarines completed since the 1961 commissioning of the ill-fated *Thresher*. The operation had been ordered by the chief of naval operations to assess the ability of the *Sturgeon* to detect the *Seawolf* as the older submarine conducted high-speed runs in a massive undersea basin. The navy also wanted to compare the capabilities of the *Sturgeon* with the *Thresher* class boats, by then referred to as the *Permit* class.

The navy wanted to ascertain the effectiveness of the targeting system for the nuclear-armed Mk-45 "Astor" torpedo. Lacking its own acoustic tracking system, the wire-guided torpedo depended on navigational commands from the launching submarine that tracked the target using shipboard sonar. What concerned the navy was that a lurking Soviet missile submarine could operate with impunity inside a submerged basin, where its machinery noises and the ping of targeting sonar would echo off the submerged walls in a confusing cacophony. If the *Sturgeon* were successful in tracking the *Seawolf* in the acoustically confusing confines of an undersea basin, the effectiveness of the Mk-45 torpedo was assured. If not, a technical solution was needed.

Under Cmdr. Edward T. Scott, the *Seawolf* would make high-speed runs inside Georges Basin, the largest and deepest of twenty-one depressions that scalloped the Gulf of Maine. This granitic basin, whose steep walls rose 1,236 feet from the seafloor, was selected as the site of the operation since its interior was a natural, underwater echo chamber that might be used as an acoustical smoke screen by a Soviet ballistic missile submarine.

Grounding

The operations in Georges Basin began on January 22, 1968, and were to continue for more than a month. All submarine operations are potentially dangerous, but this exercise was exponentially more worrisome, since the game was being played at high speed in a confined area. To avoid a collision with the basin's wall, the *Seawolf* would have to carefully plot each run so a turn could be made at the precise moment. This would prove easier said than done.

A fundamental tool in avoiding grounding was use of a low-grade sonar signal pinged downward to ascertain the depth and slope of the seafloor. Although this fathometer introduced a detectable sound into the water, its use was an essential precaution in areas proliferating with poorly charted undersea pinnacles. A sharp decrease in depth almost always indicated a submarine was approaching an undersea obstacle. It was not uncommon for submarine officers to activate the fathometer infrequently or not at all when trying to avoid detection.

For World War II–era diesel-electric submarines that could barely muster a dozen knots of submerged speed, undersea collision was not as calamitous as striking a seamount at the 20- or 30-knot speeds deeper-diving nuclear boats such as the *Seawolf* could reach. Combined with the problem of woefully inaccurate bottom contour charts, groundings had become a serious problem for the submarine force by the late 1960s. The fear of striking an uncharted seamount was the stuff of nightmares for nuclear submariners said Fred Wales, a lieutenant serving aboard the *Seawolf* at the time. Wales's own anxiety about colliding with a submerged peak was exacerbated by the *Seawolf*'s impending mission, and he wasn't the only officer sweating the assignment.

Seawolf executive officer Gus Weber accompanied Scott to a briefing that outlined the specifics of the exercise and was mortified by what he heard. The *Seawolf*, they were told, would dash back and forth inside Georges Basin at high speed while the *Sturgeon*'s skilled sonarmen attempted to track and "kill" the submarine. "What made this one different was that it involved high-speed, 18-knot runs for a long period of time," said Weber. "I looked at that and said, 'That's playing with fire.' I brought it up with the skipper and we went and talked to the squadron commander who said it had to be done in the same area [as previous tests] because they needed the same [acoustic] background."

Weber and other officers were worried about operating at high speed in the basin, where colliding with a stray granite outcropping—if not a vertical wall—might occur without near-perfect navigation. Along with the general lack of confidence about the navy's notoriously unreliable bottom-contour charts, some doubted if the *Seawolf* possessed adequate navigational technology. Any dissent was muted by the culture of audaciousness that permeated the submarine force. Cruising blindly with questionable charts was just another day at work for submariners, who were confident that leadership, skill, and resourcefulness would prevail. By January 22, the *Seawolf* was noisily racing toward the jagged walls of Georges Basin as the *Sturgeon* swam nearby like a patient, predatory fish.

At dinnertime on January 30, the *Seawolf* descended to 381 feet as its navigator carefully calculated the submarine's starting position relative to the walls of the basin. The chart indicated that the boat was a safe distance from the basin's walls, with the seafloor 678 feet below. The twin propellers of the 337-foot *Seawolf* bit into the cold water, pushing the boat to 18 knots.

As Wales was dining in the wardroom, the *Seawolf* was speeding blindly toward a granite outcropping in absolute blackness. The officer of the deck, Lt. Joseph Mueller, was on the verge of ordering the preplanned turn when the 3,700-ton submarine lurched and nosed upward.

"My chair bounced off the deck and we knew something unearthly had happened," said Wales, whose collision nightmare had come true. Wales and the other officers scrambled for their stations. "I immediately headed for the control room as we started to take a big up angle. I was hanging on against what may have been a 45-degree angle when there was another hit." As the *Seawolf* continued its forward motion with its now-smashed bow tipped upward, the underside of the stern arrived to slam into the outcropping, damaging the rudder and stern planes.

Wales pulled himself into the control room with Scott close behind as the second collision jolted the submarine. Scott coolly issued orders and called for damage reports. The captain then snatched the handset of the underwater telephone and transmitted a prearranged emergency message to warn the *Sturgeon*.

Sailors and officers throughout the submarine reported the status of their compartments and systems. The helmsman and planesman sitting side-by-side quickly reported that the rudder, stern, and bow planes were not responding. Throughout the submarine, men were securing watertight doors and checking for leaks. Miraculously, the reactor and electrical power remained online.

Across the control room, the chief of the watch stood with his hands pressed against the emergency main ballast tank (EMBT) blow switches installed during SUBSAFE work the previous year. He was prepared to send 3,000-pound compressed air screaming directly into the ballast tanks, bypassing the regular blow system, which worked in a slower fashion.

Although it might at first seem prudent to immediately blow the water from the ballast tanks during a submerged emergency, activating the EMBT blow system was actually considered a last-ditch solution. Racing to the surface at the first sign of trouble not only reeked of panic—psychological leprosy to submariners—it was also potentially dangerous. Rocketing from the depths like a cork could cause a collision with the *Sturgeon* or a surface ship. The chief would stoically wait for orders.

As Weber noted the calmness exhibited by the chief of the watch at his ballast control panel, the helmsman matter-of-factly announced that he would attempt to steer the submarine using the emergency control mode. When the helmsman found the emergency steering inoperable, he stood and calmly declared that he was shifting to his last option, the manual hand wheel behind his seat.

The chief of the watch knew that the submarine's controls were a lost cause and gently pushed the helmsman into his seat, saying, "don't worry about that." It was obvious to all that the *Seawolf* lacked operable control surfaces and was unable to drive upward—the preferred means for heading to the surface. The EMBT system, known as the "super blow," was now the *Seawolf*'s fastest means of reaching the surface.

The order came for the chief of the watch to activate the emergency main ballast tank blow system. Half a second later, 2-inch ball valves opened, sending compressed air shrieking from high pressure air flasks to displace the water in the *Seawolf*'s ballast tanks. The *Seawolf* began to rise, slowly at first, then with increasing velocity. Everyone aboard silently hoped they would not collide with a commercial ship or the *Sturgeon*.

With the boat now headed to the surface at a sharp, 35-degree angle, Scott ordered full power to the submarine's twin propellers to provide additional impetus to the *Seawolf*'s ascent. People, coffee mugs, tools, pencils, and anything else not already thrown to the deck, now slid or flew through the air. Some sailors worried that if the steep angle became more pronounced, the precious air in the ballast tanks might spill from the open bottoms of the tanks.

After an ascent that some say lasted a full minute, the submarine burst to the surface in the early-evening darkness. It was not quite fifteen minutes after 6:00 P.M. as the boat undulated with the sea swells. Miraculously, none of the crew had been seriously injured during the collision or the harrowing ride to the surface.

The crisis, however, was not yet over.

In the stern compartment of the *Seawolf*, where hydraulically powered rams as big around as a man's arm traveled through the pressure hull to operate the stern planes and rudder, the collision had created a dangerous situation. A 3-inch-diameter stern plane ram was bent, and water was squirting through watertight packing boxes where the rudder and stern plane rams penetrated the hull.

On duty in an adjacent compartment was Machinist's Mate First Class Allen "Chauncey" Leach, who initially thought the *Seawolf* had only struck a dense layer of cold seawater: "When I felt it hit in the back I knew goddamn well that was no temperature layer. I went down a

The *Seawolf*'s terrifying grounding required timbers to shore the stern plane hydraulic cylinder and aft bulkhead (right) and the rudder cylinder at upper left.

ladder and through a watertight door to where the rams penetrated the pressure hull and saw water and [hydraulic] oil flying everywhere."

Leach, joined by Quartermaster First Class Paul Chihocki, shut and dogged the watertight door behind them as they entered a blinding maelstrom. A fine mist of mustard-colored oil hissed from high-pressure hydraulic lines as seawater jetted through the damaged packing boxes. As the yellow fog settled, it coated everything with a slippery layer of 2190 TEP hydraulic oil, making the work of Leach and Chihocki thoroughly treacherous. The men slipped and fell repeatedly while struggling to control leaks.

Through the oil-smeared deadlight of the secured watertight door, Wales anxiously watched the two men who were callously, but of necessity, imprisoned in the stern compartment. Although the seawater leakage was not excessive, Wales had to ensure that catastrophic flooding would not occur before opening the door. Leach and Chihocki knew they were the *Seawolf*'s sacrificial lambs. The mist suddenly cleared and the improved visibility allowed the two struggling submariners to stop most of the hydraulic leakage.

A Broken Boat

When the fairwater bridge watchstanders looked toward the stern of the surfaced *Seawolf*, they could see the huge rudder leaning lifelessly to starboard, clinging precariously to its mounts.

Scott requested and received an assessment of the boat's condition from his officers. Three hours after the grounding, he transmitted a detailed damage report to SUBLANT and Submarine Flotilla 2. The report, classified as "Confidential," was an ugly picture. Scott reported more than a dozen areas of serious damage that rendered the submarine incapable of making its own way back to port.

While the crew survived the initial collision, their boat was on the surface in the dark in an area where strong currents might shove the disabled boat aground on nearby shoals or where it might be struck by a passing ship. The submarine needed to be towed to safety. It was decided that no civilian tugboat would be allowed on the scene of the mishap, which would be cloaked in a considerable amount of secrecy for decades. A call went out for the submarine rescue ship *Skylark*, which would not reach the crippled *Seawolf* for twenty-four hours.

When the *Skylark* finally arrived the following evening, a *Seawolf* deck gang attached a cable to the submarine's bow anchor chain. As the rescue ship slowly advanced to take up the slack, the tow cable whipped against the leg of a sailor, smashing the bone and throwing him to the deck, gashing his head. "I ended up in the chief of the boat's quarters helping the corpsman sew the guy up," recalled Sonar Technician Third Class Bob Roth. "The doc [a navy corpsman] was a real skinny guy and his hands were shaking like he was coming off a drunk. There was blood everywhere."

It took nearly a week for the crippled *Seawolf* to be towed two hundred miles to Naval Submarine Base New London. As it neared the U.S. Coast Guard lightship *Nantucket*, the submarine's battered rudder finally released its tenuous purchase and sashayed to the seafloor like a giant leaf.

Finally back at New London, the *Seawolf* was placed in a floating dry dock and levitated from the water, revealing the damaged stern. It looked, recalled Wales, like the end of a cigar savagely chewed by a giant. The *Seawolf*, he believed, had very nearly been lost.

In the decades to follow, American submarine groundings would remain a significant problem. On March 18, 1968, barely two months after the *Seawolf*'s grounding, the ballistic missile submarine *Theodore Roosevelt* struck an uncharted seamount off the coast of Scotland, causing extensive damage to its bow.

Submariners tell of numerous near-misses with seamounts while operating their fast-moving nuclear submarines during the 1960s. The fast attack boat *Skate* narrowly averted a calamity in 1962 when a chief petty officer deduced the submarine was traveling far too fast with too little information about its whereabouts. When a sounding ping revealed less than two dozen feet of depth beneath the hull, a full rise was ordered on the bow planes. The boat began a steeply angled ascent moments before it would have plowed into the continental shelf off America's East Coast. (In this case, the fathometer was also turned off.) Subsequent to that incident, officers aboard the *Skate* again lost their bearings and ordered the submarine to begin a gentle, slow-speed dive. The bow tipped downward but despite a massive application of power, the *Skate* refused to move forward. All the power of the boat's nuclear reactor was applied, and the submarine still refused to budge. The crew would soon realize that the submarine had gently nosed into a muddy incline, and after some difficulty they managed to back her out.

Incredibly, this problem has not abated with the passage of time or the infusion of technology. On October 25, 2003, the attack submarine *Hartford* grounded off Sardinia and seriously damaged the hull and stern, although full details of the damage remain unclear. Since the bathymetry charts in the area were considered accurate, the cause of this grounding was blamed on human error. While there was no loss of life and no resultant radiation hazard, the mishap created an international incident because the navy attempted to conceal the accident from the Italian government.

A far more tragic grounding occurred when the attack submarine *San Francisco* struck an inaccurately charted seamount 250 miles south of Guam on January 8, 2005. The incident killed one sailor and injured almost everyone aboard. Much of the bow was almost completely torn away, and its forward ballast tanks were badly damaged. Its emergency main ballast tank blow system was activated, but the fractured ballast tanks hemorrhaged air. Buoyancy, however, was finally achieved, and the submarine slowly ascended from a would-be grave. The submarine was very nearly lost. The *San Francisco* incident again placed a harsh light on the fact that the navy's seafloor charts remained woefully inadequate four decades after this problem was recognized. As in the case of the *Seawolf*, it was understood that taking a sounding with a fathometer would have alerted the crew to the presence of a seamount rising from the seabed.

The Replacement: USS *Scorpion*

SUBLANT was forced to strike the *Seawolf* from its list of usable submarines. Since the requirement to send a submarine to the Mediterranean did not evaporate with the *Seawolf*'s inability to deploy, SUBLANT began looking for a nuclear attack submarine as its replacement. A likely candidate was the *Scorpion*, then on its way back to Norfolk from submarine-vs.-submarine exercises known as Aged Daddy V. The Sixth Fleet was expecting a nuclear-powered attack submarine in the Mediterranean by early March, and SUBLANT would put the *Scorpion* into the breach.

When notified of this on February 2, Slattery's crew had twelve days to complete preoverseas movement (POM) preparations before departing February 15 for operations in the Caribbean, Atlantic, and Mediterranean. Slattery's boat would serve as the electric rabbit for a hunter-killer group from February 17 to February 19 in the Caribbean, followed by additional exercises near the Azores. After a stop at Naval Station Rota on Spain's Atlantic coast, the *Scorpion* would travel east through the Strait of Gibraltar, where it would come under the control of the Sixth Fleet's Submarine Flotilla 8 in Naples. While in the Mediterranean, the fast attack boat would conduct exercises with ships of the Sixth Fleet and NATO until the middle of May.

The *Scorpion* would show the flag in the Mediterranean while the *Seawolf*—now badly broken and stranded in a dry dock—was mended in a cascade of welding sparks. The *Seawolf*'s bad fortune, like all submarine mishaps, would be a cautionary tale for the *Scorpion* and its men.

4

Preparations

Although officers within SUBLANT had praised the *Scorpion*'s condition during October sea trials three months before, problems had emerged, including the vibration issue, though most were minor. Nonetheless, some *Scorpion* crew members believed the boat had numerous small problems that needed work.

Electrician's Mate First Class Andrew "Nick" Elnicki was a career enlisted sailor who served four years on the *Scorpion* and departed the boat shortly before its 1968 Mediterranean deployment. "We always had problems," recalled Elnicki in 1992. Elnicki did not consider the *Scorpion* an unsafe submarine, but scoffed at the notion that it was flawless. "We were always having to make adjustments you normally wouldn't have to make on equipment."

Elnicki had great confidence in the nuclear propulsion system on the *Scorpion*—a domain governed by the perfectionist Hyman Rickover—but less faith in the rest of the submarine. While at Norfolk Naval Shipyard for its 1967 nuclear refueling, few of the *Scorpion*'s systems outside the reactor compartment had been refurbished by shipyard personnel, recalled Elnicki. "The shipyard didn't hardly touch the [rest of the] submarine." When Elnicki departed the boat he remembers handing Electrician's Mate Third Class Gerald Pospisil a hefty stack of pending electrical work orders.

A routine chore completed in early January 1968 was a discharge test of the TLX-53A main storage battery to evaluate its ability to store and release electrical energy. The battery was a 65-ton arrangement of 126 individual cells standing 55 inches tall and 14 inches square. Inside the plastic case of each were lead plates drowned in 20 gallons of sulfuric acid diluted with water. The cells formed a single battery that could power a restart of the reactor or the submarine's emergency propulsion

42

motor. The last option was scoffed at by many nuclear submariners who believed that the propulsion endurance provided by the battery was inconsequential.

Experience with the TLX-53A battery showed it to be a safe and reliable power source. Although the *Scorpion*'s battery was nearing the end of its predicted life span, experience showed it had greater longevity than originally estimated, and its service was extended another twelve months. Some *Scorpion* sailors considered this unwise. Despite its clean bill of health by navy experts, some sailors believed the *Scorpion*'s battery was "tired" and needed replacement.

Although some distrusted the battery, not having to replace its cells was a blessing. The removal of 126 ungainly battery jars, each weighing roughly 1,000 pounds apiece, was an exceedingly tough job, as each cell had to be disconnected, laboriously lifted from the battery well, and winched through a 25-inch hatch. Installation was a reversal of this unpleasant procedure.

Despite the doubts of some, the battery fared extremely well in the January 1968 discharge test by holding 106 percent of its rated electrical charge. The discharge process, like most activities on a submarine, was potentially dangerous and carefully monitored. A hazard during discharging was the production of explosive hydrogen gas and pure oxygen, which aids combustion. The atmosphere within the submarine was monitored by hydrogen detectors, while an extensive ventilation system removed gases from the battery space.

The potential for destructive main storage battery explosions on navy submarines since 1900 was well known. One event often cited in battery safety discussions was the 1955 hydrogen gas explosion that rocked the *Pomodon* at San Francisco Naval Shipyard with blast damage and flames, killing five sailors.

If this weren't bad enough, other, more insidious hazards lurked within the *Scorpion*'s huge battery. While it would take tons of seawater to sink a submarine, it took a relatively small amount to wreak havoc on a main storage battery. Flooding of the cells by conductive seawater could cause an explosive discharge of the chemical energy, producing massive amounts of heat. Even more insidious was the infiltration of seawater into the battery cells, where the chloride in the saltwater was converted into deadly chlorine gas, which could dissolve the respiratory tract's mucus membrane. The *Scorpion*'s main storage battery, no matter its condition, was yet another component that had to be handled with great care.

The New Executive Officer

On January 5, 1968, as the *Scorpion*'s crew prepared their boat for the submarine-vs.-submarine exercises known as Aged Daddy V, Lt. Cmdr. Robert Fountain left the submarine for his next assignment. With Fountain's departure, the crew was losing an officer who served two tours on the boat. Besides being the navy's most knowledgeable line officer regarding the *Scorpion*, Fountain—some sailors grumbled—had been ruthless in his efforts to ensure that the crew was well trained. Despite his rough edges, Fountain "was the kind of officer who always brought his boat back," observed a fellow officer.

An example of Fountain's exacting style could be seen in "cleanups" of the boat that sailors considered far lengthier than necessary. Fountain was viewed by some as unemotional, unyielding, and quick to apply disciplinary measures. Others familiar with Fountain recognized him as a tough but fair officer.

The officer replacing Fountain was the boyish-looking David Bennett Lloyd, whose agreeable manner gave no hint of his prowess as a competitive wrestler. Lloyd graduated third in the Naval Academy's class of 1956, and a year later placed fifth in a class of fifty-nine officers at Submarine School.

Lloyd served on the ballistic missile submarine *Ethan Allen* for twenty-one months, followed by a year as a nuclear power instructor. In 1964 he reported to the nuclear-powered attack submarine *Skate*, which subsequently entered Norfolk Naval Shipyard for a difficult and lengthy overhaul. Lloyd couldn't have been more different than the executive officer he replaced. Where Fountain was austere, Lloyd was matter-of-fact and, some felt, more approachable. The crew quickly warmed to both Lloyd and Slattery. *Scorpion* sailors who served under the two—and whose providential departure would save their lives—later spoke well of the submarine's two top officers.

"I was very impressed after the captain [Slattery] . . . and Lieutenant Commander Lloyd came aboard," Interior Communications Electrician First Class Joseph D. Underwood told the inquiry investigating the *Scorpion*'s loss. "It was one of those deals where they just seemed to fit. They both did very well. They worked good together; they were very capable and everybody was real, real happy. It was just one of those things where everybody was tickled with them. If I had a chance I would sure serve under them again."

Lt. Cmdr. David Lloyd became the *Scorpion*'s executive officer in December 1967. Highly regarded by the crew, he graduated third in his Naval Academy class.

"Captain Slattery and the XO were outstanding people, navy people," emphasized Underwood. "[Slattery] was cautious, very calm, and very, very capable, I would say."

Sonar Technician First Class Bill Elrod, who departed the *Scorpion* with Underwood just before midnight on May 16, 1968, six days before the boat was lost, agreed with his shipmate regarding Slattery and Lloyd. "I believe that the crew, overall . . . moralewise, was a little bit more eager to do better for Captain Slattery than for Captain Lewis," Elrod would later testify. "[Slattery] was the type of man that inspired you to do the work." Elrod told the Court of Inquiry that Slattery was, simply, an "inspirational" leader.

Testimony about how the *Scorpion* operated under Lewis and Slattery had piqued the interest of inquiry board member Cdr. A. J. Martin Atkins, who previously commanded the *Scorpion*'s sister ship *Scamp*. Atkins, noting that under Lewis the *Scorpion* was said to have operated in an "outstanding" fashion, probed Elrod by inquiring somewhat incredulously, "In your opinion [the operation of the *Scorpion*] actually improved after [Slattery's arrival]?"

"Yes, sir," responded Elrod.

As Lloyd learned his way around the *Scorpion* in early January 1968, the leakage problem in the boat's main propulsion shaft seal reappeared. Norfolk Naval Shipyard bristled at the suggestion that it was responsible for the leak and successfully argued that they were not obligated to repair the seal. The rear seal replacement would be completed on February 9, 1968, by personnel from the tender *Orion*.

Aged Daddy V Exercises

On January 13 the *Scorpion* sailed south for the Aged Daddy V exercises. Despite Slattery's abilities as a conscientious commander and capable mariner, he struggled as an undersea tactician during the annual submarine warfare exercises, held during the winter of 1967–1968 in an area stretching from Florida's east coast to the Caribbean.

"Commander Slattery was—when he came aboard—suffering from a lack of experience in quite a few aspects of tactical submarining," Submarine Squadron 6 commander Jared E. Clarke would tell the inquiry. "He was an extremely competent mariner. He knew his boat extremely well and he was a capable administrator—and he operated his boat safely." The problem, testified Clarke, was that Slattery operated the *Scorpion* "below the potential of his ship." Clarke counseled Slattery on his tactical shortcomings. (Slattery may have been the victim of a problem within the submarine force of the period in which officers lost two years of tactical experience to newly requisite nuclear power training and stints as nuclear instructors.)

Slattery was digesting Clarke's criticisms of his tactical missteps when Slattery was ordered to prepare his boat for a one-hundred-day "Med cruise."

Oil and Oxygen

Following the Aged Daddy V exercises, the *Scorpion* returned to Norfolk by February 5, when it drew 370 gallons of 2190 TEP hydraulic/lube oil that served as the pale, yellow blood of its hydraulic system and as the lubricating oil for machinery and gears. The *Scorpion*'s lubrication and hydraulic systems held a total of 9,192 gallons of the oil, which could be shared if one system was running low. The hydraulic system's storage tanks held 5,145 gallons, more than half of the boat's total oil capacity.

Another important item needed by the *Scorpion* was pressurized oxygen, and on February 10 the *Scorpion* took on 210 gallons of the life-sustaining gas from the *Orion*. Another 275 gallons would be pumped aboard the boat three days later. To maintain a 21 percent level of oxygen inside the submarine, the gas was released inside the submarine using the "bleed" method, which had been around for decades. Oxygen boosts combustion at a ferocious rate, and it can even generate spontaneous combustion when it oxidizes certain materials such as petroleum or sulfur. For these reasons the pressurized oxygen posed its own hazards to a submarine.

A fatal oxygen-fed fire in the stern torpedo room of the nuclear-powered attack submarine *Sargo* on June 14, 1960, at Pearl Harbor was caused by a contractor's cracked hose. Machinist's Mate Third Class James Smallwood was fatally engulfed in an inferno that sent flames roaring from the stern hatch through which the oxygen hose entered the submarine. The vicious fire was extinguished only after seawater poured into the open hatch of the submarine's stern, which was intentionally submerged. To reduce this hazard the *Scorpion* received remotely controlled shutoff valves in 1964 to prevent the oxygen flasks in one compartment from feeding a fire in another.

The *Scorpion* also replenished its stock of "oxygen candles," an ingenious device composed of sodium chlorate and iron powder that served as another source of oxygen for the crew. When initiated, the iron is oxidized to create a self-sustaining decomposition of the sodium chlorate at 400 degrees Fahrenheit without producing flame or smoke. A single candle provides enough oxygen to sustain a hundred men for an hour. Although they produce heat and not flame, the candles were only activated inside a steel oxygen furnace.

Freon

A month before Slattery was told to prepare *Scorpion* for deployment to the Mediterranean, the crew took aboard the refrigerant gas Freon, for which the submarine had an abnormally voracious appetite. For years Freon had spewed freely from the submarine's decaying air-conditioning and refrigeration systems.

The boat's four cooling systems were among the items not repaired during the *Scorpion*'s 1967 refueling period, even though they had been in poor shape for years. Besides providing cooling to the refrigerator and frozen food lockers, the cooling systems also provided air conditioning for the crew. The navy's inability to fully repair refrigeration problems aboard submarines meant that the only solution to Freon leakage was to continuously replenish the refrigerant gas. This is precisely what the *Scorpion*'s sailors had done.

On December 31, 1967, the *Scorpion* took on 950 pounds of Freon, nearly enough to fill the 250-pound refrigerant capacity of each of its four refrigeration systems. A properly functioning set of refrigeration systems aboard the *Scorpion* should have lost a total of only 75 pounds of Freon monthly. Freon is considered hazardous only if it displaces enough air to cause asphyxiation. Studies done on the *Skipjack* class boats showed that if all 1,000 pounds of Freon were released, it would make up only a harmless 0.71 percent of the *Scorpion*'s internal atmosphere.

This calculation does not address the possibility of Freon—which is much heavier than air—pooling and displacing oxygen in smaller spaces. During the early 1960s the occupants of the control room of the diesel-electric submarine *Amberjack*—including the helmsman and planesman—became dangerously groggy when leaking Freon displaced the air. A similar event several years later prompted the issuance of an April 1966 Safetygram by the Submarine Safety Center.

The only ill effect reported on the *Scorpion* regarding its Freon-laced atmosphere was from smokers who said that the lighted cigarettes converted the refrigerant to throat-burning phosgene gas. Phosgene is highly caustic and reacts with water in the lungs to create hydrochloric acid.

The *Scorpion*'s leaky air-conditioning systems were known to have filled the boat with as much as 1,000 parts per million of Freon for short periods, and it was not uncommon to have half that concentration in the atmosphere. During a week of submerged operations without ventilating, the *Scorpion* could accumulate 350 parts per million of Freon. The normal allowable limits were seven times lower, or 50 parts per million.

Leaking air-conditioning systems had actually been a problem on the *Scorpion* dating back to 1962, its third year of operational life. Lewis, the *Scorpion*'s former skipper, complained in an April 1, 1967, letter to SUBLANT that "air-conditioning and refrigeration work has been seriously undermanned" during the *Scorpion*'s refueling and upkeep period. Lewis's complaint could do little about the shortage of skilled refrigeration personnel at Norfolk Naval Shipyard—the root of the problem. Without repairs, the coughing smokers of the *Scorpion* would simply recharge their boat's refrigeration systems and lay claim to another reason why it took guts to wear dolphins.

Slattery joined the chorus of complaints about the *Scorpion*'s air-conditioning problems when he assumed command. During his boat's subsequent deployment to the Mediterranean during the spring of 1968, he wrote letters to SUBLANT seeking extensive repair work on the Freon lines, compressors, and other components. To underscore their concerns while in the Mediterranean, Slattery and Lloyd lowered the acceptable Freon limits in the boat's atmosphere to trigger more frequent use of the extendable snorkel for ventilation. The move was intended, Elrod later testified, "to put some teeth into the refrigeration problem so they could get the system straightened out."

With the replacement of its propulsion shaft seal and completion of other work, the *Scorpion* put to sea on February 11 for two days of pre-deployment trials to ascertain her readiness. The trials went well, and the boat returned to Norfolk to take on food and a load of live torpe-does. With an angled skid on the deck of the submarine, sailors lowered twenty-three torpedoes tail-first into the forward torpedo-loading hatch. Among these were ten Mk-37 Mod 1 (wire-guided) torpedoes, four Mk-37 Mod 0 (self-guided) torpedoes, and seven Mk-14 torpedoes. Also loaded were two nuclear-armed Mk-45 "Astor" torpedoes, delivered under the watchful eyes of a U.S. Marine security detachment.

Departure Day: The Missing Sailor

Although the impending Mediterranean mission had caught the *Scorpion* by surprise, the crew managed to complete the tasks necessary to prepare the *Scorpion* for its extended deployment. On the morning of February 15, the submarine seemed ready to sail.

Yeoman Senior Chief Leo Weinbeck was perhaps the boat's hardest-working man prior to the February 15 departure—and its most reluctant. With only a year before retirement, Weinbeck had requested shore duty but was forced to report to the submarine in March 1967. "I sure wish I could get off this thing," Weinbeck wrote his wife January 10, 1968. "I'm getting too old for these kids' games."

Since much of the submarine's paperwork went through Weinbeck's typewriter, he worked all night preparing correspondence that had to be mailed before the *Scorpion*'s departure. He dashed from the boat at dawn to mail a hefty batch of official letters. The chore took longer than expected, and Weinbeck worried that the *Scorpion* might sail without him. As Weinbeck hurried back, he was heartened to see the *Scorpion* still at the pier.

Weinbeck later wrote his wife, "the ship was held up about 15 minutes because of me." He was, however, mistaken. He assumed—erroneously—that he was the tardy sailor for whom Slattery had delayed the boat's departure.

The submarine skipper's real concern was another missing sailor. Fuming on the fairwater bridge, Slattery was looking beyond the pier and waving wives for missing Sonarman First Class Bob Davis. After Weinbeck's return, an impatient Slattery held the submarine, but Davis did not appear. Slattery finally ordered the *Scorpion* to get under way.

Davis had no real complaints about being on the submarine and would later insist that he did not intentionally miss its departure. Davis's excuse for missing the boat was his girlfriend's premonition of his death aboard the *Scorpion*.

As Davis was preparing to drive to the pier, his girlfriend confronted him with her grim vision. "She said if I left the house that morning something terrible was going to happen and I'd never come back." Seeing that she had not convinced Davis, the girlfriend hid his car keys. After finding them Davis drove madly to the Destroyer & Submarine Piers eight miles away, arriving as his submarine was pulling away. Waving his arms and shouting, Davis finally caught Slattery's attention. The submarine's skipper shouted through a bullhorn for Davis to report to Submarine Squadron 6. Davis was later sentenced to thirty days' confinement in the brig at Camp Allen. Regretful over missing the *Scorpion*'s departure and depressed over his confinement, Davis saw little reason to consider his predicament a lucky break—and no reason at all to relate his plight to his father, a Florida state trooper.

After ordering Davis to report to the squadron, Slattery pointed the *Scorpion* eastward. When the seafloor dropped away, Slattery ordered the fairwater bridge evacuated and gave the command to dive. The ballast tank vents on the snout and rump of the *Scorpion* snapped open, releasing snorts of white spray. The fairwater descended until it disappeared like the dorsal fin of a shark going deep. It would soon rendezvous with Task Group 83.4 near Bermuda, where it would serve as bait for the skimmers and their helpmates, the maritime patrol planes.

The Trash Disposal Unit

While racing toward the Caribbean Sea, the *Scorpion* crew settled into its first evening at sea as Commissaryman First Class Jorge Santana prepared a superb meal of roast beef and mashed potatoes. Santana, born in Santura, Puerto Rico, and raised in Brooklyn, reported aboard a few days before the *Scorpion* sailed. He was a qualified submariner with experience on four surface ships and the diesel-electric submarine *Cubera*. Santana's realm was a cramped galley where he and three stewards had the crucial job of feeding 101 men.

Santana's galley was also equipped with one of the most worrisome items on the *Scorpion*, a trash disposal unit referred to simply as the TDU. It was little more than a vertical, 10-inch-diameter stainless steel pipe capped with a circular breech hatch inside the boat and by a Teflon-coated bronze ball valve facing the sea. To keep the breech hatch and the muzzle ball valve from opening simultaneously—a nagging worry to submariners—an interlock linkage was part of the TDU's mechanism.

Another safety factor was the care with which the TDU was operated. When enough garbage was accumulated, it was weighted, and the submarine rose to periscope depth of roughly 40 feet, where housekeeping duties such as radio communications and trash dumping were conducted. The shallower depth was an additional safety factor, since it reduced the hydrostatic pressure that could force seawater into a malfunctioning TDU.

The procedure for dumping the trash, like every activity on a submarine, was governed by procedure. While a "talker" in communication with the ballast control panel operator observed the procedure, the TDU operator opened a small valve to check for water in the breech just in case the ball valve was open. If none spewed from the valve and the ballast control panel operator gave approval, the inner hatch was opened, and weighted trash was inserted. After closing the inner hatch, the outer ball valve was rotated until the hole in its center lined up with the TDU barrel. Water pressure then flushed the garbage into the depths, and the ball valve's hole was again rotated perpendicular to the TDU barrel.

Weeks before the *Scorpion*'s February 15 departure, a new TDU muzzle ball valve had been ordered and was being fabricated at the time the boat sailed. A common problem with the ball valves was their tendency to get scratched during use, allowing minor leakage into the barrel of the TDU. Sailors were cautioned to avoid damaging the ball valve with items shoved into the TDU breech, but they were scarred nonetheless and required replacement regularly.

The presence of water inside the TDU breech from an extremely slow leak might falsely lead the crew to believe that the ball valve was open. Worse, the crew might be lulled into believing that a squirt of water from the vent valve *only* meant that the scratched ball valve was leaking harmlessly when it was fully open. This might prompt an incautious sailor to open the breech door, only to be struck by a jet of high-pressure water. Even the lowliest sailor dumping the trash had to know what he was doing, which was the rationale for making every sailor qualify as a submariner.

Bleeding Oil

As the *Scorpion* cruised to its submerged rendezvous with the hunter-killer group southeast of Bermuda, it became dishearteningly apparent by February 16 that the hydraulic system was bleeding oil at an alarming rate. Although the *Scorpion* was not in immediate danger, the hemorrhaging was so severe that the officers discussed turning back to Norfolk.

The dimensions of the leak were extraordinary for a boat on its first day away from port. While the *Scorpion*'s hydraulic system was expected to lose nearly 100 gallons of oil monthly, the submarine was gushing 50 gallons each hour, a rate that could drain the submarine's entire supply of oil within eight days.

The situation was serious, though not necessarily dangerous. Without hydraulics, the submarine's control surfaces—its rudder, stern planes, and fairwater planes—would be unusable. The problem did threaten to delay the *Scorpion*'s rendezvous with the hunter-killer group and perhaps even its voyage to the Mediterranean, unless it could be repaired by the crew.

When sailors could not locate a hydraulic leak inside the boat, a decision was made to take the *Scorpion* to the surface to inspect the hydraulic systems inside the towering fairwater. Once on the surface, the crew would enter the fairwater to inspect the hydraulics controlling the various sensor masts and the sizable hydraulic ram that controlled the massive fairwater planes. Machinist's Mate First Class Robert James Cowan clambered into the fairwater to hunt for the leak amid a maze of piping.

At 9:00 A.M. on February 17, Cowan began blocking the flow of hydraulic oil to the electronic countermeasures (ECM) mast and to the radar mast in an effort to halt the leakage. By 4:00 P.M. Cowan and his shipmates solved the problem and the *Scorpion* steamed to meet the task force that was already pinging the ocean with active sonar signals.

For the next two days the *Scorpion* assumed the role of a Soviet SSGN, a nuclear-powered missile submarine, during which it reported a series of additional malfunctions. Initially the *Scorpion* had difficulty with the tuner for its AN/BRA-19 high-frequency communications antenna.

Worse yet, the boat suffered potentially dangerous steering problems. On February 19, the last day of the Bermuda hunter-killer exercise, the *Scorpion* suffered rudder failures when the control surface shunted hard left twice during a ninety-minute period. Each time this happened, the *Scorpion* was thrown into a sharp left turn, prompting a drastic reduction in speed. The hazard posed by such a rudder failure could be especially serious during high-speed operations, since the *Scorpion* had a tendency to heel in the direction of the turn, converting the normally vertical rudder into a horizontal stern plane in the dive position. The rudder failures, whatever their cause, seemed temporary, and the *Scorpion* completed the exercise. Oddly enough, although the rudder failures were reported to the hunter-killer group, no mention was made of the *Scorpion*'s hydraulic oil leakage.

On February 20 the *Scorpion* departed the Bermuda hunter-killer exercise to participate in another free-play, antisubmarine exercise, code-named Azores HUKEX, in the vicinity of the mid-Atlantic island group. By February 25 the *Scorpion* was attempting to elude the surface ships and aircraft of the group while heading toward the Strait of Gibraltar to the south.

The *Scorpion* was released from control of the commander, Anti-Submarine Warfare Force, Atlantic Fleet (COMASWFORLANT) on February 27 to sail for Spain's Naval Station Rota, where the boat would receive supplies and upkeep.

5

Rota

Jutting from Spain's southwestern coast, the fishing village of Rota sits on the northern side of the Bay of Cádiz, 60 miles northwest of the Strait of Gibraltar. Adjacent to the village was U.S. Naval Station Rota, which began operating in 1958.

As the *Scorpion* approached Rota in darkness on February 27, its off-duty enlisted men crowded the crew's galley to watch the romantic comedy *A Countess from Hong Kong*, the implausible pairing of Sophia Loren and the brooding Marlon Brando. The 1967 film did not meet the standards of Electronics Technician Second Class James Tindol III, who lamented both the movie and his homesickness in a letter written the following day, "Baaaa, poor. No plot and no continuity for one hour and 50 minutes. 82 days to go."

Just before 6:00 A.M. on February 28, hours after the film was rewound in a clatter of celluloid, the *Scorpion* arrived outside Rota's breakwater. At sunrise, Slattery deballasted enough to bring only the fairwater above the surface. The *Scorpion* then wallowed in the swells, waiting for daylight.

When *Scorpion* finally moved through the Rota breakwater's 900-foot-wide entrance, its unique shape turned heads at the naval station, where fast attack boats were seldom seen. The *Scorpion* had the lean look of a predator as it moved past the bloated missile boats. The *Scorpion* was not a city-killer but a cannibalistic craft designed to kill surface ships and Soviet missile submarines and looked like a wolf creeping among a flock of sheep.

Once positioned near the submarine tender *Canopus*, the *Scorpion*'s hydraulically operated capstans silently rose from its smooth deck while its topside gang manually unlocked stowed cleats to allow the fastening of mooring lines. The *Scorpion* would remain at the naval station for upkeep, with the help of *Canopus*, and its crew would enjoy liberty visits in the town of Rota, with its dusty streets and Moorish architecture.

Before that would happen, Chief of the Boat Walter William (Wally) Bishop put the men to work on a "cleanup" of the submarine, after which he gathered his sailors to discuss the dos and don'ts of liberty in Spain. Some in the crew, especially those in their late teens and early twenties, were prone to boisterous behavior fueled by unwise amounts of alcohol. While a moderate amount of brawling was accepted as a rite of passage in the world of the warship and the waterfront, the *Scorpion* would soon be under the command of the Sixth Fleet in the politically sensitive Mediterranean, where it was deemed crucial to respect the sensibilities of American allies. The rules were different in the Med, and Bishop was laying down the law.

Tindol had heard it all before: "This morning we had a lecture by the COB about what we could and couldn't do over here—Don't get in trouble with the police, don't get in fights, don't get so drunk you can't be rolled easily, be back to the ship by 0800, don't go to out-of-bounds areas, and all the other usual don'ts."

Chief of the Boat

Chief of the Boat Bishop—"the COB"—was a burly, square-jawed sailor who many said was the best they had ever known. He was the senior enlisted man aboard.

Bishop was a tough-talking disciplinarian who expected his sailors to do their jobs. Bishop could singe the air with hard language as he verbally transformed a pimply slacker into a conscientious sailor. Bishop was also the intermediary between the enlisted men and the officers and was much loved for defending his sailors when they were in the right. Bishop was a mentor as well to newly arrived junior officers. Officers and enlisted men who served on the *Scorpion* shared a profound respect for Bishop.

Retired rear admiral Tom Evans was a young lieutenant aboard the *Scorpion* in 1964 when he met the formidable Bishop: "He was one of the best enlisted leaders I'd ever come in contact with and he was a great help to me while I was weapons officer. He was an immensely cool customer."

Evans had a personal reason to appreciate Bishop's unflappable nature. While operating somewhere in the North Atlantic in early 1966,

Chief James Wells leans on the heavily bearded and
well-respected chief of the boat, Walter Bishop, in about
1966. Both perished aboard the *Scorpion*.

a persistent rattle on the outside of the pressure hull prompted *Scorpion*
skipper James R. Lewis to bring the boat to the surface in darkness to
diagnose the trouble. Bishop, who was also the chief of topside operations, followed Evans up through the fairwater trunk and out a heavy
steel door onto the *Scorpion's* weather deck. The night was so black that
lights were rigged on the fairwater bridge to illuminate the deck below.
Bundled in life jackets and carrying flashlights, both men were hooked
to a deck track by safety belts, with Evans in the lead.

"I was about two-thirds down towards the water's edge at the bow
when the ship heaved up and then went down into a very deep, long
swell," said Evans. "It completely submerged me and knocked me over
the side. I was hanging on the safety line and Bishop immediately came
down the track and began hauling me back on the deck. We beat a hasty
retreat because more swells were coming."

Bishop's qualities as a leader were apparent since his earliest days on the *Scorpion*. The torpedoman's mate first class reported aboard the submarine in September 1959, three months before the *Scorpion* was launched. The *Scorpion*'s first skipper, Cmdr. Norman "Buzz" Bessac, remembered Bishop: "Walt Bishop was such a natural leader that I wondered why we couldn't just make him the chief of the boat." Bessac was prevented by regulations from promoting Bishop to chief of the boat, since the torpedoman's mate first class had not yet ascended to the requisite rank of chief.

When Cdr. Robert Young "Yogi" Kaufman took command of the *Scorpion* in 1962, the boat's hard-charging second skipper also recognized Bishop's abilities and successfully pushed for Bishop's promotion ahead of other, more senior enlisted men. Bishop became chief of the boat in July 1962 and remains famous in submarine lore for becoming a COB while still only a "first class." Wally Bishop was just the sort of man to have around in an emergency.

Upkeep

When the *Scorpion* docked at Rota, Slattery and his officers scrambled to ensure that repair work needed by the submarine was performed. In this, the *Scorpion* was indeed lucky. The dauntingly high maintenance standards applied to ballistic missile submarines were customary for the sailor-technicians of the *Canopus*.

Roughly forty work requests were submitted by the *Scorpion* for repairs. Though none was considered crucial, in the minds of the *Canopus*'s officers the number seemed somewhat high for a boat released from the shipyard only four months before.

The *Scorpion*, which nearly had to postpone its mission due to the hydraulic leak, was expected to operate in spite of problems that would not be tolerated on a missile boat. The missile boats were afforded the government's highest priority for maintenance work, spare parts, and other types of support. The *Scorpion* and the other attack submarines were left to struggle as second-class citizens within the submarine force. Heaven and earth would not be moved at the first sign of problems. The attack boats were expected to persevere despite this disadvantage.

While fast attack boats might sail with oil leaks or air-conditioning problems, the fleet ballistic missile boats were part of America's triad of nuclear deterrence and therefore sacrosanct. Not only were the FBMs important as a terrifying presence to the Soviets, they also allowed the navy to compete for funding and influence with the U.S. Air Force.

One broken component was the *Scorpion*'s Loran-C navigational system, which had conked out during the Atlantic crossing. On March 1, the day after the *Scorpion* docked, *Canopus* sailors arrived to manhandle the Loran-C through one of the boat's 25-inch hatches and also removed four pieces of malfunctioning test equipment and an equal number of electronic countermeasure tuners.

As the *Canopus*'s crew made the repairs, the *Scorpion* received 1,626 gallons of 2190 TEP hydraulic/lube oil, thirty-two times more than the *Scorpion* should have lost during the previous thirteen days. This sizable requisition of oil surprised SUBLANT material officer Cdr. Harold L. Young in Norfolk, who characterized the *Scorpion*'s rate of oil consumption as "excessive." Neither Young nor his superior, Capt. Clarence Russell Bryan, seemed aware of the *Scorpion*'s postdeparture hydraulic leakage.

While it was odd that SUBLANT was unaware of the oil leak, Slattery requested warranty work from Norfolk Naval Shipyard on January 27, 1968, to repair a leaking seal on the hydraulic piston operating the fairwater control surfaces. The shipyard pointed out that this leakage was a matter of routine maintenance and that it would not furnish any repairs. It is unknown if the leakage reported in January was the source of the massive February leakage, though it's unlikely Slattery would have departed with a 50-gallon-an-hour oil leak. Either the massive leak was a new problem, or an insignificant oil leak became far worse after the submarine sailed.

It is also possible that Slattery and Lloyd may have considered the postdeparture leakage nothing but a routine matter resolved on the fly and not worth reporting, like many problems tackled by the hardworking attack submarine crews.

The hydraulic oil mystery was possibly explained months later, when Sonar Technician First Class Bill Elrod—who departed *Scorpion* days before it was lost—revealed that the problem was the result of two leaks: one in the no. 1 whip antenna hoisting cylinder, and another somewhere in the hydraulics of the fairwater planes. "We were considering going back to have it repaired," said Elrod. It was his recollection that the "ship's force"—the *Scorpion*'s own machinist's mates and auxiliary men—made permanent repairs to the leaks and that no assistance was required from the *Canopus*.

This, however, may not have been the case. The *Scorpion* was plagued with hydraulic leaks throughout the boat, according to a SUBRON 16 officer who inspected the *Scorpion* upon its arrival in Rota. The officer observed that the submarine seemed to be suffering both from a lack of maintenance and poor morale. The officer also said the crew and officers seemed humorless and emotionally depleted.

Repair officer Kenneth Fox boarded the *Scorpion* soon after its arrival in Rota and was surprised at the number of visible hydraulic oil leaks in the submarine. "It wasn't uncommon to see hydraulic leaks on the old diesel boats but I was surprised to see them inside the *Scorpion*," said Fox. "They were catching the leaks with all sorts of things to keep them from staining or contaminating things inside the boat. I remember most of the hydraulic problems were aft [in the engine room]. There was quite a bit of hydraulic work they needed done. In fact, they needed so much hydraulic work I pulled our men off the missile boats to help them since [the *Scorpion*'s] time in Rota was limited."

Another squadron officer who helped oversee the repairs was surprised at the amount of work required. "We accepted something like forty jobs and they were supposed to be alongside the *Canopus* for about seven or eight days," he recalled.

Fox and the other officer were struck by the demeanor of the crew, who seemed subdued and somewhat demoralized. Fox, who assisted *Scorpion* engineer Lt. William Clarke Harwi, observed that the officer "seemed very tired." Harwi was among three *Scorpion* officers who had submitted their resignations.

Harwi was a 1961 graduate of Princeton University who majored in math and physics. On the occasions when Fox met Harwi he noted the officer had covered his khaki uniform with a dark blue, cotton "poopy suit," navy-issue coveralls favored by those in the engineering spaces of the submarine. Although the coveralls were originally authorized only for missile boat crews, the item became available to attack submarine sailors in 1967. The funds for their purchase were mentioned in a letter given to Slattery by Lewis when Slattery assumed command of the *Scorpion*. (The existence of such coveralls on the *Scorpion* became controversial when a body that appeared dressed in them was subsequently observed near the submarine's wreckage.)

Slattery, a New Englander usually quick to dispense quips and humorous observations, seemed in no mood for levity while in Rota. Like Harwi,

Slattery appeared somewhat fatigued. Said Fox, "The thing I remember about Slattery and the crew is that morale on the boat was quite low and the feeling was that they were long overdue for maintenance. I remember Slattery as a guy who did not smile very often."

The other officer's greatest sense of foreboding came when he was visited by a former shipmate then serving aboard the *Scorpion*.

"Sidemeat"

A *Scorpion* crew member who visited the *Canopus* several times during the first week of March was Torpedoman's Mate First Class Donald Yarbrough, who had replaced James Peercy as the *Scorpion*'s senior torpedoman. When the officer saw his former shipmate, he hailed Yarbrough into his office for a cup of coffee.

The officer had high regard for the torpedoman, whom he believed exemplified the best qualities of a sailor. Yarbrough was a thoroughly professional and unceasingly cheerful sailor. "He was naturally curious, which made him very knowledgeable," recalled the officer. "Yarbrough said hello and wanted to talk but I remember the nonverbal more than the verbal." Yarbrough's body language bespoke reticence. "When I asked a few leading questions [about the *Scorpion*] he didn't provide any verbal feedback and his facial expressions indicated the *Scorpion* was not a happy ship." Despite Yarbrough's uncharacteristically evasive behavior, his one-time shipmate had no doubt that the *Scorpion*'s torpedo room was capably run by his former shipmate.

During the inquiry, Yarbrough's qualifications and proficiency as a torpedoman would be closely examined, with Interior Communications Technician Joseph Underwood vouching for Yarbrough's professionalism. "The only basis I have for saying that is the fact that Yarbrough was always in the torpedo room," Underwood would later testify. "[For] every evolution [activity] he was there. Peercy [stood] watches on the BCP [Ballast Control Panel] and he wasn't nearly so involved as Yarbrough. [For] everything that happened [Yarbrough] was there. If there was any kind of shifting of the fish he was there. He stood his watches there and nothing moved in that compartment that he didn't know about or he didn't supervise."

As the torpedo room's "first class" since December 1967, Yarbrough was in a critical position. Though overseen by Lt. Charles Lee Lamberth—

From left are Fireman Robert Watson and torpedomen Donald Yarbrough and Robert Domanski in December 1967. Only Domanski would be alive six months later.

whose training as weapons officer began with Yarbrough's arrival—it was Yarbrough who directly managed the torpedo gang. Yarbrough's emotional balance and expertise were essential to the safety of the crew. Though Lamberth and Yarbrough were the same age, Yarbrough had the benefit of specialized torpedo training and had served in submarines twice as long. Had there been a potentially lethal problem with one of the torpedoes, it would probably have been Yarbrough to whom all eyes would turn.

Lamberth reported aboard the *Scorpion* as the main propulsion assistant in 1965 and was being trained as the weapons officer by his predecessor, Lt. John Burke. Both Burke and Lamberth submitted their resignations prior to departing on the deployment, as had Harwi and Lt. George Patrick Farrin. This was hardly unusual at the time: roughly half the junior officers of the submarine force were then choosing to resign after their initial duty obligation expired. Brutally long hours even when in port and extended periods at sea drove officers and sailors from the submarine force.

With nearly twelve years in the navy, twenty-nine-year-old Yarbrough was a career sailor. The native of Martinez, Georgia, possessed a southern drawl so thick it even amazed fellow southerners. A small man with dark, half-moon eyebrows and prominent ears, Yarbrough had a joyful outlook on life. His hilarious stories about a gambling uncle who raised fighting roosters enlivened the cramped submarines on which he served. None could remember when the irrepressible Yarbrough wasn't smiling or making others smile. Like most submariners, Yarbrough had inherited a nickname. Nearly four decades after his last conversation with Yarbrough, the officer still remembered the torpedoman simply as "Sidemeat," a slang term for bacon.

Despite his reputation as a competent submariner and torpedoman, Yarbrough was a hard-drinking sailor who occasionally got into trouble ashore. During the early 1960s, an inebriated Yarbrough once drew a crowd while amorously entwined in a parked car outside a Groton, Conecticut, restaurant. A large Connecticut state trooper dragged the small sailor from the car and held him aloft by the nape of his jumper, asking onlookers, "Does he belong to anyone?" A grinning Yarbrough looked at the spectators as his bell-bottom trousers hung precariously from his ankles. A shipmate hurriedly escorted the torpedoman back to the boat.

While serving on the *Skipjack* based out of Charleston, Yarbrough and his shipmates built their own stock car and began dirt track racing, skidding the car around the ovals ensconced in South Carolina's piney woods. Though one teammate lost a fingertip in a rollover, Yarbrough drove the battered car with abandon. "Sidemeat thought he was driving a tank," said shipmate Bobby Dempsey of their off-duty racing days.

When Yarbrough's luck did run out it was not on a tumultuous racetrack but on an ordinary street in 1967 when he broke his neck in an automobile accident. With pins screwed into his skull to keep his neck in traction, Yarbrough was incapacitated for a month. ("He looked like the Frankenstein monster," said Dempsey.) Yarbrough made a full recovery but lost his bunk on the *Skipjack* and was ordered to the *Scorpion*.

The irrepressible Yarbrough whom the repair officer had known six years before, was not present aboard the *Canopus* in early 1968. Perhaps sobered by his near-fatal car crash or made more serious by a recent marriage, Yarbrough seemed a different man. Yarbrough's reserved behavior triggered a decidedly negative view of life aboard the *Scorpion* within his old friend. Although his impression may not have been fully accurate, the officer was not alone in thinking the *Scorpion* was an unhappy boat.

As work progressed on the *Scorpion*, off-duty sailors were allowed into Rota for liberty. Tindol, despite Bishop's lecture about curbing the use of alcohol, went to Rota and drank himself into a stupor nonetheless. "I went in last night like I said I would," Tindol wrote his wife. "Sure wish I hadn't. Your husband got stoned last night. Boy did I feel bad." Tindol was so hung over he slept through a work detail and found himself being dressed down by Lt. Robert Flesch, who reported to the *Scorpion* in December 1966. Tindol soon realized that much of the crew was suffering hangovers as well: "Half the crew is recuperating and the rest are out getting bombed again. Seeing these drunks come back reminds me of how I must have looked last night."

During his stay in Rota, Tindol recognized his inability to tolerate alcohol and began noting the drunkenness among his shipmates. "Too many drunks here," he wrote during his third day in Spain. "Only three days of sea between here and Italy [and] people shouldn't be so hell-bent on getting drunk here." He concluded the letter by adding, "Darling one, its 3 a.m. and the drunks are starting to come back."

Radio Room

On March 3, 1968, Senior Chief Radioman Robert Johnson arrived in Rota from the Radio School in Bainbridge, Maryland, where he was an instructor. His assignment to the *Scorpion* eighteen days after it departed Norfolk was surprising, since the *Scorpion* already had an adequate number of radiomen aboard. Until the arrival of Johnson, Chief Radioman Garlin Denney was the senior enlisted communicator.

Johnson was a lean-faced Kentuckian who spent his first twelve years in the stark coal town of Jenkins before moving with his family to Matewan, West Virginia, another grim community. Johnson's credentials were superb. He served as a radioman for the commander in chief, Southern Europe, before becoming an instructor for three years. He then received advanced communications training and was assigned to the headquarters of the U.S. Pacific Fleet at Pearl Harbor before serving as an instructor in Bainbridge. He said good-bye to his wife, Roberta, his two daughters, and his son, and returned to sea duty.

When Johnson reported aboard the *Scorpion* at Rota, Radioman Chief Daniel Pettey instantly recognized him as his own radio school instructor. Pettey considered Johnson a top-notch radioman: "If anyone could get a message out, Chief Johnson could." No official mention exists as to why Johnson was assigned to the *Scorpion*, although the boat had experienced occasional communications difficulties since it departed Norfolk on February 15.

A possible clue to Johnson's inclusion on the *Scorpion* may have been in a letter Johnson wrote his wife the day of his arrival: "I reported aboard and found all the radiomen working. Would you believe that every piece of electronics equipment including antennas was inoperative? These boats have a radio shack that makes the old boats look sick, and not one single piece of equipment was working." Johnson's letter made it plain that the communications equipment was in miserable shape.

Tindol, who helped maintain the equipment in the radio room, wrote his wife the same day, expressing empathy for the task facing Johnson: "I rather feel sorry for him. They expect so much from him and he's not a whole lot better off than what we already have."

Although testimony provided to the Court of Inquiry in the aftermath of the *Scorpion*'s loss characterized its communications equipment as being from "good to excellent," the submarine experienced long-running problems with its AN/BRA-19 whip antenna. This telescoping whip antenna was frequently damaged when hoisted hydraulically, and its tuner had proven problematical as well. Another problem endemic to the AN/BRA-19 antenna was that saltwater leakage shorted it out.

The troublesome AN/BRA-19 antenna also picked up the radio signals for the Loran-C navigation system used to plot the submarine's position. In addition, the boat was equipped with an antenna-tuner combination known as the AN/BRA-9. If neither of these antennas was working, a pair of emergency antennas could be installed on the sail while the submarine was on the surface.

Johnson and his fellow radiomen conscientiously applied themselves to maintaining and operating the communications equipment, although problems persisted. Tindol and Johnson eventually clashed over who had responsibility for maintaining the communications equipment when the KWR-37 "Jason" decryption machine went on the blink. The argument proved acrimonious, with Tindol writing his wife, "Rather broke even in the end. Got the problem worked out on the KW-37 that started the argument . . . got through grinding my teeth and ate supper."

Departure

As the *Scorpion*'s March 5 date for leaving Rota neared, the crew rushed to finish last-minute chores. On the day of its departure, with its decrepit refrigeration system still pumping Freon inside the submarine, the crew received 950 pounds of Freon from the *Canopus* in 50-pound bottles. It marked the beginning of a pattern in which the *Scorpion*'s crew requested Freon from nearly every American warship and tender it encountered in the Mediterranean.

As the day of departure neared, Tindol was again working on the boat's electronics. He savored a small victory just before the *Scorpion* sailed when he got the Loran-C navigational system reinstalled. This triumph was immediately followed by word that the range repeater on the boat's frequently troublesome radar had failed. When the submarine finally sailed from Rota, Tindol was repairing that problem.

Despite the best efforts of the crew, the *Scorpion* found itself unable to depart Rota at 8:30 A.M. on March 5 as planned. Tindol wrote to his wife that the "nukes" handling the reactor were not quite ready and that the departure was delayed for six hours.

When the *Scorpion* finally eased away from the pier and glided through Rota's breakwater entrance, it was carrying Cdr. Kurt F. Dorenkamp, the operations officer of Submarine Flotilla 8 in Naples. While the *Scorpion* was in the Mediterranean, SUBFLOT 8 would have direct authority over the *Scorpion*, and it was Dorenkamp's job to ride the boat to Italy while briefing Slattery and his officers on the Mediterranean's "rules of the road" regarding navigation and communications protocol. (Dorenkamp would later testify that the *Scorpion*'s departure from Rota was delayed by difficulties with the boat's AN/BRA-19 antenna, conflicting with Tindol's letter stating that the problem was within the propulsion system.)

The *Scorpion*, Dorenkamp informed Slattery, would proceed at a leisurely pace in the Mediterranean, not exceeding 12 knots "unless it was an operational necessity." This restriction meant the *Scorpion* would travel at half its normal cruising speed during transit, though it could depend on its full capabilities during operations. Near the Strait of Gibraltar the *Scorpion* conducted a brief mission that remains classified. The *Scorpion* then crawled eastward past Gibraltar toward Taranto, Italy, reaching the Italian naval base in the instep of the Italian boot in four days.

During his ride on the submarine, Dorenkamp was impressed both with the *Scorpion*'s crew and its skipper, Frank Slattery. This upbeat observation stands in contrast with the impressions of Fox and others at Rota. Dorenkamp would tell the Court of Inquiry that Slattery appeared to be "a very calm, confident, and competent individual [with] complete confidence in his personnel. He told them what he wanted done and then let them do it."

6

The Mediterranean

As the *Scorpion* knifed through the Strait of Gibraltar during the second week of March 1968, a storm made the eastern Mediterranean so turbulent that the *Scorpion* felt the convulsions hundreds of feet below.

"Since leaving Spain we've done nothing but try and keep the boat upright," said Weinbeck in a March 10 letter. "Ran into one of the famed Mediterranean storms . . . even at considerable depth the boat was rocking pretty bad. Everyone came through unscathed." If those aboard the *Scorpion* interpreted the rough weather as an omen, they would have been wise to heed it. By the time of the *Scorpion's* transit through the Strait of Gibraltar, the Mediterranean had become a deadly place for submarines.

Epidemic

On January 25, the Israeli Navy submarine *Dakar*—formerly the Royal Navy's HMS *Totem*—was lost a day's sailing from Haifa. Aboard were sixty-nine sailors of Israel's fledgling submarine force. The *Dakar* foundered sixteen days after departing Portsmouth, England, where it received a refit after being purchased by Israel. The *Dakar's* disappearance, however, would not be the only Mediterranean submarine tragedy of 1968.

Just two days after the *Dakar's* loss, the French diesel-electric submarine *Minerve* sank off Toulon, killing all fifty-two aboard. Israel and France were unable to determine what precipitated the foundering of either boat. (The *Dakar's* wreckage was not located until May 1999. The *Minerve's* hull remains unfound.) Those aboard the *Scorpion* were well aware of the twin tragedies that preceded their arrival.

The submarine mishaps of January 1968 would trouble Vice Admiral Arnold F. Schade, commander, Submarine Force, U.S. Atlantic Fleet. The COMSUBLANT had overruled the commander of Submarine Squadron 12 in Key West, Florida, by forbidding one of its submarines from conducting submerged operations due to a minor mechanical problem.

Schade explained his anxieties in a letter to SUBRON 12's Capt. George Ball: "If it appeared we were getting into your hair on the details following the *Tusk* [casualty report] I can only attribute this to the intense focus of attention following the loss of *Dakar* and *Minerve*. . . . The *Seawolf* grounding has once again brought all the searchlights to bear on the problem of submarine operations and [the] safety of operations."

The outbreak of submarine disasters had not yet run its course. Before the end of the year, the secretive Soviets would lose two submarines—one on March 8 in the Pacific and another rumored lost in the Arctic Sea. The *Scorpion* would be lost on May 22. As many as 396 men perished in unrelated submarine disasters during 1968. When the *Scorpion* arrived at the Italian Navy base in Taranto on March 10, the submarine's crew had only seventy-three days to live. After spending three days in Taranto, the *Scorpion* sailed south into the Ionian Sea, a body of water between the sole of the Italian boot and the southern Balkan Peninsula. There the *Scorpion* would participate in war games with Sixth Fleet carrier groups as it stalked and was stalked in an exercise named Easy Gambler.

During a break in operations on March 20, the crew found time to celebrate an accomplishment unique to submarine sailors. After eight years, the *Scorpion* had completed its five-hundredth dive. Santana the commissaryman baked a large vanilla cake covered with white and blue icing. Adorning the cake were two images of the *Scorpion*'s teardrop-shaped hull below the inscription "Five Hundred." It also carried the dedication "To the Crew and W. W. Bishop, TMC—Plank Owner."

As part of the festivities, Slattery decided to "splice the mainbrace" and ordered that a fifth of liquor be mixed with two gallons of black coffee. This tradition evolved from the extra rum issued to Royal Navy sailors who rewove the crucial line bracing a sailing ship's mainmast. On modern American warships—where the consumption of alcohol was forbidden by regulation—this illicit tradition spliced together men rather than rope.

Machinist's Mate David Stone: Augusta Bay, Sicily

After completing the Easy Gambler exercise on March 21, the *Scorpion* set course for Sicily's Augusta Bay, arriving there on March 23. In Taranto, the submarine was not allowed to moor at the pier, owing to Italian concerns over its nuclear reactor. In Sicily it would also be banished offshore, for the same reason. American nuclear-powered submarines were a lightning rod for protests during the late 1960s and often kept out of sight to avoid aggravating Italian political tensions. The *Scorpion* would drop its mushroom-shaped anchor far from shore. Its crew could visit Sicily but only after being ferried ashore by a liberty boat.

Although each sailor anticipated three days of liberty during the seven they were moored at Sicily, the *Scorpion* still needed routine upkeep, and at least one of the repairs was major.

By the time the *Scorpion* reached Sicily, a nagging problem had become so bad it could no longer be ignored: the deterioration of a bearing in one of the boat's largest pumps. Without the assistance of a submarine tender, the *Scorpion*'s sailors made the repairs. Machinist's Mate Second Class David Stone mentioned the problem to his parents in an April 12 letter while decrying the preferential treatment given ballistic missile submarines: "The boat has been pretty good to us so far this trip as the majority of the gear is holding up, although one of the biggest pumps aboard threw a motor bearing. We repaired it in three days, a job which 75 percent of all the SSNs and 100 percent of the SSBNs would have gone to the shipyard for." (Slattery had previously sought warranty work from Norfolk Naval Shipyard on the bearings of one of the steam plant's feed pumps that operated five decibels louder after being rebuilt in 1967. The pump moved condensed water back to the steam generator, where it could be reheated to spin the boat's turbine.)

Although Stone prefaced his comments saying the *Scorpion* had "been pretty good to us," he also described the boat as something of a maintenance headache while taking a jab at the ship's officers: "We have repaired, replaced or jury-rigged every piece of equipment after 'frame 44' at one time or another and this boat hasn't been in overhaul in $4\frac{1}{2}$ years. The officers get in and do a lot of arm-waving and jaw-working. We do the work and they take the credit if anyone gets any. But we grin a little at each other 'cause we know better." (Stone's reference to "frame 44" refers to the demarcation between the nonnuclear front of the submarine and the engineering spaces that included the reactor compartment.)

Stone's comment about the *Scorpion* not having an overhaul in $4\frac{1}{2}$ years was factual. The complicated reasons behind the elimination of this overhaul would be closely studied by the Court of Inquiry after the deaths of Stone and his shipmates. The *Scorpion's* first and only full overhaul was completed on April 28, 1964. When Vernon and Sybil Stone received their son's letter in Ames, Iowa, both noted it was the first time he had complained about the mechanical condition of the *Scorpion*. His comments would leap to mind six weeks later with the *Scorpion's* fatal disappearance.

If the pump wasn't enough of a problem, one of the *Scorpion's* air-conditioning compressors "blew up" on March 27, wrote Tindol. "Now we only have three left. Hope the weather doesn't get too warm in the next few months."

An Unexpected Transfer

On March 28, two days before the *Scorpion* departed Augusta Bay, Radioman First Class Daniel Pettey's prayer was answered when orders arrived transferring him to the *Skipjack*. Pettey, who despised serving on the *Scorpion*, had spent the previous twelve months unsuccessfully trying to escape the boat.

Pettey so hated duty aboard the *Scorpion* that in 1967 he sought a transfer to the U.S. Army, where he intended to volunteer for hazardous duty in Vietnam as a helicopter pilot. To Pettey, death at the hands of the North Vietnamese Army was a reasonable alternative to the *Scorpion*. Pettey claims that many sailors were unhappy on the boat besides himself. "I wasn't an extreme case. I was just one of the run-of-the-mill guys." Considering that Pettey was a career sailor with seventeen years of service, his willingness to jeopardize his career to escape the *Scorpion* was extremely unusual.

Pettey reported aboard the *Scorpion* in March 1967 and found himself in an environment he considered toxic. "In my opinion the morale of the crew was so bad there was no morale. The men had even quit complaining. The men would work like dogs and they [the officers] would promise the men a week off and then they would break that promise."

Pettey believed the *Scorpion* was an unhappy boat, a situation exacerbated by demands made on the crew during the nuclear refueling and repair period the year before. The *Scorpion's* most frustrated sailors, claimed Pettey, were those in the engineering spaces. "They hung up a sign one time that read 'Please Don't Make Us Any More Promises.'"

Pettey, like a few others aboard the *Scorpion*, had clashed with the *Scorpion's* austere executive officer, Robert R. Fountain. The executive officer once restricted Pettey to the boat for falling behind in his studies to qualify as a diving officer. Pettey considered the action a common example of the unreasonably harsh discipline on the boat.

In contrast to Pettey's angry assessment of conditions aboard the *Scorpion* during 1967, he came to have high regard for Slattery and the new executive officer, David Lloyd. By the time he left the boat on March 28, 1968, Pettey said their leadership was having a positive effect on morale. However, Pettey's favorable view of Slattery and Lloyd was not enough to soften his desire to leave. Pettey's heart sank when Slattery asked him to delay his transfer. To Pettey's delight, SUBLANT responded by ordering him to depart the *Scorpion* immediately.

The radioman packed his seabag and flew back to the United States. A week later Pettey reported to the *Skipjack*, where he found a submarine humming with good morale and a sense of camaraderie, things Pettey did not observe during his year on the *Scorpion*. He was never called as a witness before the inquiry into his former submarine's loss.

Tindol, homesick for his wife and daughter, took envious note of Pettey's departure in a March 28, 1968, letter: "Chief Petty [*sic*] is leaving the boat tonight to go back to the States and be transferred to the *Skipjack* at Norfolk. Sure do wish I was going back too. I've had enough of the Mediterranean for a long time." The *Scorpion*, whose crew temporarily numbered 102 men with the arrival of Senior Chief Radioman Robert Johnson in Rota, shrank to 101 with the eager departure of Pettey.

Sicily

The ancientness of Sicily fascinated Electronics Technician First Class John Livingston, who found a doll for his daughter and a black beret for himself. While visiting the Augusta Bay waterfront, Livingston met a group of French sailors from the diesel-electric submarine *Flore*. "I picked up a set of French dolphins off the *Flore*, a French submarine. It's a sister ship of the one [the *Minerve*] that recently went down over here," said a soft-voiced Livingston in an audiotape for his parents.

Not surprisingly, before departing Augusta Bay, the *Scorpion*'s auxiliarymen found their troublesome refrigeration systems again running low on Freon. After a few radio calls they managed to scavenge a small amount of the refrigerant gas from an American destroyer moored nearby.

As the crew worked to fix its ailing gear prior to its departure, Tindol had more problems with the Loran-C navigation equipment, prompting him to write, "Loran-C is almost, but not quite broke and worst of all we're out of potable water. Worked on the damn Loran from noon until 9 last night. Finally gave up, got a book and went to bed." The lack of drinking water on the submarine, created by the evaporative distillation of seawater, indicated the sailors in the *Scorpion*'s engineering department were making repairs as well.

On March 30 the *Scorpion* sailed for a rendezvous with the diesel-electric boats *Blenny* and *Irex* as part of another exercise, but another mechanical problem interfered with this assignment.

When the *Scorpion* was late arriving for the exercise, Submarine Flotilla 8 radioed the submarine to ascertain why. The *Scorpion* blamed the delay on a motor-generator fire. This device, as its name implies, serves as an electric generator when its rotor is turned mechanically and as a motor when it receives electrical current. The problem went unreported until SUBFLOT 8 asked about the *Scorpion*'s tardiness. The fire appeared to have been contained by the crew with little resulting damage, since no other mention was made of the malfunction.

The exercise continued for ten days, and Slattery was pleased with the results, mainly because of the excellent training they provided his crew. In an April 18 letter to SUBDIV 62 Slattery wrote, "Ten days of services to units of TF60 between our Augusta and Naples visit may prove to be the best training we get while in the Med."

Material Condition

Like any submarine commander, Slattery was keeping a close watch on his boat's material condition, noting what systems needed repair before the boat's next deployment, especially those that might affect the submarine's safety and combat readiness. Even before reaching Augusta Bay,

Slattery drafted a March 23 "Interim Docking Request," listing work he considered essential.

One problem threatening the submarine's readiness stemmed from paint chips gushing into the interior of the torpedo tubes from a poorly painted torpedo impulse tank. The impulse tank forced water under pressure into a torpedo tube to push a torpedo on its way. The chips, complained Slattery, could damage the gaskets of the slide drain valves that drew water from the torpedo tubes when the tubes were drained for reloading.

A more massive paint job sought by Slattery included sandblasting and repainting of the hull. On April 18, more than a month after requesting the interim docking, Slattery wrote to Greene about the poor condition of the *Scorpion*'s hull: "Every day it seems more and more desirable to go into [dry] dock upon our return. During flank speed today I noted at least [a] $1\frac{1}{2}$ knots decrease in ship speed from what we were getting. I attribute this primarily to paint peeling, fouling and general hull roughening." Slattery's boat was once again losing speed after recapturing it temporarily with the polishing of its propeller months before.

"Delay of the work an additional year could seriously jeopardize *Scorpion*'s material readiness during the intervening year," argued Slattery, who warned of "potential damage to torpedo tube slide and drain valves." Slattery's other reason for aggressively seeking repairs was SUBLANT's 1966 decision to select the *Scorpion* as the subject of a special maintenance program to reduce the excessively long overhauls crippling the submarine force.

The planned availability concept, or PAV, was established to streamline the byzantine submarine maintenance process to squeeze more sea duty from its scarce and expensive fast attack boats. Recognizing the importance of this program to SUBLANT, Slattery carefully sharpened his argument by warning, "Unnecessary delay of any identified work items can permit, through normal wear and tear, the gradual deterioration of the ship to the point that the Planned Availability Concept is no longer a practicable means of overhauling *Scorpion*."

Slattery was concerned that allowing too many small repairs to pile up would nullify the overhaul experiment, which was to be something of a maintenance blitzkrieg. Hinting that the experimental overhaul could be jeopardized was perhaps the strongest card Slattery had to play. Also on Slattery's list of problems in his March 23 message was a predictable plea for repairs on the weary refrigeration system and replacement of a towed hydrophone lost during the Mediterranean operations. He also sought repairs on a tuner degrading the capabilities of the trouble-prone AN/BRA-19 antenna.

As the exercises concluded on April 9, the *Scorpion* set a course for the Gulf of Naples. On that same day, SUBLANT shipped an additional 500 pounds of Freon across the Atlantic for the *Scorpion*.

"Leper Colony"

The *Scorpion* was once again on the surface as it glided toward the Italian port city of Naples for a five-day visit. As usual, Italy's Ministero Della Marina requested that the submarine moor in the Gulf of Naples and not at the pier. This, reasoned the Italian officials, would deny local Communists a pretext for staging protests. This problem was not unexpected. The crew had been ordered not to mention the Naples visit to family members to reduce the likelihood that word of the visit might trigger anti-American protests common in the region. David Stone spoke for his shipmates when he wrote on April 12 that the banishment "makes us feel like we're a leper colony."

Mooring the *Scorpion* in Naples Harbor had physical risks as well. The surfaced *Scorpion*'s low silhouette made it hard to see, inviting collision with an unwary merchant ship, but there was a solution. For safety's sake, the *Scorpion* would moor near an ungainly craft named the USS *Tallahatchie County*, an "advance aviation base ship" (AVB) that landed personnel and equipment on beaches to establish temporary airfields for submarine-hunting patrol aircraft. The lumbering *Tallahatchie County* and the sleek *Scorpion* would rendezvous on April 10.

Neapolitan Communists would have been apoplectic had they known the truth about the *Tallahatchie County*, which scarcely raised an eyebrow while in the Mediterranean. Secretly stored in the boxy ship were two dozen Mk-34 "Lulu" antisubmarine depth bombs armed with W-34 nuclear warheads—precisely the same fission bomb attached to the *Scorpion*'s brace of Mk-45 torpedoes. The *Tallahatchie County* was actually a nuclear weapons warehouse.

A concern facing the *Tallahatchie County* skipper, Cmdr. Charles M. Walker, and Slattery was that the *Scorpion* posed a serious hazard to the aviation support ship. The *Scorpion*'s rounded pressure hull of blast-resistant, 2-inch-thick steel might puncture the *Tallahatchie County*'s ¼-inch hull of softer steel if rough seas slammed them together, particularly if the low-lying submarine surged beneath the flat hull of the *Tallahatchie County*. To prevent this, Walker's officers and sailors devised a docking plan that involved the use of a camel—a timber pontoon employed as a floating fender—and a garbage barge ballasted enough to keep the two ships separated beneath the waterline. The *Scorpion* would also be secured to the larger ship with a dizzying combination of docking lines.

When the day arrived for its rendezvous with the *Scorpion*, Walker grew worried when the *Scorpion* could not be seen on the horizon. "Then, all of a sudden, he surfaced about 220 yards from us," recalled Walker. Slattery, who spotted the ship using his periscope, decided to surprise the *Tallahatchie County* sailors with a submerged arrival.

Pistols, Pompeii, and Psychiatry

Naples, despite the anti-American nature of some of its citizenry, was not hostile to individual sailors—or their American dollars. Luckily for the sailors, Rome and its endless supply of sights were ninety minutes north by bus. Even closer were the ruins of Pompeii. Mount Vesuvius, which vomited a lethal triumvirate of rock, gas, and ash upon the city in A.D. 79, towered skyward to the south.

While the sailors made their plans, news of a particularly good bargain ashore swept the submarine. What had stirred the sailors was word that the NATO Base Exchange was selling pistols made by the famed Beretta firm at an irresistibly low price. A small sampling of letters sent home reveals the excitement created among the crew about the inexpensive pistols. Livingston, a devout Catholic and a family man, was ecstatic over purchasing two pistols with holsters for sixty dollars.

Tindol wrote his wife, "Friday I'm going to town and buy a pistol, a .22-caliber, 7.5-inch barreled Beretta—somewhat like a Luger. Can't resist it and only $24." Sonar Technician Second Class Michael Henry also fell under the spell of the marvelously crafted Beretta pistols, buying one on April 13 in the company of Tindol.

During the Court of Inquiry, no mention was made of this plethora of firearms brought aboard the *Scorpion* during the first of the submarine's two trips to Naples. Submarine officers who served during the period said sailors were allowed to return to their submarines with a legally purchased firearm. However, all such weapons were secured in the boat's small-arms locker, and it's unlikely the *Scorpion*'s cramped passageways were filled with trigger-happy sailors twirling pistols on their fingers.

Although it seems odd that private firearms would be allowed aboard a submarine where safety was paramount, sailors who could easily endanger a submarine with their technical knowledge would not be metamorphosed into a threat by the mere possession of a firearm. A subsequent review of medical records found no evidence of emotional instability among any member of the *Scorpion*'s crew.

The presence of firearms aside, it remained possible that a sailor or officer might experience the sudden onset of a serious psychiatric problem that had not before reared its head. Such problems can be caused by physically based brain disorders such as schizophrenia or bipolar illness. Even if this were the case, a crew member experiencing a psychotic episode is not necessarily driven to harm others.

The issue of emotional instability on submarines had concerned the navy since World War II. A new flurry of submarine crew studies were conducted during the 1950s and 1960s, when nuclear technologies allowed submarines to remain submerged for months instead of days while carrying city-killing missiles.

A 1967 study conducted by then-navy psychiatrist Aaron R. Satloff and published in the *American Journal of Psychiatry* determined that 3.8 percent of sailors aboard ballistic missile submarines received psychiatric care. Half of those were disqualified from submarine duty either permanently or temporarily, with 8 percent of the patients exhibiting psychotic symptoms.

To eliminate individuals who were psychologically unfit for submarine duty, applicants were given a one-hundred-question psychiatric test known as the Personality Inventory Barometer (PIB), said Satloff. There was one personality question buried inside the questionnaire that—if answered incorrectly—would end a submarine career before it began. If a sailor or officer replied affirmatively to the question "I continually seek excitement" he was shown the door, recalled the psychiatrist. It was not easy to determine how prevalent psychiatric problems were in the submarine service, said Satloff, since it was not uncommon for a sailor's lack of emotional fitness to be passed off as a "lung infection" or some other health problem.

An equally important issue aboard complex, nuclear-powered submarines—and perhaps more threatening than a psychotic sailor—was the hazard posed by a fatigued or demoralized sailor doing tedious, technically demanding work. "It's well known that if morale is poor, or there is a certain kind of tension on a submarine, [that] performance is impacted inversely," explained Satloff.

Discussing psychiatric issues in conjunction with any mishap or disaster is a slippery slope. Those with psychosis are no more likely to be violent or dangerous than "normal" people, although serious mental illness impairs judgment and can lead to a higher rate of suicidal or self-destructive behavior. A curious phenomenon of schizophrenia and bipolar depression is that both tend to appear in males between their late teens and early twenties. Of the ninety-nine men aboard the *Scorpion* when it was lost, sixty-five were younger than twenty-five years old.

Psychiatrists and psychologists were such frequent visitors aboard submarines during the 1950s and 1960s that it provoked intentionally bizarre behavior by irreverent submariners. Even Slattery would have fun with a deadly-serious, note-taking psychologist aboard the *Nautilus* during the early 1960s.

When Slattery noticed the psychologist lurking in the control room, he loudly stated, "I have this random theory . . ." As the intrigued shrink crept closer, like an entomologist approaching an undiscovered insect, Slattery grandly announced: "My random theory is that everything in the world is random and the degree of randomness is random and the unit of randomness is the 'rando.'" The clinician earnestly inquired, "When did you come up with the theory?" "I thought of it as a child," replied Slattery. Oozing with understanding, the psychologist reassured Slattery that "most fruitful thinking does occur in childhood." Slattery's shipmates struggled to keep from laughing: the "theory" was Slattery's well-worn comedy routine.

It's true enough that tempers flared, blows were struck, and threats were made among shipmates on submarines. It's also true that alcohol and drug use among submarine sailors increased during the late 1960s and the 1970s—reflecting similar behavior within American society. However, no evidence has emerged that the loss of the *Scorpion* was precipitated by a suicidal act or the inadequate actions of a demoralized or inebriated sailor.

As the *Scorpion*'s sailors made their way to the base gun store and the remains of Pompeii, the officers visited the home of Lt. William

Richardson of the SUBFLOT 8 staff, who had served on the *Scorpion* from 1962 to 1964. Richardson was enthused about meeting its officers and held a party for Slattery and his wardroom.

Richardson had considerable experience with the *Scorpion* and with submariners. At Naples he was the operational control center officer (OPCON) who kept track of all American and NATO submarines in the Mediterranean, and he sensed no problems as the submarine's officers chatted in his living room. *Scorpion* navigation officer Lt. Cmdr. Daniel Peter Stephens was a Naval Academy classmate of Richardson's. The two later dined together several times in Naples. Even in private, Richardson heard no revelations from his former classmate indicating that the *Scorpion* was a boat headed for trouble.

Collision

After being moored for five days in Naples, the time came for the *Scorpion* to depart for additional antisubmarine exercises. Stormy weather arrived on the night of April 14, and by the following morning, rain and strong winds sweeping the Gulf of Naples created the worst-case scenario dreaded by Slattery and Walker regarding the incompatible shapes of their respective hulls.

As the *Scorpion's* crew worked to release the mooring lines, the wind velocity increased, and green water surged over the low-lying submarine's weather deck. The ballasted garbage barge serving as a protective fender held its position between the ships until the stern of the *Scorpion* was forced toward the *Tallahatchie County*. Pinched between the two ships, one side of the barge tipped up and slammed down atop the *Scorpion's* hull as water surged over the barge's lower gunwale. The flooded barge quickly sank.

With the barge now gone, Slattery was concerned that his submarine might slam unimpeded into the *Tallahatchie County*. Bishop and his deck crew performed an "emergency breakaway" in which the docking lines were rapidly separated by any necessary means. The hectic effort was successful, and the *Scorpion* was soon free of the *Tallahatchie County*, allowing the submarine to distance itself from the larger ship. Much to his relief, Slattery succeeded in keeping his boat from caroming into the thin skin of the *Tallahatchie County*.

Slattery, under orders to report such incidents to SUBFLOT 8, failed to tell of the barge collision. When word of the collision filtered back to

The *Scorpion* departs the *Tallahatchie County* off Naples on April 16, 1968, after rough seas slammed its hull into a garbage barge that sank.

SUBFLOT 8's Dorenkamp, the chief of staff messaged Slattery requesting a description of the event and an assessment of its effect on the *Scorpion's* ability to conduct operations. "We were," an irked Dorenkamp would tell the Court of Inquiry, "forced to query him about it."

Counting the St. Croix incident, this was Slattery's second run-in with a barge in five months and his second failure to advise SUBFLOT 8 about a potentially hazardous incident involving the submarine while in the Mediterranean, with the first being the motor-generator fire in early April. In addition, it appears that Slattery did not report the severe hydraulic leak that appeared soon after the *Scorpion* departed Norfolk in mid-February.

Electrical Fire

Soon after leaving Naples, a near-fatal event occurred during a check of the *Scorpion's* electrical system. During the routine test, an electrical load was placed on a tie bus, a circuit that linked both halves of the boat's alternating-current power plant. The bus was also linked to the boat's aft escape trunk's shore power connection that allowed the submarine to be powered by locally produced electricity. At the time of the test, the *Scorpion* was 200 feet beneath the surface.

When a breaker was closed sending a considerable amount of current through the shore power connection, gauges on the boat fluctuated wildly, indicating there was a massive electrical short. The baffled electrician's mates immediately began tracing the problem and eventually realized the short was in the aft escape trunk, where a leaking valve flooded the trunk. The energized shore power connection had been immersed in conductive seawater.

With the *Scorpion* still submerged, the aft escape trunk was pumped dry and a sailor was sent to investigate, only to be overcome by gases generated by fire and the action of electrolysis on the seawater. The engine room's carbon monoxide level—a by-product of the burning of escape trunk steel by the potent electrical short—rocketed from 0 to 100 parts per million. Carbon monoxide molecules craftily bond with hemoglobin 250 times more efficiently than oxygen, allowing small amounts to sicken or kill.

With the gassing of the sailor, the command was given to bring the boat to the surface for ventilation. As the boat's ventilation blowers were activated, a portable blower was also placed inside the trunk to rapidly dry the shore power connection and clear any remaining gases.

When it was possible to inspect the damage, it was a sobering sight. The massive electrical short burned through heavy steel around the connection. Wrote Slattery: "The . . . connector plug was destroyed and a V-shaped notch about $1^{1}/_{2}$ inches deep and $^{3}/_{4}$ inches wide was burned into the periphery of the escape trunk penetration for the connector."

Although chastised for not immediately reporting the *Scorpion's* collision with the garbage barge, Slattery promptly notified his superiors of the electrical short. He also authored a Safetygram describing the mishap and mailed it to the Submarine Safety Center on April 20. This message was written on a special form to serve as the basis of an alert known as a Safety Note for distribution throughout the submarine force. These alerts had been issued by the Submarine Safety Center since its 1964 establishment in response to the *Thresher* disaster.

Slattery reported that dripping water would have alerted engine room watchstanders to the escape trunk's flooding if a drain valve had been left open as required. Incredibly, the crew *had* turned the wheel of the valve, but not enough to open it. The electrical short was an example of how a small problem can create a hazardous cascade of potentially lethal events, even when everything is done properly.

The *Scorpion* had been lucky. The electrical fire in the aft escape trunk caused only minor damage, and the sailor overcome by gas recovered. This potentially deadly problem had again proven the adage that naval procedures and regulations were written in the blood of sailors.

7

The Final Month

W hen the *Scorpion* departed the stormy Gulf of Naples on April 15, it intended to cover the nine hundred miles to the Turkish port of Izmir for another visit, but this was not to be. The Turkish government—also riven with anti-American sentiment—was unwilling to court controversy by welcoming the fast attack submarine.

Return to Naples

Notified at sea of this decision, the *Scorpion* was faced with a dilemma. Until the April 28 initiation of the *Scorpion's* next mission—an antisubmarine exercise dramatically named Dawn Patrol—the boat was free to rest at anchor if a location in the politically tetchy Mediterranean could be found. The only locale deemed acceptable was Naples, so the *Scorpion* made its way back to Italy's western coast.

The politically scabrous *Scorpion* would again moor far out in the Gulf of Naples, but there would be no *Tallahatchie County* for a mooring point. Despite this drawback, the *Scorpion* could find maintenance assistance in Naples. The boat developed new maintenance problems and needed technical assistance for repairs that could be provided by the Naples-based destroyer tender *Shenandoah*. Of the work requests submitted to the *Shenandoah* by the *Scorpion*, four were classified "confidential" or "secret" and not disclosed during the Court of Inquiry proceedings. None of the classified work requests, however, involved items related to the watertight integrity of the submarine.

The *Shenandoah's* utility boats would also provide liberty boat services to *Scorpion* sailors interested in going ashore, though not all were going to Naples for enjoyment. Among the revelers were *Scorpion* sailors assigned to shore patrol duty. All that differentiated them from their shipmates was a brassard around their bicep stenciled with "SP" and a twenty-four-inch oaken nightstick holstered in a white leather frog. Not surprisingly, sailors who had shore patrol duty one night were sometimes in custody the next.

On April 24, Tindol was assigned to shore patrol duty from 6:00 P.M. until 2:30 A.M. In the company of his shipmates, he strolled through Naples issuing warnings to overly rambunctious sailors and taking into hand those whose behavior had gone too far. He was appalled at the conduct of his fellow sailors. "I now know why some seamen are [always] restricted," wrote Tindol. The way they act on liberty I'm surprised they get liberty at all. Get drunk and raise hell is all they know how to do. We had to run three bunches in last night: one drunk and disorderly, one indecent exposure and one 'conduct unbecoming' USN personnel. In other words: one bunch fighting, another bunch pissing in the street, and one bunch cursing out civilians. All of them just got sent back to their ships. I sure was glad when it was all over and I could go back to the boat."

At least one *Scorpion* sailor was swept up by the shore patrol: during the eight days spent in Naples in the latter part of April, Electronics Technician Third Class Rodney Joseph Kipp was apprehended for over-staying his leave on the Isle of Capri and returned to the *Scorpion*. Lloyd and Slattery restricted the sailor to the boat.

Fouled Propeller: A Final Hull Inspection

Among the *Scorpion*'s mechanical problems needing attention during the second Naples visit was the fouling of the propulsion shaft and propeller that occurred between its original April 15 departure from Naples and its return on April 20. Help would come in the form of divers from the *Shenandoah*. The cause of this problem was hardly a mystery. Italy's waters were a hunting ground for thousands of commercial fishermen. Ships of all types regularly entwined fishing nets and hand lines around their propellers and shafts.

The nervy denizens of the *Shenandoah*'s dive locker were a self-confident group not prone to being awed by cocky submariners. In fact, the divers believed their subsurface chores were on par with those of the "bubbleheads." Said Diver Second Class Robert Sonosky of the *Shenandoah*, "We thought they had the good life; they were surrounded by two inches of steel and got paid more money. All we had between us and the ocean was a Jack Browne [face mask]."

Sonosky remembers the *Scorpion*'s problem as "rope in the stern." While preparing for their assignment, the divers ensured that their sharp, serrated knives for cutting heavy line were at hand. Leading the divers was Boatswain's Mate Chief John Yoest, a tattooed navy veteran whose naval career began in World War II.

After loading their equipment into the *Shenandoah*'s workboat, the divers soon arrived alongside the *Scorpion*, where they warily noted a considerable amount of slippery marine growth atop the submarine's stern. Yoest stepped onto the rounded hull aft of the fairwater and gingerly walked down the *Scorpion*'s slickened spine toward the stern. After momentarily losing his footing on the slimy "grass," he turned to caution his men. At that moment Yoest's feet shot from under him and he tobogganed into the water. When Yoest's fellow divers quit laughing, they donned their diving gear and plunged into the water to learn what was troubling the *Scorpion*'s propeller shaft.

Aside from Yoest's dunking, the work on the *Scorpion* was relatively routine, said diver Ronny Roe, who inspected the propeller. He found hundreds of feet of nylon line and fishing net wrapped tightly around the propeller and shaft. The *Shenandoah*'s official report to the Court of Inquiry stated that 300 feet of line had fouled the shaft, though Roe remembers that most of the entanglement was wrapped around the propeller. Tied to the line was a concrete anchor 16 inches long, 12 inches deep, and 12 inches wide.

Before cutting away the line with their saw-toothed knives, the dive team broke for lunch in the *Scorpion*'s mess room. It was here that Roe took note of a surprisingly negative atmosphere. "They had a guy on board who was a real character. He was wearing a black beret and saying how much he hated the military. 'There's nothing keeping me in this fucking navy,' he said. I actually got the feeling there was an atmosphere [of unhappiness], and a lot of people were complaining." (Roe's memory of the sailor wearing a black beret is revealing; since Electronics Technician John Livingston had purchased a black beret, the item may have been purchased by others.)

After lunch, the ensnarled rope was cut away and the concrete anchor discarded. Roe and his fellow divers conducted a "security swim" around the *Scorpion*'s hull, looking for explosive devices such as magnetically attached limpet mines, a common precaution. Roe found the hull not only in good condition but also free of sabotage. The *Scorpion*'s banishment to the harbor was advantageous for the inspection because a 10-foot-deep layer of dark green pollution existed near the piers. "Out there the water was too clear for us to miss anything," recalled Roe.

This inspection by the rough-and-ready divers of the *Shenandoah* was the fifth time the *Scorpion*'s stern area, propeller, and propulsion shaft had been examined since October 1967. And, once again, no problem was found.

Senior Chief Quartermaster Frank Mazzuchi

When the diving assignment on the *Scorpion* was made, *Shenandoah* diver Sonosky was somewhat familiar with the submarine because he knew Frank "Patsy" Mazzuchi, the *Scorpion*'s good-natured and much-respected senior chief quartermaster. Both Sonosky and Mazzuchi had homes near Norfolk and shared mutual friends.

Born in Ceprano, Italy, the two-year-old Mazzuchi arrived in Lackawanna, New York, with his mother in 1927 after his father, Tomasso Mazzuchi, had arrived the year before to find work. Immediately after the Japanese attack on Pearl Harbor, the sixteen-year-old Mazzuchi burned with desire to join the navy. Mazzuchi could join at seventeen but only if he obtained parental permission, something his protective father refused to give.

Tomasso Mazzuchi's poor English would be the son's ticket into the navy. Soon after his seventeenth birthday in November 1942, Mazzuchi arranged with navy recruiters to have the parental permission papers awaiting his father's signature. With every Italian word a lie, Mazzuchi delivered a grave warning to his father that the government needed his signature on immigration papers. Tomasso Mazzuchi, surrounded by uniformed recruiters, unknowingly delivered his son to the gentle hands of the U.S. Navy.

The Mazzuchi home was filled with grief at this subterfuge, but Frank Mazzuchi was overjoyed. Skipping his last semester of high school to attend recruit training, Mazzuchi was assigned to Motor Torpedo Boat Squadron 21 in the Pacific. By war's end, Mazzuchi had made thirty-eight PT boat patrols. His squadron was later awarded a Presidential Unit Citation. After World War II, Mazzuchi volunteered for submarine duty.

By 1968, Mazzuchi was anticipating his retirement from the navy after twenty-five years and knew he might never again see Italy. He made

The *Scorpion's* chief quartermaster, Frank Mazzuchi, center front, was a
superb navigator and a veteran of harrowing World War II torpedo boat
action.

a point of visiting Ceprano, the city of his birth, and toured Rome during the *Scorpion's* visits to Naples. While ashore, Mazzuchi realized his
Italian had withered. "Boy—is my Italian rusty—it's coming back but it
sure has left me," he wrote. "I really need some practice."

Torpedo Room Polka

When the USO in Naples offered to send a variety show to the *Scorpion*
exiled in the Gulf of Naples, Slattery accepted. In spite of the nervous
Italian government's insistence that the submarine moor far from Naples's
harbor, there was no restriction against Neapolitans visiting the warship.

What resulted was a party that was as much fun as it was crowded. It would take place the evening before the *Scorpion*'s second and final departure from Naples, on April 28. The crew was initially told the visitors would include a small number of female dancers and a few musicians. Once aboard, the troupe would entertain the crew before being treated to a formal dinner. The *Scorpion* was carefully cleaned, and every available table was set with a white tablecloth and candles.

On the evening of April 27, the crew put on their dress blue uniforms and eagerly awaited their visitors. What arrived in one of the *Shenandoah*'s flat-bottomed landing craft were twenty female dancers and a five-piece band, including an extremely short accordion player. This assemblage overwhelmed the confines of the *Scorpion*. The crew, however, managed to cram the guests and their musical instruments inside the pressure hull.

"Yesterday we pulled a first in the annals of the submarine service," Fireman Phillip Seifert wrote his mother in Madison, Ohio. "The Captain invited the USO director in Naples to come out to the boat for a visit. Well, I guess he didn't realize how small a submarine really is because he came out and brought 20 beautiful Italian girls and a band with him. Well, you can imagine what a shock that is . . . somehow we got them all below and had a big party. We had girls in the torpedo room—as in the picture—girls in the crews mess, girls in the galley; anywhere we could find room we stuck one . . . we had girls everywhere.

"Then it happened . . . the band got in the middle of the [torpedo] room and started playing polkas. Did you ever try to polka in a sardine can? What a riot. But we had one heck of a good time." Seifert then described a photograph of the scene he enclosed in his letter: "The picture was taken in the torp room. The little guy in the middle is playing the accordion. The kid that's facing this way is from Conneaut, Ohio. I didn't get in the picture. I was to the left of the camera."

Flanked by twenty-three torpedoes—including two with nuclear warheads—the diminutive accordion player was near the torpedo tube breech doors. With her back to the camera, a young Italian woman watched the party. Turning to face the camera with a gleeful look was John Livingston, the "kid" from Conneaut, Ohio. His smile was marked by a slight imperfection, the result of his younger brother Erich chipping a front tooth with a thrown shoe years before. In 1968 Erich and another brother, George, were sailors as well, serving aboard surface ships during the *Scorpion*'s final voyage.

As an Italian USO band plays in the torpedo room during a party in the Gulf of Naples, Electronics Technician John Livingston smiles back into the camera.

The *Scorpion*'s youthful sailors were giddy at having so many beautiful women squeezed into their tiny world. As the honking strains of accordion music filled the torpedo room, the sailors and their visitors danced away the evening.

As the party continued, so did the running of the liberty boat provided by the *Shenandoah* as sailors continued to come and go on liberty. *Shenandoah* Boatswain's Mate Robert Flor piloted his utility boat to the *Scorpion* while the party was in full swing. When he arrived he learned the submarine was filled with "twenty-five women and five or six musicians." As he waited for passengers, Flor was invited aboard by friendly *Scorpion* sailors. Once inside, he saw the white tablecloths and the candles. During his half-hour visit, wave action clanged his utility boat against the *Scorpion's* hull. Flor worried unnecessarily for decades that his thin-hulled craft had somehow damaged the *Scorpion.*

After dinner, the music gave way to the hubbub of farewells. The sailors then helped their guests into a bobbing liberty launch for the return to Naples.

Less than two months later, the Court of Inquiry in Norfolk wondered if the *Scorpion's* loss could be attributed to sabotage. The court eventually determined that the twenty-three-day interval between the *Scorpion's* departure from Naples and its sinking argued against sabotage. It was believed an explosive device such as a limpet mine would have detonated or been discovered long before the submarine's loss on May 22.

Navy investigators would interview divers and others aboard the *Shenandoah* who interacted with the *Scorpion's* crew during its April 20–28 stay in the Gulf of Naples. Despite these interviews, the court did not seem aware of the security swim that would have revealed the presence of a limpet mine magnetically attached to the hull. "Everybody on the ship got questioned," recalled Sonosky. "They asked: 'What did you do, what did you see?' They wanted to know if they [the *Scorpion's* crew] wanted oil and what kind of oil they drew." The questions about oil usage revealed the Court of Inquiry board's curiosity about the *Scorpion's* need to draw an excessive amount of lubricant/hydraulic oil during its Mediterranean deployment.

It also appears that the Court of Inquiry was unaware of the April 27 visit to the boat by the roughly two dozen Italian entertainers twenty-five days before the *Scorpion* foundered. Neither Elrod nor Underwood mentioned it in the declassified portions of their testimony, and it is not included in the "Findings of Fact" released by the court. In any case, a saboteur jammed shoulder-to-shoulder with sailors aboard a submarine would have little opportunity to commit sabotage.

Since the submarine returned to Naples somewhat unexpectedly, it made it less probable that a sabotage operation could be concocted and executed on such short notice. Even America's implacable foe of the period, the Soviet Union, might see more risk than gain in such a plot. It was only natural for grieving and angry relatives of the *Scorpion's* crew to later suspect foul play as a reason behind the mysterious foundering of the boat. Pearl Seifert, whose son told of the visit by the Italian entertainers, long wondered if a saboteur had been among them.

The possibility of sabotage, like so much guesswork about what destroyed the *Scorpion*, can't be proven or disproven. It seems preposterous that the *Scorpion* was destroyed by a lively group of entertainers armed with nothing more dangerous than an accordion and a brass section.

Dawn Patrol and OUTCHOP

On Sunday morning April 28, the day after the party, the *Scorpion* put to sea for its last Mediterranean exercise. The Dawn Patrol operations would take place for twelve days near the island of Crete, where the *Scorpion* would serve as prey for antisubmarine forces of the Sixth Fleet and those of NATO allies.

After departing Naples, the submarine veered south through the Strait of Messina before setting a course for the eastern Mediterranean and the Aegean Sea. At the outset of the exercises, the *Scorpion* submerged and remained so for the entire exercise. When the exercise ended at noon on May 10, the *Scorpion* was positioned near Crete, nearly 1,800 miles east of the Strait of Gibraltar. The submarine had performed well. "We have been extremely successful in our endeavors and it will certainly mean many 'kudos' for the Skipper when this exercise is evaluated," wrote Leo Weinbeck.

Even the somewhat jaded sailor Tindol found the performance of his skipper and the other officers impressive. "We've done real well on this last operation," said Tindol on May 10. "[We] sank 12 ships and [have] not gotten caught once. How about that? The khakis are getting better. Some day they might even get good enough to keep from getting killed in the first 10 seconds at war—if this thing ever went to war." These observations indicated Slattery was getting the knack of undersea warfare tactics, a shortcoming for which he had been previously counseled by his superiors.

Not all the *Scorpion's* encounters with warships during Dawn Patrol were congenial. The Soviets, who had bolstered their naval presence in the Mediterranean during the previous twelve months, located the *Scorpion* and harassed the submarine for some time. A letter written by Torpedoman's Mate Third Class Robert Violetti claimed the submarine was shadowed by a Soviet destroyer for two days near Crete. At one point the *Scorpion* surfaced only a hundred feet from the Soviet destroyer. "I can't say much about this incident other than United States fighters [aircraft] came to our aid," wrote Violetti to his mother in Broomall, Pennsylvania. "It took us two days to get rid of that big tin can." The Soviet warship then kept pace with the surfaced *Scorpion* "with every gun trained" on the moving submarine, according to Violetti's account. His mother, Luella, was greatly distressed by her son's letter, lifted by helicopter May 10 from the *Scorpion* as it prepared to depart Cretan waters.

Weinbeck also may have referred to the *Scorpion*'s attempt to elude Soviet antisubmarine surface ships in the crystalline waters of the Aegean Sea when he wrote on May 9, "Here we are just off the island of Crete playing games with the bad boys."

It was a common practice for Soviet spy trawlers or warships to move dangerously close to American submarines to obtain photographs or electronic intelligence. Soviet vessels would also drive straight toward American warships in a dangerous game of chicken. The latter practice infuriated American naval officers and endangered the crews of both ships. The results of these confrontations could be collisions, or more frequently, an exchange of angry messages. The game eventually became so dangerous that both sides sought to reduce these confrontations with the 1972 Incidents at Sea Agreement. Whatever the full details of the *Scorpion*'s encounter, the submarine departed the waters near Crete without damage.

On May 10 a message was received by the *Scorpion* giving it authorization to move west, toward the Strait of Gibraltar. This order was welcome, since it heralded the start of their journey home. It also contained instructions ordering the *Scorpion* to serve as a target along the way for antisubmarine forces. The order to head west meant the crew was a step closer to the CHOP, or "change in operational control," which would return them to SUBLANT's authority.

Little is known of the *Scorpion*'s activities during the 1,800-mile voyage between Crete and the Strait of Gibraltar. When the submarine passed through the Strait of Gibraltar on the night of May 16, it had spent six days on that journey.

Things were now looking up for the *Scorpion* crew. Once the boat dashed into the Atlantic, it would place itself on a route known to navigators as a "great circle track" because of the curved appearance of the course when drawn on a flat Mercator projection. As the submarine glided past Gibraltar, the talk among the crew was that the *Scorpion* was only a week away from Norfolk, a rumor that was off by four days.

Unexpected tragedy and a secret mission would intervene to slow the *Scorpion*'s return to Norfolk. Instead of returning May 23, the *Scorpion*'s return to Norfolk would be reset for May 27.

Emergency Leave

As the *Scorpion* churned across the Mediterranean toward the Strait of Gibraltar, Interior Communications Electrician Joseph Underwood began coughing up blood. For days the problem had worried Chief Hospital Corpsman Lynn Thompson Saville, who was unable to diagnose the problem.

Underwood's health presented a dilemma to Slattery because Underwood's symptoms were consistent with tuberculosis or some other dangerously contagious respiratory infection, which posed a medical risk to all 101 men remaining aboard.

Slattery also knew that releasing Underwood would require a detour to the nearest warship or naval base. As Slattery and Lloyd considered their dilemma, the arrival of messages from SUBLANT at 7:47 P.M. GMT on May 16 settled the matter: the wife of Sonar Technician Bill Elrod had given birth prematurely, and the infant had not survived.

It was the worst news a sailor could receive 3,000 miles from home. Slattery wasted no time approving the transfer of both Elrod and Underwood. (Faced with the necessity of releasing Elrod from the *Scorpion*, it made sense that Underwood should go as well.) Slattery understood Elrod's situation, since Slattery and his wife, Dorothy, had experienced the death of an infant son eight years before. The word went out to a subdued crew to write what would be their final letters home, since a mailbag would be taken off along with the two departing sailors.

Weinbeck hurriedly penned a few lines before the *Scorpion* met the tug. Like Slattery and Elrod, Weinbeck had experienced the deaths of children. "Just got word we'll be meeting a tug boat off the cost of Spain to transfer two of our men—one for emergency leave and one for medical reasons," wrote Weinbeck. "The fellow going on emergency leave is flying back to Norfolk—his premature baby boy died today. Feel kinda sorry for him. Told him of our two children buried in Arlington and he seemed to brace up somewhat knowing that things like this have happened to other people. As of midnight tonight we were to leave the Mediterranean and head for the barn. Sure will be nice to be back in the good ol' USA."

Tindol, whose detailed letters home were something of a diary, provided a similar description of the solemn evening: "This letter comes as a result of Bill Elrod's baby dying this morning. We're just through the Straits of Gibraltar. A tug will meet us at 12:30 and Elrod will transfer to it, go to Rota and catch a flight to the states. Underwood—you met his wife—is going for TB tests."

Shortly after midnight, just outside the breakwater of Rota's harbor, the *Scorpion* broached into the night air. The fairwater's hatch was undogged and the bridge watch clambered up the dripping trunk as sailors extended and locked the port and starboard running lights. A navy harbor tug drew closer as the throb of its deep-throated, 2,000-horsepower engine vibrated in the darkness.

As the tug pressed its gracefully swept gunwale against the *Scorpion's* hull, the two departing submarine sailors stepped aboard. A sack containing hurriedly written letters and seven official messages were passed to the tug. Had tragedy not intervened, the last letters from the *Scorpion* would have been those lifted by helicopter from the submarine six days before.

Sturgill, a sailor who missed American hamburgers and worried about his soldier-brother going to Vietnam, barely got his letter in the mail sack before it was hauled up on deck. His final note, dated May 17 instead of May 16—possibly because he finished it near midnight—mentions the transfer of Elrod but not of Underwood. Homesick and convinced the *Scorpion* would dock in Norfolk on May 24, Sturgill vowed to his family: "I'll see you by the 25th at the latest."

The tug, with its cargo of two subdued *Scorpion* sailors, a sack of mail, and a sheaf of official messages, chugged toward the lights of Rota. In its wake lay a submarine whose crew now numbered ninety-nine.

As the tug moved away, the submariners unlocked and stowed the *Scorpion's* running fairwater lights, slammed the boat's vaultlike fairwater doors that led to the deck and the fairwater planes, and sealed the watertight hatch leading to the fairwater trunk. The ballast tank vents were cracked just enough to allow the submarine to settle only slightly beneath the surface. The dive was halted at periscope depth, where a "rough trim" was obtained by delicately adding and removing water from trim tanks along the keel. The *Scorpion* then dove a bit deeper as the trim was checked and adjusted. Once the officer of the deck and the diving officer of the watch were satisfied that the boat was balanced, the submarine dove to the depth it intended to use and accelerated toward its final mission.

By this time, the sailors were aware that their hopes of returning to Norfolk by May 24 were misplaced. The *Scorpion* had been given a secret reconnaissance mission that would delay their arrival until May 27. All aboard believed their arrival home was now only ten days away.

Secret Mission

Before leaving the Mediterranean, the *Scorpion* was assigned one last mission during its return to Norfolk. It was not a terribly mysterious mission, nor would it be particularly dangerous, aside from the ordinary hazards of operating a 251-foot ship under water. The *Scorpion* was to observe an operation designed to solve fundamental problems plaguing Soviet naval forces. Geography, and the USSR's status as an international pariah, had worked against the Soviet Navy extending its reach. Its fleets were widely separated and seldom granted basing privileges by other countries. America, on the other hand, had a plethora of allies around the world who were deeply distrustful of the Soviets and eager to provide bases to the U.S. Navy. In case of war, Soviet ships would have to make a suicidal dash through nautical choke points under constant surveillance.

To counter this detection problem and compensate for being denied access to foreign harbors, the Soviets began experiments in which a flotilla of support vessels would provide a midocean base in the Atlantic for warships. This concept could conceivably extend Soviet naval capability across the globe, free its ships from geographic confines, and keep it from being enslaved by the wintertime ice that plagued its northern ports. Open-ocean maintenance was fraught with hazards, including dangerously rough weather, but the U.S. Navy wanted to learn if the Soviets had found a way to make it work.

Also operating in the region was a Soviet flotilla conducting "hydroacoustic operations" that included two hydrographic survey ships, a submarine rescue ship, and a submarine. Of the craft in the flotilla, one of obvious interest to SUBLANT, was a Soviet guided missile submarine carrying the NATO designation Echo II. Introduced in 1962, the Echo II was armed with eight nuclear-tipped surface-to-surface cruise missiles. These weapons, with a range of 300 nautical miles, had been given the NATO code name Shaddock. The submarine was also armed with antishipping and antisubmarine torpedoes.

Slower and noisier than the *Scorpion*, the Echo II boat would most likely be outclassed by the *Scorpion* in an undersea showdown. (Although many have speculated that an undersea duel resulted in the destruction of the *Scorpion*, U.S. Navy antisubmarine forces reported that no Soviet ships were within 200 miles of the *Scorpion* at the time of its loss.)

Though the *Scorpion* was initially directed toward Spain's Canary Islands, off the northwestern coast of Africa, to observe the Soviet maintenance operations, the attack submarine was operating in the vicinity of the Azores, 900 miles west of Portugal, by May 21. Also operating in the area around the Azores and the Canaries were patrol planes and surface units of the navy's Anti-Submarine Warfare Force, Atlantic Fleet (ASW-FORLANT). These forces were participating in operations known as Bravo 20 and were also conducting surveillance of Soviet naval activities.

This surveillance operation by ASWFORLANT is shrouded in mystery. The Soviets, in an apparent effort to conceal their activities near the Azores, conducted their operations only at night. This forced ASWFORLANT to cancel its daytime aircraft surveillance and operate in darkness with P-3 Orion aircraft flying out of Lajes, on the Azores island of Terceira.

"Whatever they [the Soviets] were doing they would not do in the daylight, but rather at night, and we wished to detect this," ASWFORLANT operations officer Deming W. Smith later told the Court of Inquiry. The *Scorpion's* path of return to Norfolk curved through the very area placed under tight scrutiny by ASWFORLANT's patrol aircraft. Despite the *Scorpion's* proximity to the Bravo 20 operations, it was never detected by aircraft-dropped sonobuoys or destroyers. Smith surmised that the *Scorpion* avoided detection by departing the area at a cautiously slow speed to minimize its sound signature.

Smith also dashed speculation that the *Scorpion* was subjected to enemy attack by professing that ASWFORLANT patrols could guarantee a 100 percent probability of detecting an enemy missile launch between May 16 and May 27 in the area of the Bravo 20 operations. This was a curious statement, since the Soviet Navy would not introduce a rocket-propelled, antisubmarine homing torpedo known as the SS-N-14 Silex until 1969, the year after the *Scorpion's* loss.

It's interesting to note that Smith made it clear that the area under surveillance by ASWFORLANT included a portion of the *Scorpion's* intended route. The dates of the surveillance missions also coincide with the *Scorpion's* own mission, raising the question of whether ASWFORLANT and the *Scorpion* were pursuing the same prey. In any case, ASWFORLANT was not informed that the *Scorpion* was near the Azores until the attack submarine was reported overdue on May 27.

Radio Silence

That ASWFORLANT was not notified of the *Scorpion's* presence is hardly surprising. SUBLANT sought to keep the *Scorpion's* whereabouts absolutely secret. For this reason, on May 16 the submarine was placed under

SUBLANT's Operational Order 2-67, which required it to exercise strict radio silence. While a coded message transmitted by the *Scorpion* might not be susceptible to decoding, the radio signal could reveal a submarine's location, and the extension of an antenna created a risk of visual or radar detection. Due to Operational Order 2-67, the *Scorpion* would transmit only a single message between May 17 and its disappearance.

By 11:00 P.M. on May 21, the *Scorpion*'s secret operation had been completed. In the darkness just west of the Azores, the boat rose to periscope depth in a calm sea beneath partly cloudy skies. After listening for sonar returns and making a radar and periscope sweep to ensure that its fairwater would not be struck by an approaching ship, the submarine slowed to roughly seven knots, raised an antenna, and attempted to contact the Naval Communication Station in Rota. By the time the *Scorpion* began transmitting, it was after midnight on May 22.

The *Scorpion* intended for Rota's communications station to relay its messages to SUBLANT and was calling specifically for the station in Spain. After an hour of unsuccessfully trying to reach Rota, the Naval Communications Station in Nea Makri, Greece—2,000 miles to the east—intercepted the signal and offered to relay the messages to Rota, which would forward them to SUBLANT.

At first Nea Makri heard a ship transmitting in code under the sign "NJ," a generic call sign that could be used by any NATO warship. (The *Scorpion*'s voice call sign was "Brandywine.") Only when a communications link was firmly established, at 1:02 A.M. GMT on May 22, did the station in Nea Makri learn it was in contact with the *Scorpion*. The submarine then flashed a coded signal that meant "I have one immediate message." At 1:05 A.M. GMT, communications were abruptly lost. The radioman in Greece began trying to restore communications and managed to do so at 1:31 A.M. Once the Nea Makri station was again in contact with the *Scorpion*, the radioman in Greece warned, "I'm being interfered with extremely." (This problem was caused by either atmospherics or signal interference from another ship on the same frequency.)

This began a two-hour communications session—a period considered "unusually long"—as the submarine transmitted a considerable number of messages. By 3:03 A.M. GMT, the *Scorpion* had finished transmitting. The messages sent by the *Scorpion* did not reveal any mechanical difficulties, nor did they indicate problems with pursuing or harassing Soviet warships. Among the messages sent by *Scorpion* to SUBLANT was its position as of one minute past midnight GMT on May 22. Adding the hour it spent unsuccessfully trying to reach Rota, the *Scorpion* was near the surface and transmitting for a total of 3½ hours.

Although a submarine ordinarily establishes its own movement plan, SUBLANT selected the *Scorpion's* return route. Following it assiduously would return the *Scorpion* to Norfolk at 1:00 P.M. on May 27. Both Greene at Submarine Division 62 and Clarke at Submarine Squadron 6 were informed of this. The arrival date, however, would not be released to family members until May 24. Instead of traveling willy-nilly across empty stretches of ocean, warships adhere to strict movement plans as closely as possible. Doing so provides a simple but effective means of predicting a warship's approximate location without exchanging radio messages.

The Court of Inquiry board speculated if the *Scorpion* increased its speed to compensate for slowing during the 3½-hour radio transmission. During the communications process the *Scorpion* was probably traveling no faster than 7 knots, or less than half its normal transit speed of 18 knots. This meant the *Scorpion* would have fallen two hours behind schedule. The board members knew the boat faced increased hazards at higher speeds if it accelerated to make up for lost time. Should a stern plane failure throw the submarine into a sudden dive, higher speed allowed the crew less recovery time before reaching the hull's collapse depth.

Although increased speed would have heightened the hazards faced by the *Scorpion* in case of a control malfunction, it appears the submarine may have been traveling no faster than 18 knots at the time it was lost. Only twelve hours of travel at 21.5 knots—a relatively minor speed increase—would have allowed the *Scorpion* to make up for time lost during the lengthy radio transmission. Since the *Scorpion* sank roughly thirteen hours after it communicated with Greece, it may have already compensated for lost time.

However, if after its last message the *Scorpion* slowed to check its charts or conduct repairs (actions the submarine did take while crossing the Atlantic in late February), it may have been forced to travel at a higher rate of speed to make up for lost time. In any case, it was important that the *Scorpion* arrive in Norfolk no later than May 27, since the boat needed a number of minor repairs. One reason for the rush was the last-minute surveillance mission assigned to the *Scorpion* that delayed its original arrival in Norfolk by two full days.

Despite the *Scorpion* operating under an ironclad admonition against transmitting messages, it was still expected to extend an antenna to passively receive daily broadcasts. Even though it was barred from transmitting, messages were sent to the *Scorpion*. SUBDIV 62's Greene transmitted two messages requesting replies from Slattery after May 22 on the off-chance that the *Scorpion* was no longer practicing radio silence. When no reply was received, Greene correctly assumed that the *Scorpion* remained under radio silence. Neither Greene nor his staff had any reason to sound an alarm over the *Scorpion*'s silence, even though the submarine and its crew were already lost.

"I was not concerned for the safety of the ship for the reason that neither myself nor COMSUBRON 6 had been informed that the ship had been taken off COMSUBLANT OPORDER 2-67, which prohibits her transmitting," Greene later testified. "There was confusion in our mind as to whether she was able to transmit or not. When I did not receive the replies to those messages I made the assumption that she considered that she was not able to transmit under the provisions of COMSUBLANT OPORDER 2-67."

SUBLANT's boss, Vice Admiral Arnold F. Schade, also testified that his command did not expect to hear from the *Scorpion* following its receipt of the submarine's May 22 transmission that included its position report.

One newspaper report has claimed that Schade ordered a hush-hush search for the *Scorpion* on May 24, two days after the submarine was lost and three days before its failure to arrive prompted the largest search in U.S. Navy history. In reality, neither Schade nor his staff had reason to assume the *Scorpion* had been lost. As the first witness before the Court of Inquiry on June 5, 1968, Schade told the court: "I might point out that submarines operating under special order, once they give their departure report—their course and speed and indicate their arrival report . . . we do not expect to hear from them."

So it was that on May 27, 1968, dozens of wives, children, and girlfriends would wait in the rain for a submarine and ninety-nine men who would never arrive.

8

Waiting in the Rain

In the predawn hours of May 27, the Norfolk area was savaged by a
wild storm. Shingle-peeling winds gusted to 52 miles per hour, carrying away awnings and toppling trees. Massive vertical winds known as
downbursts fell like giant pistons to flatten crops. The scene flickered in
spasms as jagged veins of lightning zigzagged across the sky.

As the feeble, gray dawn arrived, it was apparent the storm had lost
none of its strength and showed no signs of weakening. The storm had
fomented the sheltered waters of Hampton Roads into whitecap-tipped
waves. It was a poor day to be at sea off the Virginia Capes. On the day of
the *Scorpion's* expected arrival, an oil tanker lost steerage and was shoved
hard aground off Virginia Beach.

Experienced submariners knew the storm would be merciless on the
Scorpion as it made its way into Hampton Roads on the surface. The submarine could endure rough weather when surfaced, but not easily. Lacking a V-shaped hull like a surface ship or older, diesel-electric boats, the
rounded, teardrop hull of the *Scorpion* rolled like a branchless log in rough
weather. On the surface, even in moderate seas, the *Scorpion* was a 251-foot
carnival ride, capable of making the most experienced sailors wretchedly
seasick. While some within SUBLANT thought Slattery might radio in
to delay his arrival due to the weather, no such call was received. With
the *Scorpion* operating under orders to maintain radio silence, no news
was taken as good news.

Despite the ungodly weather, Allie Brueggeman, like dozens of other
wives, dressed her children and huddled them into cars for the drive to
the Destroyer & Submarine Piers to wait for the *Scorpion*. Fog accompanied the storm, and the gusting winds drove the rain horizontally, ob-
scuring any chance of spotting the *Scorpion* at a great distance. Although
some officers consider families at the piers to be a dangerous nuisance,

turning out to greet their sailors was an age-old tradition. The wives and children, after all, had contributed their loved ones. The navy had provided only the submarine.

Mazzuchi's wife, Geneva, arrived with their three daughters and son. Knowing how proud her husband was of their son, Tommy, and his achievements in the Boy Scouts, Geneva Mazzuchi made sure he was wearing the crisp new Boy Scout uniform he had earned by being the top fund-raiser for his troop.

Another wife waiting with her was Lois Saville, whose husband was Chief Hospital Corpsman Lynn Saville. The couple's two daughters and son were attired in new clothes she made for the occasion. Of those awaiting their husbands, Lois Saville may have been the most appreciative of her spouse.

Lois Saville was the daughter of a violent, alcoholic father and a victimized mother, and her childhood was one of chaos and brutality. She watched as her drunken father flung her pregnant mother into a doorknob, inflicting mental retardation upon an unborn brother. Child welfare workers eventually took Lois from her parents and shuttled her among fourteen different foster homes until she took a job and left foster care at seventeen.

While living in Washington, D.C., during the late 1950s, she met Lynn Saville, a navy corpsman stationed at Bethesda Naval Hospital. Marriage followed, and the couple began the nomadic life of a sailor's family. After his duty at Bethesda, Lynn Saville served on a succession of surface ships before volunteering for submarine duty in 1965. He reported to the Scorpion in September 1967. Lois Saville did not worry about her husband returning to her and their children from the Mediterranean simply because she could not imagine her life without him.

Other family members, distant from the sprawling naval station, awaited the return of a family member aboard the Scorpion as well. One was Danish immigrant Axel Christiansen, who was uncharacteristically anxious about the safe return of his son, Machinist's Mate Mark Christiansen, a married sailor with a son and daughter. The source of the elder Christiansen's unease was a haunting dream he had May 22, the date of the Scorpion's last radio transmission. In the phantasm Christiansen's twenty-six-year-old son paused at a fence while trudging away in a snowy field. Before disappearing into the sterile landscape, Mark Christiansen solemnly turned to his father to issue a single instruction: "Take care of my children."

Top left: machinist's mate John Houge. Middle row from left: machinist's mates Robert Smith, Robert Chandler, James Wells, and Mark Christiansen. The figures on the right and the lower left are unidentified.

For some families, waiting for the return of a submarine was a familiar routine. The eldest sailor aboard the *Scorpion* was Steward First Class Joseph Cross—the lone African American on the boat. The *Scorpion* was the eleventh submarine and the third fast attack boat Cross had called home. As they had many times before, his wife, Anna, and a young son awaited his return.

Cross's World War II exploits were the only ones that could rival those of Mazzuchi, the former PT boat crewman. As a young man, the Louisianian had endured eight harrowing Pacific war patrols, and for his valor was awarded a Bronze Star with a "V," indicating the decoration was earned under fire. (It is said that while serving on the submarine *Halibut*, the sharp-eyed Cross spied a Japanese warplane in time for the surfaced submarine to dive to safety.) The steward reported to the *Scorpion* in July 1967 at age forty-six.

In the days before the *Scorpion*'s anticipated arrival, Ruthann Hogeland returned to Norfolk with her young son and her newborn daughter to welcome her own husband, Electronics Technician Richard Hogeland.

According to his wishes, Ruthann would wear a brightly colored dress so he could more easily spot her on the crowded pier. The couple had last seen each other in January, when her husband received emergency leave for the birth of his daughter.

Like many of the wives eager to show off growing children and to get reacquainted with their husbands, Allie Brueggeman went shopping for new clothes for her children. She wanted her twin sons and daughter to look their best for her twenty-five-year-old husband, Machinist's Mate James Kenneth Brueggeman. A favorite clothing item bought for toddler sons of *Scorpion* crew members was a sailor's outfit.

Of the wives who were waiting at the pier, one that was never comfortable being part of the navy "family" was Beth Houge, the spouse of Machinist's Mate John Richard Houge. The couple considered navy life so stratified that they believed it reduced the enlisted personnel and their families to second-class citizens. In spite of her disenchantment with the navy, she was still a navy wife eager for the return of her sailor. When the *Scorpion* arrived, she, too, would be at Pier 22 to greet her husband.

Submarine Missing

The unrelenting storm made noon as dim as dusk, and the absence of shadows in the dim light gave the impression that time was standing still. As 1:00 P.M. approached—the expected time of the *Scorpion*'s arrival—the submarine had yet to come into view.

Even before its arrival time, SUBLANT officers were puzzling over why they had not received a call from the *Scorpion* to request docking assistance in the form of a tugboat. Even more worrisome was why the *Scorpion* had not radioed to warn SUBLANT of its tardiness, since Slattery knew women and children would be waiting in the atrocious weather. The worried officers knew that even if the *Scorpion*'s only problem was with its radio communications, the submarine should have arrived on time.

COMSUBLANT Schade departed Norfolk days before the *Scorpion*'s anticipated arrival to observe operations aboard the recently commissioned fast attack submarine *Pargo*, then operating out of New London. Had he been given the slightest hint that the *Scorpion* was in trouble, Schade would have undoubtedly remained in Norfolk to oversee any necessary rescue operations. His presence on the *Pargo*, however, hardly meant he was incommunicado. The submarine could easily communicate with SUBLANT's headquarters in Norfolk, which would soon have reason to transmit an urgent message to Schade.

As 1:00 P.M. passed, a terrible realization sank in among the SUBLANT staff. Some recall officers being thrown into a momentary shock as they realized that the *Scorpion* might be in trouble. It was time to notify Schade, who had the authority to proclaim a "Submarine Missing" or "SUBMISS" alert. Schade immediately initiated a search for the *Scorpion*, but he did not instantly declare an "EVENT SUBMISS," as the alert was known in navyspeak. This alert notifies rescuers to rush to the last known position of a missing submarine. This reticence may have been because the last position report transmitted by the submarine was—by May 27—five days old and most likely useless.

As he issued directives, Schade ordered the *Pargo* south at flank speed toward the Virginia Capes. The initial search would be just east of Norfolk, where the shallow continental shelf might halt the descent of a stricken *Scorpion* before it reached crush depth. Patrol aircraft would scour the *Scorpion*'s projected path farther out at sea. All knew that if the *Scorpion* sank far from shore, where the shallow continental shelf fell away to the deep ocean, there was no hope for its crew. Schade noted ruefully that the coming search efforts would have to contend with the atrocious weather that meteorologists indicated would persist for days.

At 1:15 P.M., COMASWFORLANT was ordered by Schade to launch two search flights along the *Scorpion*'s path of intended movement. It was hoped by all that the submarine, unable to communicate but otherwise intact, was stranded on the surface. Flight plans were hurriedly prepared, and maritime patrol aircraft were fueled and given preflight checks. The first aircraft lifted off from Bermuda and climbed into the sky at 5:13 P.M. Norfolk time. The second roared into the still-forbidding sky from Norfolk Naval Air Station thirty-two minutes later.

The navy's submarine-hunting patrol aircraft of the period were the relatively new P-3 Orion, powered by turboprop engines, and older P-2V-7 Neptune, a World War II–era design with an odd combination of propeller engines and jet engines. Both could loiter for nearly twelve hours while their crews used radar, sonar, eyesight, and magnetic anomaly detectors to hunt for submarines.

The effort would commence off the Virginia Capes, a broad area east of the entrance to Chesapeake Bay bracketed by the headlands of Cape

Charles to the north and Cape Henry to the south. A call also went out for submarine rescue ships, whose rescue chambers might mean the difference between life and death for a crew trapped in their submarine on a shallow section of seafloor.

A submariner based at New London noted a goodly number of submarines tied to the piers on the morning of May 27. By the following morning, nearly every pier in New London was empty as every available ship was looking for the *Scorpion*.

As Schade and the *Pargo* raced to a location designated Point Alpha—where ships and submarines were gathering for the search—the decision was made at 2:15 P.M. to officially declare an "EVENT SUBMISS."

The question as to why EVENT SUBMISS was issued one hour after it was realized the *Scorpion* was overdue has never been fully answered, though it probably had much to do with the fact that Schade was initiating the search while hoping the *Scorpion* might appear.

A Lack of Candor

As the search for the missing submarine lurched to life, nearly a hundred wives, children, and girlfriends continued their sodden vigil, oblivious to the navy's growing concern over the submarine's fate. A vague announcement was made stating that the submarine had been "delayed" and that everyone should go home. Although it might be stretched to qualify as a half-truth, it was mostly a lie, and it would not sit well with the families in the years to come.

The navy's lack of candor and its perceived insensitivity in dealing with the families generated long-lasting bitterness among many wives. Just hours after being told of a "delay," the wives would be enraged to learn that the news media, tipped off regarding the true concerns of SUBLANT, had been preparing stories on the *Scorpion's* disappearance while the wives waited, uninformed, in a driving rain. Some wives felt as if the navy considered their presence at the pier nothing more than an embarrassing public relations problem.

In fairness to the officers of SUBLANT, they did not know what had happened to the *Scorpion* and may have been hesitant to announce their assumptions, even though a search had already been launched. Simply revealing that Schade was initiating a search would have been an incendiary announcement, though an honest one.

Preventing a panic on the rainy pier among a group that included pregnant wives and children does seem sensible. In hindsight, it probably would have been far better to gather those awaiting the *Scorpion* in one place and explain the situation as fully as possible. This may have sparked an emotionally charged scene, but it was preferable to what happened: spouses hearing the terrible news on televisions and car radios, or receiving panicked phone calls from acquaintances who had.

Another reason why the navy may have hesitated to announce that the *Scorpion* was missing may rest in a false alarm raised eight years earlier when the *Scorpion* was erroneously declared missing on September 16, 1960, while operating near the British Isles. On September 17, 1960, a startling headline in the *New York Times* declared, "Radio Contact Is Lost with Atomic Submarine." The following day it was realized that the *Scorpion* was *not* missing and that confusion over communication schedules had triggered a false alarm.

Some have even suggested that Schade intentionally delayed issuing a SUBMISS alert to avoid bad publicity. This is patently absurd. Although the failure to inform the families of the *Scorpion*'s status as a missing submarine was shortsighted—if not myopically callous—not even the biggest fool in the navy believed that news of the *Scorpion*'s disappearance could be concealed.

Determined Dead

As radio signals and telephone calls alerted the rest of the navy to news of the *Scorpion*'s failure to arrive, some *Scorpion* family members continued their vigil at the pier as the afternoon faded to dusk, still unaware of the developing efforts to find the *Scorpion*.

Although many drifted home at the urging of officers who assured them that the submarine was merely delayed, others remained in their cars, believing the *Scorpion*'s appearance was imminent. As children napped and wiper blades rhythmically swept windshields, wives strained to glimpse the approaching submarine until they, too, folded their expectations and headed for home. Believing the submarine was only delayed, all remained confident that the *Scorpion* would eventually make its appearance.

On the morning of the *Scorpion*'s anticipated arrival, Kathy Karmasek helped her sister-in-law Barbara Karmasek dress her brother's two young sons in white sailor uniforms before driving the 20 miles to Norfolk. Not only was Kathy Karmasek eager to see her brother, Torpedoman's Mate Second Class Donald Karmasek, she also had recently become engaged to *Scorpion* commissaryman Michael Gibson.

After three hours at the pier, the women decided to end their vigil and drive back to Portsmouth, Virginia.

Beth Houge also heard the navy's vague explanation about the *Scorpion* being delayed and eventually made her way home as well. "Obviously they hadn't heard from them," said Houge. "But for them to say the *Scorpion* was out at sea and waiting for the weather to break was not true."

Soon after tired wives walked through their front doors and turned on televisions, they were overwhelmed by reports that a search was being mounted for the "delayed" *Scorpion*. Many remember anchorman Walter Cronkite on the CBS *Evening News* stating flatly that the *Scorpion* was "missing."

Kathy Karmasek arrived at her sister-in-law's trailer home in Portsmouth at 4:00 P.M.; the television was not switched on. Kathy fell asleep on the sofa but was soon awakened by pounding on the door. Kathy and her sister-in-law found a clutch of *Scorpion* wives in a state of near panic after hearing that the *Scorpion* had been declared missing. Kathy Karmasek then realized she may have lost not only a brother but her fiancé as well.

In naval argot, "missing" is a precise term meaning that the *Scorpion* could not be located and was most likely in serious trouble. The word "missing" also provided succor to those not willing to contemplate something worse. What the experienced navy wives feared most was a declaration that the submarine was "lost," meaning that the ship and its men had been claimed by the sea.

Another desperate hope clung to by the families was how long the sailors could survive if the *Scorpion* was helpless on the seafloor. Many wives knew the sailors could survive for a considerable period in a stranded submarine; this allowed some of the wives to maintain a positive attitude. They gathered in small klatches to reassure one another and hope for the best.

Although it was surmised that the *Scorpion*'s sailors might last for days if not weeks using oxygen sources on the submarine, their life span might be jeopardized most by their supply of lithium hydroxide crystals used to absorb exhaled carbon dioxide. A hefty but finite supply of the crystals was carried aboard the submarine for just such emergencies. If the trapped sailors were unable to cleanse the air of carbon dioxide using its atmospheric scrubber or the crystals, the sailors would eventually experience convulsions and unconsciousness, followed by death.

If the *Scorpion* lost buoyancy due to a temporary flooding problem that sent the boat to the bottom but not below collapse depth, there was a chance the men aboard could be rescued, but only if the submarine was quickly located. For this reason SUBLANT searched for the *Scorpion* as if its crew were awaiting rescue.

If the *Scorpion* was lying intact on the seafloor, the crew would have released one or both of its messenger buoys tethered to the submarine by stainless steel cables. Located on the bow and stern in cavities between the outer fairing and the pressure hull, the buoys were released by hand, using mechanisms inside the escape trunks. Once they bobbed to the surface, they could transmit an emergency signal. What was supremely worrisome to SUBLANT was that no such signal had been received.

A myth would emerge claiming the *Scorpion*'s crew tack-welded the messenger buoy covers closed prior to its Mediterranean deployment to prevent an accidental release of the buoys. Others have claimed the submarine left its buoys behind: "I saw them lying on the pier after they sailed," swore one submariner.

It was true that submarine messenger buoys were tied down or their hatches welded in place for touchy patrol operations inside Soviet waters, but the Mediterranean cruise was not the type of operation in which an accidentally released buoy could imperil the crew. Furthermore, disabling the messenger buoys could not be done at the discretion of Slattery. Lt. Cmdr. John E. Allen, SUBLANT's engineer officer, testified that the *Scorpion* neither sought nor was given permission to lock down its messenger buoys for its Mediterranean deployment. Furthermore, said Allen, the messenger buoys had been inspected just prior to the *Scorpion*'s departure and were found to be fully operable.

Underscoring the relatively innocuous nature of the *Scorpion*'s deployment to the Mediterranean was the fact that the *Scorpion* was not carrying the two scuttling charges ordinarily issued for sensitive operations in Soviet waters.

Despite the wishful thinking of those who wanted the *Scorpion* to return, reality was tinged with far less hope. While remaining outwardly hopeful, Schade and every other submariner knew the *Scorpion* was probably lost with all hands. Had a single, unforeseen malfunction triggered another, more serious problem? Had a mechanical malfunction been made worse by an incorrect recovery action? The permutations were too numerous to calculate.

By the end of the day on May 27, nothing was known except that the *Scorpion* was overdue. If SUBLANT had known precisely when the submarine ran into trouble, the boat's movement report would have allowed the navy to quickly deduce its general location. Lacking that crucial piece of information, searchers assumed the submarine could be anywhere along a curved, 2,500-mile route between Norfolk and the Azores. Without better data, the search for the *Scorpion* might have to cover 250,000 square miles of ocean. Unless a more precise location of the *Scorpion* could be refined, finding the submarine was an insurmountable challenge.

As the search for the *Scorpion* entered its second full day, it was not forgotten that the sailor's families would need the men's pay. On May 29, the navy officially declared the men "missing" to allow the pay of the sailors to go directly to their wives and other dependents. On May 30, Schade transmitted this announcement to all commands within SUBLANT, though he did so in the most considerate way possible. He sought to reassure all that the search had just begun and stated, "this action is based on considerations to minimize financial hardship and in no way affects continued SAR [search and rescue] operations."

Schade also described the extent of the search: "While search results to date have not been encouraging, I wish to assure you that we are not giving up. Air searches are being employed continuously and are covering an area 20 miles either side of [the] entire *Scorpion* track. A five-ship surface search element and a five-submarine search element are each moving eastward along *Scorpion*'s track systematically covering a 50-mile front. Special search elements are concentrating on shoal areas to the south of the Azores and along the approaches to Chesapeake Bay. Other search elements are investigating reporting sightings of debris, oil slicks, floating objects, etc. Every credible clue is being pursued."

As the days dragged on, neither an oil slick nor floating debris that could be associated with the *Scorpion* was found. Schade and the rest of the navy soon recognized that while the search would continue for the missing submarine, it was not realistic to perpetuate the belief that the crew was alive.

On June 5, after nine days of searching, the navy changed the status of the men from missing to officially dead. This triggered an operation in which casualty assistance calls officers (CACOs) were selected and briefed on how to notify the next of kin. Ordinarily, CACOs assisted the family in setting up funeral arrangements, but with the loss of the *Scorpion*, no bodies had been recovered. CACOs were also the official bearers of the condolences of the navy and were to be available to resolve problems or issues regarding pay and benefits.

The job was a tough one. Officers were instructed to be helpful and understanding, but to firmly use the word "dead" when informing the families of their loss to encourage the necessary acceptance of a brutal reality. They were also to avoid becoming personally involved with the dependents beyond their official duties. The CACOs were to provide a strong but temporary shoulder.

The following day, ninety-nine "Report of Casualty" forms were typed by navy clerks in a clatter of monotonous finality. This form—also known as Department of Defense Form 1300—is nothing more than a military death certificate. As required by regulations, a total of ten copies were delivered to the next of kin. Relatives would need the documents when applying for insurance benefits and settling the affairs of a husband or son.

When Barbara Powell received her husband's death certificate, it was a single sheet of paper upon which the navy explained the fate of twenty-four-year-old Donald Powell in fifty-three words:

MISSING TO DETERMINED DEAD—Died June 5 as a result of the loss of the *Scorpion* which was last heard from on May 21, 1968, and became overdue at 1300 27 May 1968 at Norfolk, Va. Determined to have died 5 June 1968 under Section 9 of the Missing Persons Act, as amended.

His DD-1300 did go on to mention that Powell was born in Oxnard, California, on August 13, 1943, and that he entered the navy on November 5, 1965. His monthly pay was $223, including his incentive pay. It did not mention that Powell reported aboard the *Scorpion*—his first submarine—just four months before the boat was lost.

Machinist's Mate David Stone's parents and sister were having dinner in their home in Ames, Iowa, as the television murmured in another room. Laura Stone, who adored her older brother and who would follow in his artistic footsteps, was joking with her parents when word of the *Scorpion's* disappearance echoed through the house. The family was stunned into a state of collective shock from which it would not soon recover.

Stone's articulate and mannerly mother, Sybil, was particularly close to her son. She had given birth to David during her husband's own World War II service as a naval aviator. While living in half of a sweltering Fort Lauderdale bungalow due to wartime housing shortages, Sybil took her infant to the beach to escape the heat. David had been their only child for a decade until the birth of his sister Laura in 1954. The Mediterranean mission was to be his last, and the machinist's mate was making plans to attend art school while contemplating marriage to his girlfriend, whom he called "Bunny."

When official word of her son's death arrived, Sybil Stone suffered such a deep shock that it took more than thirty years for certain memories of that period to return. The Stone family became a small, inviolate entity unto itself, comforting one another and deflecting any further hurt the world could send their way. Laura Stone, who was fourteen when the *Scorpion* failed to return, was profoundly affected by her brother's loss.

Months after the *Scorpion* disaster, when the painful thoughts of their son's death had receded to a deeper place, a delivery truck pulled up unannounced to the Stones' house.

"I've got a grave marker from the navy," the deliveryman matter-of-factly told Sybil Stone. "Where do you want it?" Sybil Stone drew herself up and, in an uncharacteristically rude tone, demanded the driver take it away. "I don't want it here," she said firmly. She knew full well her son was dead and needed no further reminders of the tragic fact.

Lois Saville had heard the early reports announcing the *Scorpion* was missing and disregarded them, horrified to think that they might be true. Hoping for the best, she chose instead to wait for an official explanation about her husband's whereabouts. Soon after that stormy day at the pier, she looked out her window and saw an impeccably uniformed man walking toward her home. The woman, who had already weathered so much, knew she could not endure the message carried by the solemn officer knocking at her door.

Lois Saville suffered an emotional collapse. Navy doctors prescribed sleeping pills. Slipping into despondency, she attempted suicide with the sedatives. Limp as a marionette whose strings had been cut from above, Lois Saville was rushed to the psychiatric ward of Norfolk Naval Hospital, where the sedatives were pumped from her stomach. Brought back from the edge of death, the distraught woman was placed under a suicide watch.

As her mind cleared from the shock of her husband's death, she realized she might lose custody of her three children, as her mother had once lost custody of her. Lois Saville then found the courage to drag herself from the miasma of depression. When her husband's $10,000 Servicemen's Group Life Insurance benefit arrived, she bought a home near her in-laws and went on with her life.

Even the most experienced navy families had trouble coping with the loss of loved ones on the *Scorpion*. Navy captain Robert Odening, a combat veteran of World War II and Korea who served as the head of the Naval Ordnance Laboratory during the mid-1960s, was the father of Lt. (j.g.) Michael Odening, the *Scorpion's* youngest officer. Neither Robert Odening nor his wife, Georgia, could have foreseen that their son would die at sea in a peacetime disaster.

Michael Odening was a 1966 graduate of the Naval Academy who reported aboard the *Scorpion* on February 13, 1968, just two days before it sailed.

"My wife, Georgia, took it very, very hard," said Robert Odening of the loss of their twenty-four-year-old son. "She didn't take care of herself afterward and was doing a lot of drinking, which she hadn't done before. She was trying to drown her sorrows. She was diagnosed with cancer in 1971 and died a few years later. We had three other kids but she couldn't recover from the loss of Michael."

Camp Allen, Naval Station Norfolk

Late on the night of May 27, as the shocking news of the *Scorpion's* disappearance rippled across America, Sonarman Bob Davis was asleep in his cell at the Camp Allen brig at Norfolk. The *Scorpion* crewman had been sentenced to thirty days' confinement for not being aboard his submarine when it departed on February 15.

A Marine guard told Davis his submarine was missing and that the duty officer wanted to see him in his office. The officer knew that the sailor's parents believed their son was still on the *Scorpion* and realized they would be unnecessarily distraught by news of the submarine's disappearance. "He knew I hadn't told them of my situation," said Davis. "I called and it turned out that my father, who was then with the Florida

Highway Patrol, had come across a *Scorpion* sailing list with my name still on it and was pretty upset."

His anxious girlfriend's attempt to hide his car keys, and Slattery's refusal to go back for him as he shouted from the pier, were two events that had preserved Davis's life. The navy could have sealed his fate by flying him across the Atlantic to meet the submarine at Rota, as it had done for Johnson, the senior chief radioman. Instead, the navy decided to make an example of Davis with thirty days' confinement and a demotion.

In its punishment of Davis, the unyielding navy had sentenced the sonarman to life.

Joseph Underwood

After the June 6 memorial service, the time came for Interior Communications Electrician Joseph Underwood to be assigned to another submarine. He had heard they were going to assign him to the *Shark*, another of the *Scorpion*'s sister ships, and he spoke to his pregnant wife, Diane, about it.

"It freaked me out," said Diane Underwood. "We had quite a talk about it. He said if he didn't go they might put him in the brig for six months. I told him I didn't care, because when he got out, I'd still have a husband."

Shortly afterward, an officer asked Underwood, "What do you want to do?" Underwood didn't even have to think about his reply: "I want to be on the IC [interior communications] gang on the *Orion*, sir." Less than ten months later, Underwood left the submarine tender and the navy for good.

During the 1980s, Underwood joined the Iowa Army National Guard with his son Steven. On April 23, 1988, while the two were hiking during a weekend drill in Des Moines, Joseph Underwood collapsed. The former submarine sailor was declared dead of heart failure at age fifty.

Bill Elrod, Underwood's companion during the nighttime transfer from the *Scorpion* outside Rota, would continue in the submarine service, become a chief of the boat, like Bishop, and retire after a long career. He would be haunted by the loss of the *Scorpion* and find himself rankled and intruded upon for years by questions from many who wanted him to tell them why the boat had been lost. Elrod had no answer for his interrogators, only grief for his dead shipmates.

A Total Net Savings

For reasons that may never be understood, U.S. Navy budgetary personnel—on the heels of America's second-worst submarine disaster—blithely announced in December 1968 that the loss of the *Scorpion* and its crew was a fortuitous "total net savings" to the navy of $9.2 million.

It appeared that the navy had found a silver lining surrounding the terrible cloud of the *Scorpion* disaster. The submarine's much-delayed full overhaul and pending SUBSAFE work—which were no longer required—could be stricken as expenses. Furthermore, the navy revealed that it was no longer obligated to pay the active-duty salaries of the ninety-nine men who were lost.

This news was contained in a report detailing how the navy intended to reduce expenses by $992 million during the 1969 fiscal year. Soon after, the navy was roundly criticized for its callousness. This prompted a less-than-comforting explanation by the navy, which pointed out that the loss of a ship and its personnel were never considered "budget reductions." Only the planned expenditures eliminated by a tragedy, said the navy, was a "savings in a budgetary sense."

It was a distinction that did little to endear the navy to the families of the *Scorpion*'s dead.

9

The Initial Search

With SUBLANT lacking even a rough idea of the *Scorpion*'s location, its only option was to conduct a classic surface search using a 100-mile-wide line of ships to retrace the *Scorpion*'s 2,500-mile path of intended movement from its last known position south of the Azores to its destination of Norfolk, Virginia.

If the *Scorpion*'s wreckage were on the floor of the Atlantic—an ocean whose depth averaged 12,000 feet, with topography that ranged from abyssal plains to rugged mountain ranges—the difficulty of finding an object 50 feet shorter than a football field in pitch darkness was stupefying to contemplate. To experienced naval officers the effort seemed like an exercise in abject futility.

Despite these realities, it was recognized that the *Scorpion*'s ninety-nine men might be alive. While the chances of this were exceedingly thin, the navy could not scrimp in its efforts to find the submarine. If nothing else, a thorough search could confirm what seemed apparent to many—that the *Scorpion* sank and could not be found. Decades later, a submarine officer who eagerly participated in the initial search admitted that the effort was probably doomed from the start: "Looking back, it was probably hopeless," he said. "Our early attempt to find the *Scorpion* was just the politically correct thing to do."

If nothing else, a legitimately strenuous effort to find the boat would reassure families while also complying with the American military ethos that no serviceman was willingly abandoned, even in death.

At the Pentagon, as at Norfolk, hopes were not high. As word about the *Scorpion* spread in the late afternoon of May 27, the SUBMISS/SUB-SUNK team slowly gathered in the National Military Command Center, a space commonly referred to as the "War Room." Some officers and scientists were notified by telephone of the crisis; others heard the news on

114

their car radios while driving home. One of these commuters was the chief scientist of the Deep Submergence Systems Project (DSSP), John Craven, who turned his car around and headed for the Pentagon.

Craven knew he would be a key player in the hunt for the *Scorpion*. The son of a naval officer, the youthfully rebellious Craven had entered the navy as an enlisted man in World War II, serving as a helmsman on the battleship *New Mexico*. The brilliant young man then gained an advanced engineering education at some of America's most prestigious schools under navy sponsorship and acquired his doctorate in mechanics and hydraulics from the University of Iowa in 1951. Craven then went to work at the David Taylor Model Basin, where he and his colleagues sought answers to better hull designs.

During the mid-1950s, Craven was dispatched to New London, where he helped find a solution to the problem of hydrodynamic flutter that appeared when the nuclear-powered fast attack boat *Nautilus* operated at high speeds. Craven's star rose, and a few years later he was selected as the chief scientist of the Special Projects Office, which developed the submarine-launched Polaris missile, one of the nation's most important national defense projects.

Craven subsequently gained the title of chief scientist of the Deep Submergence Systems Project, which oversaw a number of mostly secret programs. One was the development of an improved deep submergence submarine rescue vehicle, whose need was underscored by the *Thresher* disaster. Another DSSP responsibility was the highly secret effort to utilize submarines and specialized vehicles for conducting undersea espionage and for seafloor recovery of Soviet hardware, including spent ballistic missiles.

Craven was an elegant raconteur with a persuasive manner who had achieved godlike status within the navy's scientific bureaucracy. While he had many influential supporters, those who were less than charmed by Craven were quick to note that his prodigious talents coexisted with an equally substantial ego.

When the *Scorpion* was lost, it would be the talented and well-connected Craven who would be in charge of the scientific team designated the Technical Advisory Group (TAG) that would oversee the scientific effort to investigate the disaster. Craven, though considered a bit too glib and too much of a self-promoter by some, was also widely respected by many. He was masterful at overcoming bureaucratic hurdles and knew how to obtain the best scientific talent inside and outside the navy to study a complex problem. He had been adroit at expediting a blizzard of projects during the Polaris missile development effort and would apply the same prodigious skills to the hunt for the *Scorpion*.

Also at the command center was Capt. Willard "Bill" Searle, who was the navy's supervisor of salvage (SUPSALV). After an initial briefing, Searle rose to make a phone call. He had the responsibility of notifying Hyman Rickover, head of the Naval Reactors Branch, that a nuclear-powered submarine had been lost. Rickover's curt reaction was classic Rickover. The small white-haired man matter-of-factly told Searle, "Well, accidents do happen." The phone clicked and the conversation was over. Searle knew precisely what Rickover was saying and agreed with his observation; there was nothing else to say.

Needle in a Haystack

Searle returned to the meeting to discover how little hope was held out for finding the *Scorpion*. It seemed that many believed the navy had seen the last of the submarine. "There was zero confidence that we would find the *Scorpion*'s wreck," said Searle, who listened as ranking navy officers expressed their doubts about the chances of locating the submarine or its crew. "They [the admirals] were pessimistic, very pessimistic," recalled the SUPSALV.

Even Searle, who had rubbed shoulders with the navy's eggheads at the Office of Naval Research and the Naval Research Laboratory and understood better than most the deep-ocean search capabilities of the period, was not fully convinced that the *Scorpion* could be found. Like Craven, Searle had played roles in helping to locate the *Thresher* in 1963 and in the recovery of the missing hydrogen bomb lost offshore from Palomares, Spain, in 1966. At the time, few had been willing to lay odds on either of these efforts succeeding. Nonetheless, both the *Thresher* and the bomb were found, but only after considerable effort, false starts, and frustration—despite the fact that the general locations of both were known.

Searle, whose enlisted sailor father spent World War I hunting U-boats in the Atlantic, had the job of salvaging navy ships and clearing hulks obstructing harbors. Although he lacked the equipment to perform a deep-ocean search for the *Scorpion*, his office would fund other navy organizations that did.

As Craven and the naval officers planned their strategy, 150 miles south, SUBLANT continued to organize its search as May 27 descended into darkness.

As with any highly charged activity conducted in haste, the early hunt for the *Scorpion* was marked by confusion and missteps. Rear Adm. L. G. Bernard, commander of Submarine Flotilla 6, was ordered to serve as senior officer of the search force aboard the rescue ship *Petrel*, and his staff hurriedly reported aboard at 9:45 P.M. As they did so, the diesel-electric submarine *Chopper* intercepted a message that sounded like a distress call from the missing *Scorpion*. This welcome news was flashed to Submarine Squadron 12, which telephoned SUBLANT. The *Petrel*, carrying a submarine rescue chamber and highly trained rescue divers, was ordered to delay its departure as the authenticity of the message was established.

After twenty-six minutes, the *Petrel's* skipper was informed that the *Chopper* had been mistaken and the message had not come from the *Scorpion*. The hunt for the submarine was still on. In darkness, the *Petrel's* skipper ordered full power to its diesels as it sliced across Hampton Roads and charged into the storm-tossed Atlantic beyond.

As the *Petrel* headed for the Virginia Capes, its communications equipment immediately proved faulty, rendering the ship unacceptable as the flagship for the rescue operation. On the following day, Bernard and his SUBFLOT 6 officers attempted an at-sea transfer to the guided missile frigate *Standley*. Sea conditions were still so rough that they prevented the transfer. The *Petrel* and the *Standley* turned west for a sheltered rendezvous at Lynnhaven Roads. On May 29 at 5:00 A.M., Bernard was finally able to transfer safely to the *Standley*, a full two days after the search began.

Despite such missteps, by the end of the first day of searching, Schade and his subordinate officers had organized an impressive pickup force of submarines, surface ships, and submarine rescue ships. They also obtained additional aircraft from COMASWFORLANT, the coast guard, and the air force.

By 7:30 P.M. on the day the *Scorpion* failed to arrive, a dozen Orions and Neptunes were in the air in addition to the original two dispatched by Schade. These were soon joined by two coast guard C-130s from Elizabeth City, North Carolina, and three air force C-130s from the 55th Aerospace Rescue and Recovery Squadron in Bermuda. Although the C-130s were equipped with rescue swimmers and life rafts, they were not equipped with sonar and magnetic anomaly detection equipment for locating a submerged submarine. It was, however, possible for their crews to visually locate a crippled boat or its crew on the surface during daylight. Schade wanted the sky flooded with airborne searchers, and he was getting his wish.

The navy's maritime patrol planes were uniquely equipped to hunt submarines beneath the water. One tool employed by the Neptunes and Orions was the magnetic anomaly detector, a boom that protruded from the tail of the aircraft for sensing subtle changes in the earth's electromagnetic field. Electronic countermeasure systems detected and located emanations from radars or communication systems and provided the direction of their origin. In addition, advanced radars on the aircraft sought microwave signal returns from surfaced submarines or antennas that might be jutting just inches above the waves.

Perhaps the best search tools possessed by the patrol planes were sonobuoys that could be parachuted into the ocean, where their transducers could pick up sound energy transmitted by a submarine's machinery—or perhaps the eerie sound of a sailor tapping against a disabled submarine's hull—and transmit the data to the patrol plane circling above. In wartime this information would direct a depth bomb toward an enemy submarine, but in the waning days of May 1968, it was hoped that such data might save the *Scorpion*.

Despite the technical wizardry at their disposal, the navy patrol plane crews prided themselves on their ability to spot activity on the surface with what they jokingly called the "Mark-1 Eyeball." Neptunes and Orions from as far away as Sigonella, Italy, and Lajes, Azores, were ordered to sweep the Atlantic by air as Schade directed a surface search for the *Scorpion*.

Neptune sonarman Donald Dockendorf and his fellow crewmen tossed box lunches and ham steaks aboard their aircraft at Sigonella when ordered to take part in the search for the *Scorpion*. Dockendorf was anointed the "hawkeye" on his Neptune—the crewman with the best eyesight—and crawled into the aircraft's cramped Plexiglas nose, where he spent hours looking for signs of the missing submarine. Dockendorf could visualize the terror of being alone and in trouble in the water. "Of all the experiences I had it was perhaps the one that had the most impact on me of all," he said of the *Scorpion* search. "It was a gut-wrenching time. I would go to the bow of the aircraft and get eyestrain looking for them because we knew people were in trouble. Against all odds, we were looking for the proverbial needle in a haystack."

Aside from the ships that were officially part of the search, other naval vessels traveling in the vicinity of the *Scorpion*'s route were ordered to look for the submarine or its debris. Despite the harsh weather that extended its malevolent reach far into the Atlantic, crews eagerly interrupted their journeys to prowl the tumultuous waters for signs of the submarine or its crew.

The *Walworth County*—a landing ship, tank, or LST—carrying 200 tons of equipment for a U.S. Marine Corps infantry battalion was directed to take part in the search while returning to the East Coast from Rota, Spain. The slow-moving ship established a zigzag pattern as its crew watched for signs of the submarine. When a crew member spied flotsam on the storm-tossed water, the wallowing *Walworth County*—whose flat-bottomed hull made it hard to handle in rough weather—struggled to approach the floating debris field, which measured 50 feet by 30 feet.

Harry Draper, a boatswain's mate on the LST, tried unsuccessfully to snag some of the debris as the ship took 25-degree rolls. The order was given to lower a utility boat to recover items that might be from the *Scorpion*, but the rough conditions defeated that effort as well. Draper and his shipmates were troubled by what they had seen. Among the debris rising and falling on the swells were rubber thong sandals, used by warship sailors as shower shoes. The crew of the *Walworth County* wondered if they had spotted personal items belched from the innards of the *Scorpion* during its final moments. The navy would later conclude that not a single piece of debris seen or recovered during the search could be identified as belonging to the submarine. The sad reality is that the Atlantic has always been a convenient garbage dump for passing ships, and there was no shortage of refuse for the searchers to examine.

During the first segment of the "initial search," Schade ordered thirteen submarines and ships to position themselves 8 miles apart and to retrace the *Scorpion*'s track from the Virginia Capes to the edge of the continental shelf, a process that took three days. Known as the "close-in search," it focused on the shallower waters near the coast, where the *Scorpion* might be lying on the seafloor with its hull still intact.

During this shallow-water effort, the *Pargo* and the rescue ship *Sunbird* worked in tandem to locate uncharted wrecks using sonar and divers. A total of five unidentified wrecks were located by *Pargo*'s BQS-6 and

BQS-8 sonars, although one was immediately recognized as too small to be the *Scorpion*'s. Divers from the *Sunbird* descended to the others, confirming that two were sunken merchant ships and a third was a barge. When the divers descended to inspect the fourth object they were stunned to find the remains of a Nazi U-boat sent to the bottom a quarter century before. Finding a submarine hull gave the searchers confidence that the shallow-water search could locate the *Scorpion*. SUBLANT would later claim that the search had a 100 percent probability of locating the *Scorpion* on the surface, and a 94 percent chance of locating the submarine if it were on the shallow seafloor off the Virginia Capes.

The largest search involved a north–south line of five surface ships and five submarines spaced 8 miles apart that was launched May 28 to trace the *Scorpion*'s path of intended movement from the Virginia Capes to its last known position west of the Azores. The force traveled 2,235 miles at an average speed of 13 knots. Despite the violent weather and resultant poor visibility, it was believed that the radar employed on the ships would have located the surfaced *Scorpion* even if the lookouts failed to see it.

By May 29, no fewer than forty-one surface ships and submarines were involved in the search. This number would eventually climb to fifty-one vessels of various types. So large was this flotilla and so great were the distances covered that the fleet oiler *Waccamaw*, riding low in the rough water because it was filled to capacity, followed the flotilla to refuel the ships. In addition, a growing number of Neptunes and Orions were flying over the *Scorpion*'s path. (A total of 265 search flights would be conducted during the ten days of the initial search.) The search was the largest ever conducted by the navy, dwarfing even the famous 1937 effort in the Pacific to locate the aviatrix Amelia Earhart and her navigator, Fred Noonan.

Eager to capitalize on civilian observations in the mid-Atlantic, the navy even began contacting merchant ships known to have been in the vicinity of the *Scorpion*'s route home. One ship that particularly interested the navy was the German motor vessel *Unitas*, which reportedly traveled near the *Scorpion*'s position at the time of the submarine's last message. When contacted, the officers of the *Unitas* reported that they had seen nothing.

On May 30 at 12:26 A.M. Norfolk time, a radioman aboard a Neptune patrol aircraft reported intercepting yet another supposed call from the *Scorpion*. When informed of this, SUBLANT kept its enthusiasm in check due to the false distress call received by the *Chopper* on May 27. This latest call, however, seemed like the real thing. The Neptune had picked up a voice transmission in which the *Scorpion's* actual voice call sign was used. The message was brief: "Any station this net, this is Brandywine." Running dangerously low on fuel, the Neptune was forced to withdraw from the search and return to Norfolk. Another Neptune took its place to listen for additional radio calls. No fewer than six navy ships in the area heard the original call as well. Of these, the fast attack boat *Lapon* managed to obtain a directional fix on the signal, which originated north of the *Scorpion's* path of intended movement.

When journalists got wind of the "Brandywine" radio call, news of this hopeful sign ricocheted around the world. Suspiciously, the message lacked the distinguishing characteristics of a legitimate submarine distress signal. The navy soon determined the transmission was either a hoax or a radioman on a search ship thoughtlessly using the *Scorpion's* call sign as part of a test. It was also determined that eight civilian ships known to operate in the area also used the "Brandywine" call sign. The source of this message was never located, and managed only to provide relatives of the *Scorpion's* crew with a brief but false moment of encouragement.

As hopes of finding the *Scorpion's* crew alive diminished with each passing day, an additional search effort was ordered from Forbes Air Force Base in Topeka, Kansas. Between June 3 and June 4, an aircraft from the 1370th Photo Mapping Wing conducted four photographic flights using "false-color, infrared film" that could record heat on the ocean's surface. There was hope that this method might reveal a plume of heat rising from the sunken *Scorpion*, generated perhaps by its still-operable reactor. It was essentially a last-ditch effort. The photographic mission covered 2,000 lineal miles of ocean but found nothing.

With its sailors and officers exhausted from fighting the bad weather while constantly on watch, the flotilla of search ships arrived near the Azores June 4 without having seen any sign of the *Scorpion* or its crew. What the search effort confirmed was that the *Scorpion* and its men were not on the surface, and most likely not trapped on the seafloor near shore.

On June 5 the chief of naval operations, Adm. Thomas H. Moorer, had the unhappy task of publicly saying what many officers had concluded ten days before, when the *Scorpion* failed to return. The *Scorpion* and her ninety-nine men, he announced, were presumed lost. Realizing that the navy still needed to know why the disaster occurred, Moorer added that the search efforts would continue.

Ordinarily, America would have been transfixed by such tragic news, but not at this moment in its history.

On June 5, 1968, the declaration that the *Scorpion* was considered officially "lost" was but a raindrop in a deluge of bad news. On the morning of Moorer's announcement, America was digesting the realization that Democratic presidential hopeful Robert Kennedy had been assassinated the previous night in the kitchen of a Los Angeles hotel. Reeling over the April 4 assassination of civil rights leader Martin Luther King Jr. in Memphis and the steady drumbeat of American deaths in Vietnam, Americans were becoming inured to tragic news.

Given that the navy lost only 1,629 men killed in combat during the entirety of the Vietnam War, the unexpected loss of ninety-nine men far from combat during the same period was a singularly grievous disaster. But the *Scorpion* tragedy—fodder for scandal in normal times—was soon crowded to the back pages. As the great depths of the Atlantic were hiding the *Scorpion*, America's disquiet also blurred public focus on its demise.

Nonetheless, an aura of mystery surrounded the *Scorpion*'s disappearance, since there seemed to be no clues as to how or where the submarine was lost. Some relatives wondered if the crew had been forced to the surface and then taken prisoner by America's archenemy, the Soviet Union. The father of one *Scorpion* officer, unable to comprehend how the submarine had been lost, insisted for decades that this was the only explanation, a fantasy that might mean his son would once again return.

What disturbed many is that the boat had not even transmitted a distress call.

None of these things surprised experienced submariners. A nuclear submarine ordinarily operates in a sunken state, so a major problem such as flooding, fire, or a stern plane failure is either quickly resolved or it is not. If the crew outwits the problem, they survive and do not need to make a radio call; if not, the boat and its men are lost.

Submariners were inculcated with the attitude that they were one with their boat. Obsessing on how best to escape the submarine in case of trouble was considered a poor use of a submariner's mental energy. Within the culture of the submarine service, the subject of abandoning a submarine is treated with nothing less than outright derision. Officers and sailors who served aboard the *Scorpion* scoff when asked about life rafts carried on the submarine. "There was a life raft somewhere, but it was such a problem to get it out of the boat we never considered using it," said one former *Scorpion* officer.

Bobbing to the surface of the open ocean after departing a sunken submarine through one of its two escape trunks was not much of an option, since submariners would need to be rescued within minutes or hours in cold or even moderately cool waters, respectively, due to the threat of hypothermia. Although submariners trained to ascend from submarine escape trunks, bringing the boat back was the best way of surviving.

The surface search for the *Scorpion* was already being scaled back after June 4, when patrol aircraft and ships received instructions returning them to their normal duties. Moorer, however, had not lied when he said the search would continue. The truth of the matter—not revealed at the time—was that the hunt for the *Scorpion* had only just begun.

Within twenty-four hours after the *Scorpion's* failure to arrive, the navy believed it might have obtained acoustic evidence that the submarine was lost approximately 450 miles southwest of the Azores. The early sea and air search had not been a cynical, $2 million exercise conducted merely to make the navy look compassionate. As Schade directed the initial search, he was aware of the secret, parallel effort to pinpoint the place where the *Scorpion's* wreckage would most likely be found. Because the underwater sounds could not immediately be linked to the *Scorpion*, the mammoth surface search effort was conducted until the navy was absolutely sure the *Scorpion* and its crew could not be rescued.

Nonetheless, scientists and knowledgeable naval officers who reviewed this preliminary acoustical data knew they had the first genuine clues regarding the *Scorpion's* mysterious disappearance.

Despite this breakthrough, five more months of grueling work would be required to locate the missing submarine.

No Disfiguring Effects

Ruthann Hogeland, the widow of *Scorpion* electronics technician Richard Hogeland, now alone with their ten-month-old daughter, was tormented by her worry over the precise way in which her husband died.

Mrs. Hogeland heard of Capt. George F. Bond, a navy doctor and an expert on deep-diving techniques who in 1957 pioneered the science of saturation diving, a technique that acclimated divers to great depths using a pressure chamber. In desperation, she wrote Bond a letter pleading for information on what exactly happened to her husband when the *Scorpion* sank. Not long after the navy announced that the *Scorpion* had been found, Mrs. Hogeland received Bond's reply.

Bond, once a physician in rural North Carolina before entering the navy, was known as a kind man. He had become somewhat famous during the 1960s due to his involvement in the Sealab program, in which saturation divers lived in deep, underwater habitats. By 1968 he was working in the Deep Submergence Systems Project with John Craven as the assistant for medical effects.

Bond gently explained to Mrs. Hogeland that the collapse of the hull at crush depth would flood the submarine instantly. "This flooding is accompanied with a massive increase in air pressure within the boat," wrote Bond. "It is this high pressure air which is the immediate cause of the death of the crew. Physically, the effect is to collapse the lungs instantaneously, compressing the great vessels leading to and from the heart, and producing cardiac arrest and death in a matter, not of seconds, but of milliseconds. Under these conditions, no member of the crew would have any knowledge of the disaster prior to instantaneous death."

Bond assured Mrs. Hogeland that she could ignore press reports harping about the instantaneous superheating of the *Scorpion*'s interior due to the rapid compression of the air, something Bond said he had never experienced in flooding tests to which he subjected himself. (Despite his reassuring words, Bond had obviously not subjected himself to pressures equal to the monumental ones capable of collapsing the *Scorpion*'s hull.)

Finally, Bond addressed the widow's concerns about the state of her husband's remains in the great depths. He assured her that the collapse of the hull and the instantaneous flooding of the submarine would have "no disfiguring effects on the body of the victim, since the human body is basically fluid and incompressible. I am afraid that this answer to your letter has sounded cold and clinical. This is not the case. In our outfit, when the bell tolls for one, it tolls for all; we share your grief."

What Bond did not say in his genteel letter was that the crew was undoubtedly aware of the problem that threatened their lives in their final minutes or moments. While they may not have been cognizant of their deaths, few would not know it was approaching. As for "disfiguring effects," Bond was speaking only to the impact of great hydrostatic pressure on the human body. He did not detail the horrific injuries done to human tissue when hull steel collapsed into the submarine at near-supersonic speed, violently shoving heavy machinery about the boat. Bond also made no mention of the scavenging sea life that exists on the seafloor, who consume lifeless organisms that precipitate to the bottom.

To Bond's credit, he tried, within the bounds of kindness, to give a grieving woman some comfort based on his medical knowledge. Despite its politeness, the gist of the letter was clear: Electronics Technician Hogeland and his ninety-eight shipmates were no more.

10

Death Rattle

A jangling telephone disturbed the 3:00 A.M. darkness as Gordon
Hamilton slept at the navy's SOFAR (sound fixing and ranging)
station on St. David's Island, Bermuda. As he roused in his darkened
office, Hamilton knew the call couldn't be good news. The Lamont Geological Observatory scientist recognized the voice of J. W. Smith, a program manager at the Office of Naval Research.

Smith, whose office funded the SOFAR station, gave Hamilton the
bad news: the *Scorpion* and ninety-nine men were overdue and probably
lost at sea. Smith's dreadful announcement caused Hamilton to antici-
pate Smith's next question: "Is there anything strange on your records?"

The "records" about which Smith had asked were audiotapes and
diagrams of sounds picked up at Atlantic Ocean SOFAR stations managed by Hamilton. These stations used hydrophones to listen for high- and
low-frequency sound energy carried on the SOFAR channel, commonly
called the deep-sound channel, a focusing layer of water that could prop-
agate sound for thousands of miles. Located 3,000 feet beneath the surface, the sound channel traps an acoustic signal and keeps it from being
refracted or absorbed by the surface water or the terrain features of the
ocean floor. The signal bounces between the roof and floor layers of the
channel with little loss of energy.

The discovery of the SOFAR channel was made just prior to World
War II by Hamilton's boss, William Maurice Ewing. This revelation occurred when Ewing heard the signal from an underwater dynamite explosion while pressing his ear to the hull of a research ship. A farm boy
prodigy from Lockney, Texas, who earned a Ph.D. in physics from Houston's Rice University in 1931, Ewing quickly became one of the world's
most influential figures in earth science. He established the groundwork
for understanding the stunningly important concept of plate tectonics

126

and helped pioneer deep-ocean photography. With his former student J. Lamar Worzel, Ewing conducted the basic research that made it possible to use the SOFAR channel as the transmission medium for the navy's vitally important Sound Surveillance System (SOSUS), used throughout the Cold War to track Soviet submarines.

As a professor of geology at Columbia University, Ewing established the SOFAR station for the navy in Bermuda, where he installed Hamilton as its director soon after World War II. An inventor, a workaholic, and a prolific scientist, Ewing established Columbia University's Lamont Geological Observatory in 1949.

Aside from government-sponsored research for various defense projects, the primary function of Hamilton's SOFAR station was to assist the U.S. Air Force in using the deep-sound channel to pinpoint its ballistic-missile impact locations in the Atlantic. Test missiles carried small explosive charges to generate the needed acoustic signal, known as a "SUS" (signal, underwater sound) charge. When the missile struck the water, its charge detonated at sufficient depth so the sound would enter the deep-sound channel and reach the hydrophones of various SOFAR stations. When the signal's arrival time at each station was determined, the location of the signal source could be triangulated.

What gradually developed was the Missile Impact Location System (MILS), an element of what was then called the Eastern Test Range, a U.S. Air Force operation for tracking missile flights using both radar and underwater sound. As part of this effort, SOFAR stations were established along the western Atlantic, including one on the idyllic island of Fernando de Noronha, off the coast of Brazil. The southernmost SOFAR station was in the middle of the South Atlantic on the lonely island of Ascension. With one unofficial exception, all Missile Impact Location System stations were west of the Mid-Atlantic Ridge.

Both knew what Smith meant by the word "strange" when he asked Hamilton about signals in the context of a missing submarine. Smith was referring to the unique acoustic signals that accompanied the collapse of a submarine's pressure hull. The death rattle of the *Scorpion*, if captured by SOFAR hydrophones, was the only means of locating the submarine, and Smith knew Hamilton was the man to talk to when something went missing in the Atlantic.

If adequately clear acoustic data could be obtained from several SOFAR stations, it might be possible to pin down a general location for the *Scorpion*, thought Hamilton, but if it occurred east of the Mid-Atlantic Ridge, with its mountains and massive gorges, the sound might well be blocked from radiating west, toward the Eastern Test Range SOFAR stations.

Hamilton, however, had an ace up his sleeve: a secret Missile Impact Location System station masquerading as an oceanography laboratory for the study of sea life. Just four years before, Hamilton established a SOFAR outpost in the fishing village of Puerto Naos, on the island of La Palma, the westernmost volcanic outcropping of Spain's Canary Islands. It was perfectly positioned to hear most anything that took place east of the Mid-Atlantic Ridge.

The La Palma facility didn't officially exist as part of the air force's MILS network. It had been built on the cheap with ONR funding in 1964, using locals and American college students. It was just the sort of makeshift and enterprising effort that Ewing and his protégé Hamilton were masters at. The small complex was connected to the Atlantic's depths by hydrophone cables that ran past unconcerned European tourists sunning on the black sand of La Palma's western coast. Hamilton and his associates built and operated the station without telling the Spanish government its true purpose. This small bit of diplomatic skulduggery was considered necessary to avoid Spanish objections or worse—excessive demands for compensation.

The facility's Ampex, reel-to-reel audiotape recorders and 12-inch seismograph drum recorders were fed acoustic data by a pair of broadband hydrophones. The station's job was to record the sounds that reverberated toward La Palma's sloping, undersea mountainside. To create positive relations with the local population, the electrical generators of the facility supplied electricity to beachgoers at night. Running the Puerto Naos operations was retired air force lieutenant colonel Peter Greene, a hard-drinking expatriate referred to by the locals as "Don Pedro Greene." A sign outside the SOFAR station in Spanish and English invited the public to listen to the sounds of sea life courtesy of Columbia University's Lamont Geological Observatory making the tourists part of the subterfuge. Hamilton successfully argued for the establishment of the La Palma facility when the air force first proposed to splash test missiles east of Barbados, the easternmost island of the West Indies. He believed that having a SOFAR station in the Canaries would ensure that missile impact sounds would not be blocked by the rugged terrain of the Mid-Atlantic Ridge.

One problem with the La Palma station was that radio communications with the distant island were unreliable. Early in its operation, Hamilton feared La Palma would not receive messages notifying it to turn on its recording devices for an incoming missile splashdown. His simple solution was to order that the station's audiotape and seismograph recorders be left on constantly. The facility, whether manned or not, would record any sound that reached its hydrophones day or night. This would later be crucial in the quest for the *Scorpion*.

Immediately after ending his conversation with Smith, Hamilton attempted to call Puerto Naos by radio. Although the Canaries were three hours ahead of Bermuda, Hamilton's early morning radio call to the station arrived before the daily 8:15 A.M. replacement of the audiotape and the seismograph paper. While he waited for the La Palma station's technician to arrive, Hamilton checked the seismograph drum recordings and the audiotapes at the Bermuda station but found nothing usable.

A few hours later, Hamilton made contact with La Palma and asked the technician on duty to look at the six daily recordings between May 22 and May 27. The technician immediately saw a group of unusual sounds that reached La Palma's hydrophones on the evening of May 22, just sixteen hours after the *Scorpion* completed its final radio broadcast. Hamilton ordered the audiotapes and accompanying sound diagrams—recorded on electrocardiogram paper preferred by Hamilton—flown immediately to Washington. The technician gathered the half-dozen 16-inch reels of audiotape covering a six-day period and the corresponding paper recordings and caught the first available flight.

Not surprisingly, Hamilton had received a similar call five years earlier, when the *Thresher* sank off New England on April 10, 1963. The submarine's hull had imploded after passing its crush depth, and Hamilton was asked to use his missile impact expertise in the search for the *Thresher*. He analyzed several types of acoustic data, including sounds picked up by the extremely secret SOSUS system, and was able to contribute to the *Thresher*'s eventual discovery. Unfortunately, in the case of the lost *Scorpion*, the SOSUS system would be of little help, since it failed to pick up easily distinguishable signals related to the submarine.

If the sound of the *Scorpion*'s hull imploding was recorded at just one location, it would at least provide the approximate time of the *Scorpion*'s loss and allow searchers to correlate its location with the boat's path of intended movement. A physicist could tease out the time of the original acoustic event mathematically. Underwater sound slows and accelerates depending on water temperature, salinity, and density. The denser the water, the faster sound travels. Because of this, an underwater sound can travel the same distance to different locations and arrive at different times.

If the precise time of the *Scorpion's* loss could be determined and then compared with the submarine's movement plan, an approximate location of the submarine's wreck site could be plotted. This would be helpful, but still far too imprecise to effectively help the effort to locate the wreckage. However, if the *Scorpion's* death throes were recorded at two or more locations, it would allow scientists to triangulate their point of origin. The La Palma signals seemed promising, but another set of signals acquired at a different location was essential. Unfortunately, signals obtained from Eastern Test Range SOFAR stations along the Canadian, American, and South American coastlines were as indistinct as the SOSUS recordings. The South Atlantic SOFAR station on Ascension also failed to obtain a discernible signal.

Fortunately, there was one more group of hydroacoustic listening stations in the Atlantic. This deeply secret system was operated by the air force's Technical Applications Center (AFTAC), whose hydrophone arrays were designed to pick up high-frequency sound signals for monitoring Soviet nuclear weapons testing.

With most of the SOFAR, SOSUS, and AFTAC stations positioned in the western Atlantic, navy scientists knew they might not record the *Scorpion's* implosion if it occurred east of the Mid-Atlantic Ridge. This incomprehensibly huge, undersea rift zigzags like a scar down the Atlantic seafloor's abdomen, with escarpments and seamounts blocking the deep-sound channel. Hydroacoustic energy can be absorbed, reflected, or refracted by such underwater baffles. If the sounds of the dying submarine were generated east of the Mid-Atlantic Ridge, there was only one hope of acquiring the signals: Hamilton's clandestine SOFAR station. Even then, undersea mountains between might still block the signal, depending on where the *Scorpion* ran into trouble.

When the audiotapes and the seismograph representations of the La Palma hydroacoustic signals arrived in Washington on May 29, they were immediately reviewed by Alan Berman, head of the Naval Research Laboratory. Helping Berman was Art McClintock, of the NRL's Underwater Sound Division. Armed with the well-defined, high-energy acoustic signals recorded at La Palma, they compared them with sounds received from other hydroacoustic stations. Berman noted a suspicious signal re-

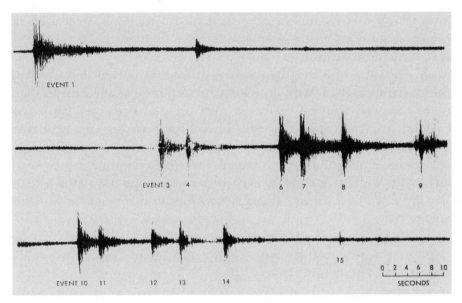

The fifteen sounds emitted by the dying *Scorpion*, miraculously obtained through a series of coincidences, were essential in locating its wreckage.

corded by the AFTAC facility in Argentia, Newfoundland, that corresponded with the La Palma signals. He circled the nearly imperceptible squiggle on the lofargram (low-frequency and analysis recording diagram) and passed it to McClintock, who confirmed that it was the same signal picked up at La Palma.

The signal detected at La Palma was an acoustical Rosetta stone that allowed Berman and McClintock to identify the second signal. With the Argentia AFTAC data, Hamilton had enough receiving stations to plot the origins of the sounds. Armed with the Argentia signals, Hamilton and scientist Brian Patterson began analyzing the data just as they would when locating a missile impact. They soon produced a series of approximate locations from which the sounds were believed to have originated. It was immediately obvious that the time and location where the sounds originated corresponded to the *Scorpion*'s plan of intended movement.

Hamilton had indeed captured the *Scorpion*'s final sounds, but locating the wreckage of the *Scorpion* would prove much more difficult.

A general search box was established that encompassed a 144-square-mile area in which a handful of high-probability locations were identified. The area of the Atlantic where the *Scorpion* was believed to have sunk was roughly 450 miles southwest of the Azores, 11,000 feet beneath the Atlantic. What would be known as the "focused search" for the *Scorpion* would now begin.

To further refine Hamilton's triangulation, the survey ship *Compass Island* was dispatched to the location considered the most likely position of the *Scorpion's* demise. Once there, the *Compass Island's* crew detonated calibration charges at great depths to recheck the signal arrival times. The charges confused both Craven and Hamilton, since larger and larger charges had to be employed to mimic the signal picked up at La Palma and by the AFTAC station. Craven began wondering if a sizable explosion was the initial acoustical event signaling the demise of the *Scorpion* and its crew.

Eventually, a secret position designated "#4" would be chosen by Hamilton as the *Scorpion's* most likely resting spot. Position #4 would prove to be amazingly accurate.

Fifteen Underwater Sounds

The *Scorpion* and its crew died on May 22, 1968, at precisely 6:22 P.M. Greenwich Mean Time. The mechanical groans of the doomed *Scorpion* were torn from the submarine in fifteen signals during a 190-second period. There could be no doubt that the sounds were directly related to the loss of the submarine. The second acoustic signal occurred twenty-six seconds after the first, and the third acoustic event took place sixty-five seconds after the second one. The remaining twelve signals occurred sporadically during the remaining ninety-nine seconds.

One other intriguing signal on Hamilton's recordings occurred twenty-two minutes before the "acoustical train" of fifteen sounds, but it could not be positively correlated with the *Scorpion's* loss, reminding Hamilton and the other scientists that the Atlantic was alive with thousands of sounds bouncing through the deep-sound channel.

At first glance, the fifteen blips looked like erratic heartbeats wildly scratched on Hamilton's electrocardiogram paper. At 1 inch of audiotape per second, it had taken 16 feet of iron oxide–coated plastic tape to magnetically record the ruination of the submarine. In Bermuda, Hamilton and Patterson studied the La Palma signals, carefully looking for small clues in the squiggly lines. Hamilton believed that the first of the fifteen sounds had some of the attributes of a signal generated by an underwater explosion, although it lacked a "bubble pulse frequency." This phenomenon is ordinarily created when water displaced by an explosion's high-pressure gas bubble repeatedly claps together in a process measured in milliseconds.

Whether the first sound in the *Scorpion's* "acoustical train" was caused by an underwater explosion was an argument that had only just begun.

USNS *Mizar*

At the moment when the *Scorpion* was declared missing on May 27, the Naval Research Laboratory's scientific ship USNS *Mizar* was heading to Norfolk Naval Shipyard for repairs and modifications. The ship's scientific team had just completed a sixty-day mission studying manganese nodule accumulations on the floor of the Atlantic. When its repairs were complete, the *Mizar* was scheduled to depart for a secret five-month mission in the Pacific, an operation made unusual because the *Mizar* had not left the Atlantic since being acquired by the NRL five years before. (Curiously, when a massive effort was made by the CIA to recover a Soviet submarine in 1974 using the specially built *Glomar Explorer*, the cover story was that the ship's owner, Howard Hughes, intended to recover manganese nodules.)

It has been speculated that the *Mizar's* next mission in the Pacific may have been related to the March 8, 1968, loss of the Soviet diesel submarine *K-129*. The guided-missile boat exploded and sank 750 miles northwest of Oahu in 16,500 feet of water, killing all ninety-eight aboard. The Soviets had no idea where their *Golf II* class submarine was but the Americans did, perhaps using the same underwater sound methods that allowed scientists to determine the *Scorpion's* general location. Thanks to an NRL scientist named Chester "Buck" Buchanan, the *Mizar* was uniquely prepared in terms of personnel and equipment to locate and photograph the Soviet submarine if ordered to do so.

Other events, however, would intrude on the *Mizar's* Pacific mission. While pressing toward Norfolk, the personnel of the *Mizar* listened to radio traffic about the missing *Scorpion* and wondered if the *Mizar* might be pressed into the search. Indeed, at 9:00 P.M., the *Mizar* received a message from the NRL ordering the research ship to forgo its planned repairs; the crew would instead make the ship ready to assist in the *Scorpion* search.

On the morning of May 28, the *Mizar* arrived in Norfolk. Buchanan, head of the NRL's Ocean Engineering Branch, soon arrived in Norfolk to assume command of the *Mizar*'s search effort. For the next five days, the *Mizar* bustled with activity as truckloads of gear arrived for installation. Buck Buchanan's boss Berman, John Craven, and Columbia University's Hamilton were certain the SOFAR signals acquired at La Palma belonged to the *Scorpion*. It was up to the *Mizar* and its personnel to carefully troll the area with its towed camera sled.

The *Mizar* now had the look of a ship preparing for war instead of a research mission. Because precise navigation would be crucial in conducting a deep-ocean search, the *Mizar* received installation of an AN/SRN-9 satellite navigation receiver. Since security also was a concern, a cryptographic communications system not ordinarily carried aboard the *Mizar* was added.

At 11:00 A.M. on June 2—six days after the *Scorpion* failed to return—detailed mission orders were hand-delivered to Buchanan from Schade containing Gordon Hamilton's latest and most refined estimates on the *Scorpion*'s position. Buchanan then turned the bow of the *Mizar* toward the open sea. It would not return for five months.

Chester "Buck" Buchanan

Buchanan, who was known to everyone as either "Buck" or "Bucky," was an irrepressibly cheerful man imbued with the tenacity and resourcefulness essential for scientists who work at sea. After World War II service as a naval officer, Buchanan came to the NRL as a sonar researcher. By the early 1960s he had become a pioneer in deep-ocean search technology and techniques. One of his innovations was a towed vehicle equipped with cameras and lights. What Buchanan called his "fish" was equipped with sensors, including a magnetic anomaly detector, sidescan sonar, and cameras. These sensors, if working properly, would send a signal by cable to the *Mizar* reporting the presence of a steel object disrupting Earth's magnetic field. A sidescan sonar return also would confirm the presence of an object. The still cameras could then make a visual record of the object. Buchanan's greatest feat was learning how to gracefully maneuver the vehicle at the end of three miles of braided steel cable.

Like SUPSALV Bill Searle, Buchanan knew most navy officers had little faith in Hamilton's SOFAR triangulation or his own proven towed-sled search techniques. However, Buchanan had already located a fast attack submarine believed lost forever in the deep ocean.

The day after the *Thresher* sank in 1963, Buchanan put together a search plan with which he proposed to find the submarine and that was quickly approved. The navy loaned Buchanan a ship for towing his sled during 1963 but it lacked the power and maneuverability to maintain precise towing paths against the wind and current. Due in large part to the inadequacy of the towing ship, the *Thresher* remained unfound in 1963. Knowing that the navy's eagerness to locate the *Thresher* had temporarily given him leverage, Buchanan boldly asked for a more capable research ship with twin screws that would allow him to maneuver by applying separate power levels to each propeller. The navy—under immense political pressure to explain the scandalous loss of the *Thresher*—initially balked, but then bowed to the insistent Buchanan.

The scientist was told to pick out a ship from the "mothball fleet" in Washington's Puget Sound Naval Shipyard. Buchanan's choice was the oddest ship in the reserve fleet. Originally built for the navy's Military Sea Transport Service with a double hull reinforced against ice, the *Mizar* transported supplies to U.S. Air Force scientific stations in Greenland and Antarctica before being retired.

In maritime terms, the five-year-old ship was virtually brand new. The *Mizar* also was equipped with Buchanan's requisite twin propellers and a diesel-electric drive, which meant he could individually adjust the thrust of each to ensure a precise towing pattern. The ship's double hull gave it remarkable buoyancy and allowed for the subsequent installation of an open "center well" in the lowest deck through which the towed camera sled could be lowered and retrieved.

Returning to the *Thresher* search site with the *Mizar*, Buchanan managed to photograph the submarine's hull and debris field in late June 1964. It was the first deep-ocean wreck ever located, and the find cemented Buchanan's reputation as a pioneer in deep-ocean search, a discipline still in its infancy during the early 1960s. While much would be made of the RMS *Titanic's* discovery two decades later by Robert Ballard, Buchanan's 1964 feat was, at the time, unparalleled.

After finding the *Thresher*, the *Mizar* was taken into a shipyard at Savannah, Georgia, and fitted with its center well. This was done by cutting a sizable opening through the bottom of the hull and shuttering it with hydraulically operated doors to keep rough water from splashing on the well deck when it was not in use. The opening allowed a winch operator in a separate compartment to lower a towed camera sled into the sea without being exposed to atrocious weather. The entire operation was observed by the winch operator on closed-circuit television. Also added was a barnlike structure that rose from the foredeck to enclose the work area below, a unique feature jokingly referred to as the "Elephant House."

The winch operator, who raised and lowered the camera sled, also was responsible for controlling the depth of the sled in "flight." Although the *Mizar* had many eccentricities—the hydraulic doors would heave up and down in heavy seas, sucking air loudly throughout the ship—it was a good tool for deep-ocean exploration. Although he was one of several NRL scientists who used the navy-owned ship, Buchanan always considered it his own.

Point Oscar

By June 10, Buchanan and the *Mizar* were in position 450 miles southwest of the Azores at a location designated Point Oscar. Buchanan's strategy was to determine his own position as accurately as possible so he could make precise "runs" while not missing an inch of the seafloor. Being off by just a few dozen feet on a sled run could mean bypassing the *Scorpion's* wreckage entirely. This had to be done while the *Mizar* crawled at 1 knot, fighting the current and the wind. Behind the *Mizar* was a 1-ton sled at the end of 15,000 feet of cable being "flown" 30 feet above the seafloor.

A trio of sonar transducers installed while in Norfolk beneath the *Mizar's* hull would help the ship keep track of its towing paths. One transducer would transmit a "greeting" to sonar transponders planted on the ocean floor, while the other two received response signals to keep Buchanan apprised of the camera sled's position. Positional awareness was crucial to avoid redundant sled runs and to keep the towing path no wider than the swath covered by the sled's magnetometer, sonar, and cameras. In addition, should the *Scorpion* be located and photographed by the sled, the precise location of the submarine's wreck would be known.

Unfortunately, once the *Mizar* began combing the designated search area, everything went wrong.

The *Mizar* is pictured with its "Elephant House" and its unusual crow's nest. Camera sleds were lowered internally through the hull of the ship.

Navigational systems of the period were problematical and—mysteriously—the *Mizar*'s hull-mounted sonar transducers only received signals from the navigation transponders at one-ninth their effective range of 18,000 feet. Adding to the search effort's woes, the magnetometer and the sonar could not be used simultaneously. This problem doubled the number of sled runs, since a sonar run would have to be followed by a second over the same path using the magnetometer, a glitch that was eventually corrected. However, when the sidescan sonar was used, it identified almost everything as a submarine hull, creating more problems than it solved.

Buchanan depended on the magnetometer to sense when seafloor objects were disrupting Earth's magnetic field before commanding the camera to begin snapping pictures. At other times, an "open eye" method was used in which the camera methodically snapped photographs of the seabed for five minutes every fifteen minutes. Shooting photographs occasionally rather than constantly aggravated Buchanan, who believed visual observation was superior to sonar, and even the usually reliable magnetometer. The only sled equipped with wide-angle cameras for covering a wide swath of seafloor lacked adequate film capacity to allow it to take photographs using the open-eye method. Photographs were snapped at intervals to give the sled's cameras ten hours of frugal use before their one thousand frames of film were exhausted. Time and again 15,000 feet of stainless steel cable was reeled in, the sled was raised from the water by a lifting cradle, and the cameras were reloaded. Once serviced for another run, the sled was splashed into the Atlantic.

On June 26, just 16 days after beginning its runs over the search area, the towed sled delivered a photograph of a 30-inch-long piece of twisted metal pipe whose shiny appearance indicated it was new to the seafloor. Remarkably, the artifact was photographed during one of the rare "open eye" periods of camera operation. The find occurred on only the ninth sled run. The image of the contorted piping should have been a victorious moment, but the navigational system failed to provide a position that could be correlated with the photograph of the pipe. When numerous tries failed to reacquire the piping, the *Mizar* continued its search elsewhere. When the *Scorpion* was finally located, Buchanan saw his mysterious piece of mangled pipe once again and realized it had only been 200 feet from the main sections of the *Scorpion*'s shattered hull. Unfortunately, that discovery would not happen for another eighteen weeks. The initial find was a testament to the expertise of both Hamilton and Buchanan.

A deeply frustrating problem for Buchanan was the sidescan sonar system, which had proven unreliable and misleading. Many days were spent pursuing sonar returns that had nothing to do with the *Scorpion*, including boulders dropped long ago by wandering icebergs. Finding something on the seafloor two miles below was like pecking at a narrow, lighted swath of seafloor through a two-mile-long soda straw. Except for a few short breaks when other scientists took over, Buchanan would not take his eye off that soda straw as he and his men continued to hunt for the *Scorpion*. As they did so, the days turned into weeks.

In preparation for the *Mizar*'s third search cruise, which began on August 14, a new sidescan sonar system was deployed. Unfortunately, the ticklish game of keeping the sled from striking the seafloor finally tipped against the winch operator when the 2,000-pound vehicle slammed into the bottom—if not a rocky outcropping—damaging the new sonar. In its quest for the *Scorpion*, the *Mizar* team couldn't seem to get a break.

In addition to the technical problems, Buchanan was beset by bureaucratic headaches. Although a well-meaning gesture by COMSUBLANT

Schade and the navy, the periodic arrival of navy captains as "on-scene commanders" aboard the *Mizar* during its search cruises provided little real assistance.

Of the six submarine force officers who served as on-scene commander, only one did so twice, since they were rotated roughly every three weeks so they could return to their commands. Just as an officer was getting the hang of the search effort, it was time for him to depart. Buchanan served as chief scientist four times, while another scientist held the position twice. Only one NRL scientist served as chief scientist for a single cruise. The submarine officers who were officially in command of the search operation were unfamiliar with the techniques and technology employed by Buchanan and the NRL. Buchanan found himself being ruled alternately by committee, by the whims of COMSUB-LANT, or by the on-loan search commanders.

Last Chance

After three months of searching, the *Mizar* was still dutifully pulling its camera sled like a huge fishing lure festooned with gadgets. It was now early September 1968, and for the general public, the *Scorpion* story was a fading memory. Gordon Hamilton had further refined his calculations about the *Scorpion*'s location, but a bureaucratic mix-up had delayed their delivery to Buchanan by nearly thirty days. When that foul-up was resolved, Buchanan used the data to adjust his search.

As the *Mizar* began its fourth month of sled runs with Buchanan confident he was closing in on the wreck with Hamilton's help, frustration grew among the navy's brass. Vicious weather would soon dominate the mid-Atlantic, forcing the *Mizar* back to port. Pressure was building within the uniformed side of the navy to halt the search until better weather appeared, in the spring.

Craven, the chief scientist of the Special Projects Office, and the man in charge of the technical aspects of the *Scorpion* search, understood the reliability of the science behind Hamilton's SOFAR calculations and had complete faith in Buchanan. Craven, backed by Rear Adm. J. C. Donaldson, director of the Fleet Operations Division, argued vociferously that the *Mizar* was in the right location conducting precisely the right type of search. Craven was an adroit bureaucratic infighter who could shepherd a complicated program through the shoals of institutional indifference, and he fought to keep the search for the *Scorpion* going as long as possible. "John was a high-level bullshit artist," observed Hamilton. "By that, I mean he was a first-class facilitator."

Despite Craven's effective lobbying, Buchanan grew increasingly concerned that the efforts of his team would be halted before they achieved success. SUBLANT, he knew, was prepared to halt the search after the fourth cruise ended, on October 7, to allow the *Mizar* to refit. Buchanan was horrified. As the search progressed, he had slowly learned the nature of the seafloor topography and was convinced that if he had enough time he could overcome technical glitches preventing him from reacquiring the area where Buchanan believed the *Scorpion* was located.

Buchanan could feel the hot breath of a disenchanted bureaucracy as he spent $50,000 a day in present-day dollars on a search that had discovered only a 30-inch piece of unidentifiable pipe, rocks, bizarre sea creatures, and ocean floor ooze. Buchanan, however, wanted to conduct a fifth cruise, to concentrate on solving a crippling navigational issue— the malfunctioning navigational sonar transducers. Only a deep-water search would allow the necessary tests and adjustments. In addition, the *Mizar* could conduct a final series of search runs. The navy, pinched for money and frustrated by the lack of results, was not receptive.

"The navy said, 'We won't pay for it anymore!'" recalls Naval Research Laboratory director Alan Berman. "After three or four months the navy was convinced we were barking up the wrong tree." The navy was losing patience with Buchanan's unlimited forbearance. "Buck was a devotee of the raster scan," said Berman, referring to Buchanan's desire to precisely cover every inch of the search area, as he had once plowed fields as a farm boy in Onward, Indiana. "What bedeviled Buck were the navigation systems of the day."

With operating funds for the research ship depleted and the navy grumbling to halt the search until spring, Berman decided to illegally pay for a final search cruise with NRL monies allocated for other activities. This action might be construed as a felony by a stuffed-shirt accountant, but Berman believed Buchanan needed to resolve the technical problems before restarting the search in the spring.

With Craven's influence and Berman's creative accounting, both prevailed in obtaining navy permission for a final search cruise. More than three decades later, Buchanan remained deeply touched by Berman's confidence: "NRL stepped in and said, 'We have faith in Buck. We'll pay for it.' It was frightening to think they had that much faith in one fellow."

Sled Run 74

The last search of 1968 would begin on October 16 and end on November 2. Berman hoped success would crown his fiscal sleight of hand, though he would settle for Buchanan's resolving the technical problems that plagued the effort. To help the *Mizar*'s team locate the *Scorpion* with the camera sled, Buchanan carefully studied the bottom charts and soundings to fully understand the terrain where *Scorpion* was believed to be.

Buchanan was fascinated to see the treacherous nature of the seafloor they were searching. If Hamilton's calculations were right, it appeared the submarine was lying inside a 12-mile-wide volcanic caldera. This formation was the remnant of a once-active volcano long ago formed by a geologic "hot spot" through which lava penetrated Earth's mantle. As the tectonic plate on which the volcano sat moved east and away from the hot spot, the volcano died. Its molten lava dome either erupted in a massive explosion due to the infiltration of seawater, or it simply collapsed after cooling, to form a massive hole. After creeping a centimeter a year for untold millions of years, the volcano arrived beneath the place where the *Scorpion* suffered its fatal mishap.

This caldera was of such great geologic antiquity that its southern wall had crumbled, creating a massive opening. With one side gone, the once-circular crater had the appearance of Rome's Colosseum, prompting the searchers to dub it "the stadium." Buchanan believed that halfway down the caldera's 1,000-foot wall, on a somewhat level expanse of silty muck, were the torn remains of what the *Mizar* and its crew had sought for nearly half a year. To help understand how to navigate over and around its rugged rim, Buchanan ordered a model of the caldera constructed using sheets of sculpted cardboard whose rough edges were smoothed over with a slathering of plaster of Paris.

As the *Mizar* headed back to the search area on October 14, the weather had worsened. As they began to diagnose problems, Buchanan and his team realized why the hull-mounted sonar transducers were not functioning at long range: they were installed upside down. This embarrassing mistake, which had plagued the search for months, was quickly corrected, and the *Mizar* was immediately able to conduct more sled runs at greater distances without interruption.

As the search team ironed out more wrinkles, Buchanan concentrated his test runs on the area where he believed the metal piping was photographed during sled run 9 on June 26. Making east–west runs, the *Mizar*'s crew held on to whatever they could as the ship was battered by powerful winds and high waves with the arrival of cold-weather storms. Gusts clocked at 44 miles per hour fought the crew's efforts to keep the *Mizar* on a straight path, although the onetime supply ship's diesel-electric propulsion and twin screws met the challenge. "It was, without a doubt, the worst weather I have ever seen," recalled Buchanan.

During run 74 on October 28, the magnetometer registered a series of magnetic anomalies, while the sled's sidescan sonar also indicated close-range contacts with objects on the bottom. The civilian crew of the ship skillfully wrestled the *Mizar* as the wide-angle cameras snapped away. After the 35mm still-picture film was exhausted, the sled was reeled in and the exposed film from its cameras was developed for analysis as the sled was hurriedly prepared for run 75.

When the hundreds of negatives were reviewed from sled run 74, small bits of debris, including wire and tubing, could be seen. It was obvious to Buchanan that it was *Scorpion* debris, but it was not unique enough to be conclusive evidence. By the time of that discovery, sled run 75 was already under way. When the film supply was exhausted, the sled was reeled from the deep and its film whisked to the darkroom. Buchanan knew in his bones that he had conclusive photographs of *Scorpion* wreckage with this sled run. With no time to waste, the sled was then prepared for sled run 76. Buchanan wanted as many photographs as he could acquire. It was the least he could do for Berman, who was risking prison to keep Buchanan and the *Mizar* at sea.

At 3:00 A.M. on October 29, Buchanan and the latest on-scene search commander, Capt. James T. Traylor, were reviewing the photographs from sled run 75 along with photographer John Zambon when the trio identified debris that could only have originated from the *Scorpion*. Jubilation swept the ship. With but five days left on the "research cruise," Buchanan's team found what many thought was lost forever.

The only real challenge left was locating major segments of the hull or other unique components that would prove conclusively that the *Scorpion* had been located. Other discoveries might also provide crucial insight into how the disaster occurred. Buchanan and his team were electrified with enthusiasm.

The readied camera sled was lowered for run 76 as the *Mizar* lurched in the stormy sea. Steel cable whined off the winch, and the run began with a sense of confidence that precedes imminent victory. Buchanan and his group believed they knew precisely where to tow the sled to photograph the major portions of the *Scorpion*'s hull.

As the vehicle snapped photographs there was a sound inside the winch room as loud as a gunshot. The shaft that turned the cable drum had snapped, allowing the winch to spin as cable disappeared into the angry ocean. At the moment of the winch failure, mechanical engineer Ernie Czul was "two decks down in the guts of the *Mizar*" when someone noticed the numbers on the cable footage counter moving in a blur. "The winch has gone berserk and is spinning uncontrollably," thought Czul, who ran up two flights of stairs to see cable screaming off the drum. Another NRL engineer, Wilbert Jones, had designed the winch, and Czul knew the mechanism well. Czul had to engage the emergency brake, a 3-inch-wide, 15-foot-long belt of rubberized asbestos and steel that looped around the edge of the cable drum.

Czul gripped the brake's handle with both hands and hesitated for half a moment as he wondered what would happen before pulling for all he was worth. As the brake band tightened around the end of the spinning drum, Czul was engulfed in a cloud of hot smoke and soot from burning rubber. The winch had stopped cold. Czul remembers that nearly 16,000 feet of ⅝-inch steel cable had played out. Short of losing a camera sled, the worst thing that could happen would be to have the winch fail. It appeared that both events had occurred. On the verge of triumph, catastrophe had crowned the efforts of the *Mizar*'s team.

All, however, was not lost. Buchanan and his team immediately engaged a slower, 10-horsepower reserve motor and began reeling in the cable. The camera sled, miraculously, was still attached. Once recovered and repaired, it could perform more photographic runs.

When the submerged sled approached the surface, the winch operator pulled the vehicle into a submerged carriage that stabilized the sled to keep it from being banged about as both were raised through the center well. As the 10-horsepower motor strained, the 1-ton sled and the heavy carriage slowly emerged. What was not known was that the sled's cable connection had been damaged during its fall to the seafloor. Just as the sled and carriage left the buoyancy of the seawater, the extra weight snapped the damaged cable connection, and the sled began an 11,000-foot free fall. The sled and its promising images of the *Scorpion*'s debris field landed near the doomed submarine it had found.

The *Mizar*'s crew was dumbstruck, but Buchanan had already formulated a backup plan and wasted no time putting it in motion. Before the
sled had been lost, Buchanan assumed that it might be unusable, and
ordered that a second, less capable sled be prepared. Its components were
in poor condition, and it lacked wide-angle cameras and sidescan sonar,
but it had ordinary still cameras and a magnetometer—the two items
that Buchanan trusted most of all. After two days of feverish repairs, the
newly functional camera sled was lowered into the caldera.

Runs 77, 78, 79, and 80 were all successful, photographing most of
the submarine's main components, whose unexpected condition provided
a surreal horror show in the grainy, black-and-white images. The bow of
the *Scorpion* containing the torpedo room was relatively intact, contra-
dicting the theory that a massive internal torpedo explosion had destroyed the submarine, although it was sheared from the submarine's hull.
The aft section of the hull, containing the reactor compartment and the
engine room, was in a configuration that was completely unexpected: 50
feet of the stern were drawn forward inside the pressure hull, and much
of the operations compartment had disintegrated. The rudder and stern
planes protruding from the stern looked like the tail of an aircraft jutting
from a cylindrical hangar.

The sail-like fairwater had sheared off when much of the *Scorpion*'s
operations compartment amidships had either imploded or been ripped
to pieces during the descent. The fairwater was lying on its port side, with
its starboard fairwater plane pointing to the surface. The bow had dug a
sizable crater upon impact with the seafloor, and the aft portion of the
boat, containing the remnants of the operations compartment and the
stern, was lying atop the seafloor ooze. The $48 million *Scorpion* looked
like a toy broken and then carelessly discarded by an angry child.

Somewhat surprisingly, what did not appear in any of the camera sled
photographs of the *Scorpion*'s debris field were bodies.

On October 31, CNO Thomas Moorer announced that the *Scorpion*
had been located "about 400 miles southwest of the Azores in about
10,000 feet of water." Moorer recounted the efforts of 6,000 men in the
air and at sea who looked for the missing submarine. "It is hoped," said
Moorer, "this new evidence will enable the navy to ascertain the cause
of the loss."

After accumulating thousands of debris field images, Buchanan and
Traylor were ordered to board a P-3 Orion patrol aircraft at Lajes Field in

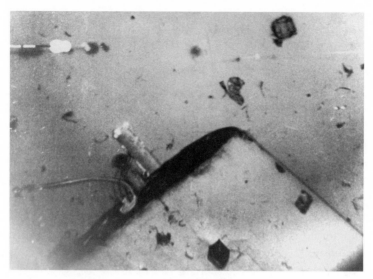

A *Mizar* photograph of the *Scorpion*'s detached fairwater reveals several masts in raised positions, indicating the submarine may have been near the surface when stricken.

the Azores with their photographs, for a nonstop flight to Norfolk. It was late on November 6 when Buchanan and Traylor entered Conference Room 3 at the Supreme Allied Commander Atlantic (SACLANT) headquarters in Norfolk, where the Board of Inquiry was assembled. The court was briefly reconvened so Traylor and Buchanan could be sworn in. A select group of 750 photographs accumulated during the last five photographic runs were then admitted as evidence before the court. (The *Mizar* took a total of 143,000 photographs during the entire search.) The board members asked a few questions of both men, and the court was adjourned. It would be reconvened at a more sensible hour for a new round of testimony.

In the predawn hours of November 6, 1968, in a move that was a gesture of the navy's gratitude for finding the gravesite of its men, Buchanan was flown home to Washington like a dignitary.

The farm boy from Onward, Indiana, had found his second lost submarine in five years. He hoped it would be his last.

11

Controversy

Even before the *Scorpion* was located and photographed, John Craven formulated a scenario about its demise with a theory as elegant as it was controversial. The master poker player studied the fifteen underwater sounds of the *Scorpion*'s descent into blackness and deduced that the submarine had destroyed itself with its own torpedo. Some believed Craven had cleverly unraveled the mystery. Others thought the poker player was holding an empty hand.

Based upon Hamilton's analysis of the SOFAR signals, Craven developed the startling assumption that the initial sound was an explosion. He further postulated that the fourteen remaining sounds occurred progressively farther east as the submarine sank. This—to Craven, anyway—indicated that the *Scorpion* turned sharply from its westerly course and traveled east during its final moments.

His focus on this scenario strengthened when he learned that a sharp reversal of course was a means of inactivating a hot-running Mk-37 torpedo by triggering its anticircular-run switch. Adding credence to this was the *Scorpion* torpedo gang's nervous handling of the Mk-37 hot-running torpedo the previous fall. What intrigued Craven was the possibility that a hot-running Mk-37 prompted the *Scorpion*'s change of course—an assumption that remains hotly disputed. When this failed—and with the fully armed weapon still in the torpedo tube—Craven believed the self-guided torpedo was launched, only to return and strike the *Scorpion* a traitorous blow.

Torpedomen and submarine officers familiar with the Mk-37 who doubt Craven's hypothesis insist that a long list of safety features on the torpedo, including the anticircular-run switch, would reliably prevent the weapon's exploder mechanism from detonating the warhead if it had turned against its own submarine. The weapon could also be programmed not to detonate at the launching submarine's depth, and it was not supposed to arm until it reached a distance specified by the torpedomen.

However, the torpedo gang's panicky behavior during the December 5, 1967, hot run strongly questioned the notion that established weapons procedures were always followed on submarines, particularly during an emergency. The personnel situation aboard the *Scorpion* had changed dramatically since the inadvertent activation of the unarmed Mk-37. Donald Yarbrough, an unflappable career torpedoman, had replaced Peercy in December 1967 as the *Scorpion's* senior enlisted torpedoman.

Although torpedoes carried during patrols were fitted with warheads, the warhead exploder mechanisms on only one or two Mk-37s were configured to make them capable of detonating the warhead's HBX-3 high explosive. It was policy for submarines to carry at least one Mk-37 torpedo configured as a "warshot"—an antisubmarine weapon ready for launch. This meant that the torpedo's Mk-19 exploder mechanism received a detonator (igniter) charge, and the tetryl-filled booster it triggered to touch off the warhead's high explosive.

If a hot-run torpedo turned and exploded against the *Scorpion*, this meant that two rare malfunctions had occurred at the same time: the inadvertent activation of the warshot's powerful silver-zinc propulsion battery, and the failure of the anticircular-run switch to disarm the weapon after a turn of at least 180 degrees. It also indicates that those launching the weapon did not give it preset instructions restricting how far from the submarine it should arm itself or restricting the depth at which it could detonate. (If the weapon was malfunctioning, the torpedo's vacuum tube electronics may not have properly warmed up to allow the input of such instructions.)

Another possibility obviating many of these safety procedures was the accidental detonation of the weapon inside a torpedo tube or the torpedo room before it could be disarmed or discarded. An obvious cause of accidental detonation was a fire that could "cook off" a rack-stored torpedo. If a torpedo room fire had detonated a warhead, the Court of Inquiry could only guess as to the cause of the blaze. Any fire would have to be relatively intense while also defying the firefighting efforts of a well-trained crew for five or ten minutes.

Although fairly resistant to heat and shock, HBX-3 could be detonated accidentally. If exposed to heat above 170 degrees Fahrenheit for an extended time, the chemical properties of HBX-3 change, rendering it dangerously unstable. At 176 degrees Fahrenheit the explosive will melt, and in cook-off tests, in which torpedo warheads were heated to 450 degrees Fahrenheit, HBX could detonate, though not necessarily with full force. Although these issues were discussed at the *Scorpion*'s inquiry, an internal detonation of a Mk-37 torpedo did not seem to captivate the interest of the board or Craven.

In his effort to establish "probabilities" related to his scenario that a malfunctioning torpedo returned to strike the *Scorpion*, Craven requested the assistance of Lt. Cmdr. Robert R. Fountain, the submarine's former executive officer. Craven wanted Fountain to go through a simulation at the David Taylor Model Basin, and he personally drove Fountain from Washington, D.C., to the Maryland facility. Fountain, as baffled as everyone else by the loss of the submarine he departed nearly five months before, was eager to help.

Without being told what would happen, Fountain dutifully responded to a variety of scenarios by issuing commands and directing responses as he would if he were commanding the *Scorpion*. "They went through this business of a hot run in the torpedo room," recalled Fountain of his afternoon with Craven. "'You're the CO,' they said, 'what would you do?' So I gave a series of orders of what I would have done to turn the ship if the gyro had not been caged [inactivated]. They brought me back and that's all I ever knew."

During the simulation, Craven observed and timed Fountain's actions and believed the steps taken by the skilled submarine officer matched those he postulated were executed by the *Scorpion* in response to a hot-running torpedo. Craven also believed he could match the time of key underwater sounds to the *Scorpion*'s final movements, and its descent to crush depth where its various tanks imploded.

Craven's focus on scenarios related to a torpedo explosion was important, since he had a key role in shaping the investigation into the loss of the *Scorpion*. As director of the Technical Advisory Group for the inquiry, Craven "took a major lead in directing the operational analysis, particularly coordinating the study by NSRDC [Naval Ship Research Development Center] personnel, and in establishing a priori probabilities," according to a navy report on the effort to locate the *Scorpion*. In short, Craven guided the effort to come up with explanations for how the *Scorpion* was lost. Accomplished, respected, and convincing, Craven's opinions carried a great deal of weight with the Court of Inquiry.

Ultimately, the court's controversial findings, contained in the Opinion section of the Findings of Fact, listed a torpedo explosion at the top of its list of most likely causes of the *Scorpion*'s loss, reflecting Craven's considerable influence. Craven has recently claimed that authors and journalists have falsely attempted to cast him as the progenitor of the hot-running-torpedo theory. "They're imputing to me a conclusion that I have not publicly made," complained Craven in 2003. "That happens all the time. My experience is that they [the Court of Inquiry] paid too much attention to my testimony. They opted out for some sort of torpedo thing. What can I say?"

Craven's claim of being a victim of his own believability must come as a shock to naval officers and others who rallied around his analysis at the time of the disaster and afterward. Despite his latter-day protestations, Craven's convincing arguments played a major role in the court's preference for speculating that a torpedo mishap was the cause of the *Scorpion* disaster.

The proposal that the *Scorpion* was destroyed by one of its own torpedoes was met with a decidedly grim reception from several corners. Many submarine officers who spent a good portion of their careers handling and launching the Mk-37 were unswayed by Craven's theory, including Fountain. COMSUBLANT Schade and his boss, the commander in chief of the U.S. Atlantic Fleet (CINCLANTFLT), Admiral Ephraim P. Holmes, dismissed this scenario as well. Their resistance to it may have kept the torpedo theory from being declared the official cause of the *Scorpion*'s loss. Naval Ordnance Systems Command—responsible for the development and testing of undersea weapons—realized the *Scorpion* disaster was being laid at its feet and apparently balked at this notion as well.

While distancing himself from his torpedo theory, Craven simultaneously claims that the navy's Naval Ordnance Systems Command waged a campaign against any theory that implicated its torpedoes.

"The torpedo thing was completely resisted by BUORD, not because they were evil or wrong but because they're human beings," claimed Craven. "They have to ask, 'Have I done all I could do keep that boat from going down?' You're reluctant to pass that along because of that thing in the human brain called denial. Remember this—nobody in this world wants to admit to themselves that they've made an error that resulted in the loss of a submarine with all the men on board."

Craven lays the supposed cover-up of the story behind the loss of the *Scorpion* at the feet of perfidious human nature embodied by Naval

Ordnance, an organization that had been a target of distrust within the submarine force since World War II. Despite the passage of a quarter century, NAVORD was still spoken of resentfully within the submarine force, whose tightly knit members have long memories. This rancor developed when the former Bureau of Ordnance failed to diagnose a series of complicated problems with various exploder, guidance, and depth control components on the Mk-14 torpedo during the first two years of the war, a lapse that severely hampered the navy's undersea war against Japan. Ill will still lurks in the hearts of submariners over this outrageous failure, in no small part because the Bureau of Ordnance initially blamed the poor torpedo performance on cowardly and inept submarine commanders.

Introduced in 1956, the Mk-37 also had its problems, particularly after it was equipped with the Mk-46 silver-zinc primary battery in 1959. However, during twelve years of duty in the U.S. Navy—and numerous other NATO navies—there appears to be no documentation that the Mk-37 torpedo equipped with the Mk-46 battery caused damage to a host submarine.

In giving the accidental-torpedo-explosion scenario a prominent place in the court's Opinions section of the Findings of Fact, the board members credited "key facts and technical opinions presented to the Court by expert witnesses which are cardinal in estimating the most probable scenario for the loss of SCORPION." These "key facts"—the supposed explosive source of the *Scorpion*'s initial death throes and the *Scorpion*'s presumed turn prior to its loss—would be called into serious doubt by subsequent studies requested by none other than Craven prior to his 1970 retirement from the navy.

While the initial acoustic event did not have a bubble pulse—a characteristic of underwater explosions—it was nonetheless deemed to be "cataclysmic in nature," a view the Court of Inquiry didn't change once photographs failed to reveal any internal or external torpedo blast damage. Because it was simply accepted that a torpedo explosion caused the initial acoustic event, the court believed that a blast originated "forward of frame 44," which included the operations compartment and the torpedo room. Following this explosion, the board opined, "Uncontrollable flooding occurred which filled the hull before reaching crush depth."

These initial assumptions support the theory that a "cataclysmic" event—a torpedo detonation—created a pathway for the sea to flood the

Scorpion. Assuming that the submarine was flooded by torpedo blast damage, the court originally concluded, "The main pressure hull did not collapse into any compartment." This assumption was made because the *Scorpion's* four internal bulkheads could only withstand sea pressure at a maximum depth of 300 to 500 feet. The flooding of any one compartment below that depth would result in the sequential failure of these bulkheads well before the boat reached the crush depth of its external pressure hull.

This assumption was rendered somewhat unbelievable soon after the *Mizar's* photographs indicated that the pressure hull in the vicinity of the operations compartment and stern experienced massive implosion damage due to hydrostatic pressure, an event that could not occur if the submarine had flooded.

Even after the imagery of the hull was reviewed, the court still believed that an explosion may have precipitated the loss of the *Scorpion*. It was also speculated that a torpedo explosion inside the torpedo room was a possibility, though the condition of the hull argues strongly against this. The torpedo room—although rather cleanly sliced from the rest of the hull—was remarkably intact. Expert testimony at the Court of Inquiry was unanimous in the belief that the detonation of a Mk-37 warhead would have caused a "sympathetic" explosion of all twenty-one conventional torpedo warheads, totaling 9,163 pounds of high explosive. Damage from such a blast would have been unmistakably catastrophic.

While a "low-order," fire-induced detonation also was considered as the source of the first noise by Craven and the court, this is a somewhat vague hypothesis. A low-order detonation can be any amount of explosive energy below the full blast potential of an explosive. (Under some conditions, high explosives also can deflagrate or burn rapidly, generating great heat without the massive shock wave that actually causes damage.) The blast considered by the court, therefore, was potent enough to sink the submarine, but unable to generate a bubble pulse—something of a fine balance.

Craven remained convinced that an explosion rocked the *Scorpion*. He believed he was bolstered by Hamilton's discovery that replicating the submarine's death sounds recorded at La Palma required surprisingly large explosive charges.

Although some have attempted to compare the acoustic signals of the August 12, 2000, loss of the Russian submarine *Kursk* to those of the

In 2002, Gordon Hamilton recalled his efforts at deducing the *Scorpion*'s general location using signals from a hydroacoustic station that didn't officially exist.

Scorpion's demise, there are few similarities. (The Russian submarine's signals were handily acquired by numerous land-based seismometer stations across Europe.) It was readily seen that the *Kursk* was sunk by two internal weapons explosions, with each generating a distinctive bubble pulse. While Craven argued that the bubble pulse missing from the blast that sank the *Scorpion* was "vented" into its hull, it's interesting to note that the *Kursk*, with its double-hull construction and twice the internal hull volume of the *Scorpion*, was incapable of gulping the smaller, initial bubble pulse of its first explosion or the bubble pulse of the second, larger detonation.

Despite early claims by some Russian naval officers that the *Kursk* collided with an American attack submarine lurking nearby, the Russian Navy later admitted that the ill-fated boat had been rocked by internal explosions, something far from apparent in the loss of the *Scorpion*.

Simulations

Craven commissioned special computerized studies at the Naval Ship Research Development Center (NSRDC) during the summer of 1968 to simulate his hot-running-torpedo scenario and other possibilities.

A computer program was devised with all the known variables to check the validity of data supplied by Craven's studies. More than ten thousand simulations were run.

The problem with this effort was that the results of the tests were governed by variables based largely on speculation. Gabriel Santore, a mechanical engineer with the Submarine Hydrodynamics and Submarine Motion Group at the NSRDC who conducted the simulations, was unenthusiastic about Craven's hypothesis. Referring to the torpedo theory as the "Craven effort," Santore told the inquiry, "I will say that the thrust and objective of the effort was to attempt to lend some credence and some validity to the acoustic data."

This seemed to put the Court of Inquiry president, Vice Adm. Bernard L. Austin, on the defensive, since the "acoustic data" to which Santore referred were the signals upon which Craven was basing his torpedo theory. Austin asked Santore, "Are you saying that you find the scenarios as proposed hard to follow?"

"I think they are highly speculative," responded Santore, who believed the simulations neither proved nor disproved Craven's theory. "I think things like this are possible, but I don't know how to defend any of it."

Court member Dean A. Horn followed up Austin's question to Santore, "I don't believe the intention was to ask anybody to defend or destroy. What we were trying to do is see whether or not it was in the realm of possible, potential, or ridiculous."

"The variables are there for you to juggle and you juggle these variables and each one will give you a solution," said Santore, hinting for the second time that any speculative scenario was subject to manipulation.

NSRDC research physicist George Chertock, who had given the simulation task to Santore, also seemed to scoff at the unnecessary grandiosity of the effort: "We can make estimates but we don't need a precise computer to do this. We can do this by scratching our heads and coming up with our best guess."

Chertock told the court that the studies were originally ordered by Craven to ascertain the size of a hole resulting from a torpedo striking the *Scorpion* amidships, and the hole's hydrodynamic effect on the boat's glide path to the bottom. Had a Mk-37 torpedo struck the *Scorpion*, testified Chertock, the resulting damage would be considerable—and obvious: "According to our best judgment, this would cause . . . an enormous hole, something on the order of [redacted] feet in diameter. All I'm trying to say is that it is a very, very large hole. Once this occurs, the subsequent event [glide path] cannot be calculated with any precision. It cannot be calculated with any confidence because the flooding rates are uncertain."

While Craven's extensive efforts using computer simulations to reveal the *Scorpion's* last moments came under fire by those conducting them, he also stirred disagreement by using similar methods to predict precisely what the submarine was doing at the moment it sank.

"The scenarios developed by Dr. Craven . . . were debatable," said an official postmortem of the effort to locate the *Scorpion's* wreckage prepared for the chief of naval operations. "In particular, these scenarios which had the *Scorpion* going from west to east did not have the concurrence of COMSUBLANT and CINCLANTFLT. In fact, the whole notion of establishing rather complicated scenarios is somewhat controversial."

The report, titled *The Scorpion Search, 1968: An Analysis of the Operation*, pointed out that the *Scorpion* wreck was close to where Hamilton's predictions originally placed it, without factoring in detailed suppositions about the *Scorpion's* reversal of course. In the years since, Craven has maintained that the submarine's wreck site was close to where his hot-run scenario placed the submarine.

Craven's various theories about a torpedo explosion had a number of weak points, although the resourceful and brilliant scientist was always prepared to counter his detractors with convincing scientific logic. One of the most damning complaints about Craven's torpedo explosion theory was that the initial acoustic signal marking the *Scorpion's* location lacked the clear indications of a "bubble pulse," the acoustical phenomenon that is ever-present in underwater explosions well below the surface. Underwater explosions instantly create a distinctive bubble that pushes the water outward, only to have it reverberate repeatedly as the bubble rises.

Craven believed that the lack of a bubble pulse was explainable. If an explosion penetrated a submarine's hull, he reasoned, the high-energy gas bubble might have been swallowed by the submarine's interior. The possibility also existed that a detonation at or near the surface would vent into the atmosphere, or its acoustic energy would be reflected and refracted by the underside of waves. Craven commissioned Hamilton to conduct tests confirming this theory, and Hamilton successfully did so by detonating explosives adjacent to steel containers that indeed swallowed the explosive bubble pulses.

While Hamilton and Craven's tests indicated that small amounts of explosives could penetrate a thin-walled container and cause the absorption of the bubble pulse, the warhead of a Mk-37 torpedo contained 330 pounds of potent HBX-3 explosive, and the hull of the *Scorpion* was 2 inches of magnificently strong HY-80 steel.

Experienced Naval Ordnance Laboratory researchers maintain that a bubble pulse invariably followed the detonation of a torpedo when it struck the hull of a fully submerged target submarine. The only way a sizable explosion could fail to create a bubble pulse, they said, was if the blast occurred near the surface, where the energy vented like a geyser into the air or was refracted by wave action. This, of course, lent weight to the hypothesis that the *Scorpion* was at or near the surface at the time of an explosion—which was supported by the raised positions of several fairwater masts on the detached fairwater in the debris field.

Although Hamilton's investigation tended to support portions of Craven's hot-run-torpedo theory, even Hamilton doubted that the acoustical data could reveal the *Scorpion* turned eastward, toward Europe, a key portion of Craven's hypothesis. The acoustical data, insists Hamilton, were not clear enough to reveal such a small change in movement. "All I'm saying is I didn't analyze it in that kind of detail because I didn't think it was worth it," Hamilton would say thirty-four years later. "John Craven made a big story out of it, but that's John."

No Incontrovertible Proof

Every conceivable scenario would be considered, from control plane failure to collision, but the one involving torpedoes seemed so elegantly complete in so many ways that Craven enjoyed discussing it whenever the subject arose. He presented the theory to the Court of Inquiry's seven members and obviously convinced its president, Vice Admiral Austin, of its plausibility. When the Court of Inquiry issued its Findings of Fact—a fifty-four-page document reporting the basic determinations of the inquiry—the various methods by which a Mk-37 torpedo could detonate and destroy the *Scorpion* were listed as "the most probable causes" in the Opinions section. The court also qualified its speculation as to the possible causes of the disaster, saying, "there is no incontrovertible proof of the exact cause."

When the navy did announce the findings of the Court of Inquiry on January 31, 1969—which stated essentially that the navy lacked sufficient evidence to arrive at a conclusion—it did not reveal the court's speculation about a torpedo mishap. Ignoring the angst of the families and their hunger for information, the navy would not release the Findings of Fact from the inquiry until October 1993, a quarter century after the *Scorpion* disaster.

Austin, the respected president of the inquiry, apparently remained favorably disposed toward the belief that one of the *Scorpion's* own torpedoes was at the heart of the disaster. When interviewed in 1975 by Jack Kestner of the *Norfolk Ledger-Star*, Austin said the navy didn't release the opinions of the court because they were only "theories," adding, "it does not preclude our having had a pretty good idea of what happened, but it still was something we couldn't be 100 percent sure about." Although the court's opinions about what caused the disaster would remain secret for another eighteen years, it's obvious that Austin was referring to the still-secret torpedo theory that topped the court's list of possible causes.

The controversy about Craven's theory even rated a mention in the official navy report recounting the efforts to understand the reasons for the disaster. The report states that the "conclusion by Dr. Craven . . . which was not shared by COMSUBLANT or CINCLANTFLT, is derived from the theory that the *Scorpion* suffered a hot torpedo run in the tube and turned [redacted] to actuate the anti-circular run device in the Mk-37-1 torpedo."

Despite all the scientific polemics over the loss of the *Scorpion*, there was, however, something decidedly worrisome about the Mk-37 torpedo, or more specifically, the cantankerous battery that powered it.

"A Goddamn Bomb"

The Mk-37 antisubmarine torpedo was one of the world's earliest smart weapons. It was designed to pursue and kill enemy submarines using an acoustic homing system while being propelled by a battery of exotic design. Although the torpedo was packed with 330 pounds of high explosives, its battery and not its warhead may have presented the greatest hazard to its users.

When Craven's tenacious belief that a hot-running Mk-37 torpedo played a role in the loss of the *Scorpion* appeared in a 1993 *Chicago Tribune* article, it came to the attention of Charles Thorne in Silverdale, Washington. Thorne, then seventy-two, had been the technical director of the Weapons Quality Engineering Laboratory from 1964 to 1981 at the Naval Torpedo Station in Keyport, Washington. Even after twenty-five years, Thorne was tormented over the loss of the *Scorpion* because he believed the navy failed to protect its doomed crew. One job of the Weapons Quality Engineering Laboratory was to test the Mk-37 torpedo's propulsion batteries to ensure that they met specifications. Thorne believed that faulty Mk-46 propulsion batteries had slipped through the system during the late 1960s.

Thorne and his personnel tested the Mk-46 batteries by exposing them to extreme cold and heat and then shaking them violently before they were activated to determine if they could generate adequate electrical power. Some batteries fared well, while others broke apart during vibration testing or simply failed to generate adequate voltage in the required amount of time.

What worried Thorne were several Mk-46 battery fires that occurred during testing that were indelibly etched into the memories of Thorne and his coworkers.

A particularly bad blaze occurred on February 12, 1966, when a Mk-46 battery exploded and burst into flames while being vibrated on the shaker stand. One side of the battery's plastic casing flew off in a blast so forceful it shook the building. Flames licked at the testing room's tall ceiling and filled the space with heavy, sooty smoke. An electrical engineer rushed in with a dry chemical fire extinguisher but soon retreated, with his skin burning from the caustic, potassium hydroxide electrolyte. As the battery burned, some of the 48 pounds of government-supplied silver used in making its plates melted and dripped to the floor. "The thing was a goddamn bomb," said the engineer, who was amazed that no one was seriously injured.

Later, after the fire was out, an inspection revealed that a foil diaphragm had failed, allowing electrolyte to partially fill the battery cells, triggering the explosion and flames.

Thorne had become concerned about this and other incidents involving batteries produced by Whittaker Power Sources Division. Samples from lots of Mk-46 batteries from various manufacturers were tested, and if any was defective, the entire lot was considered suspect and returned to the manufacturer. Due to a severe shortage of batteries for Mk-37 torpedoes during the mid-1960s, batteries from what Thorne considered a defective lot had been sent to the fleet before testing. (Actually, hard-to-manufacture Mk-46 batteries had been in short supply going

A Mk-46 torpedo propulsion battery that caught fire and burned ferociously while undergoing testing during the 1960s.

back to the late 1950s.) At the urging of Thorne, the commanding officer of the Naval Torpedo Station at Keyport, Capt. James L. Hunnicutt, wrote a letter to NAVORD in late April or early May 1968 warning of the fire problem just before the *Scorpion* was lost.

Craven, whose torpedo theory had been excoriated by critics within the navy during 1968, believed that Thorne's 1994 letter explained how the warhead of a Mk-37 torpedo could have been overheated to the point of detonation *inside* the *Scorpion*. Craven, still clinging to the belief that the *Scorpion* turned east in its final moments, incorporated the battery fire hypothesis into a revamped version of his original torpedo theory. Craven believed the control room incorrectly assumed that a hot run was the problem and turned the submarine to trigger the torpedo's anticircular-run switch, when a torpedo battery fire was the actual problem.

Over the years, Thorne and his coworkers became passionate over this issue as they discussed it among themselves while wondering about the possibility of a cover-up. However, if faulty Whittaker batteries entered the submarine force during late 1967 or early 1968, there is a question as to whether these batteries had enough time to end up on the *Scorpion*. The submarine took on torpedoes between February 12, 1968, and its departure three days later. The batteries would have had to enter the navy's inventory, been issued to various commands, mated to torpedoes, and then delivered to the *Scorpion* before mid-February. In addition, the paper trail for the *Scorpion*'s torpedoes seems to have gone cold, since the records for each of the *Scorpion*'s weapons are said to have gone down with the submarine.

Although Thorne's letter to Craven seemed to contain a revelation about bad torpedo batteries, the navy had been having problems with the Mk-46 battery since their development during the 1950s. The Keyport facility only started testing the battery components in 1965, introducing Thorne to these issues.

In a curious twist, the commander of the Naval Ordnance Laboratory during the early 1960s was Capt. Robert E. Odening, whose son was Lt. (j.g.) Michael Odening, the youngest officer aboard the *Scorpion* when it was lost. A June 25, 1964, letter by the senior Odening to the Naval Underwater Ordnance Station in Newport, Rhode Island, detailed the results of Mk-46 battery testing since 1959. Among the failures Odening noted was a 1959 electrolyte leak in one battery during vibration testing.

Electrochemical engineer Frederick M. Bowers, who went to work for the Naval Ordnance Laboratory in 1955, struggled with the problems of the Mk-46 battery for thirteen years prior to the loss of the *Scorpion*. During the early 1960s, Bowers was at the Naval Torpedo Station in Newport, Rhode Island, watching a representative of a battery manufacturer cut into a malfunctioning Mk-46 with a hacksaw. As the factory representative penetrated the casing, Bowers was surprised by a 4-inch-diameter jet of blue flame shooting from the battery's casing. "When you have a fire like that, the chemical energy in the battery is being removed [as fire and heat] in an uncontrolled fashion," said Bowers. "We pushed it outside so the fire engine could spray water on it."

Bowers, who served as an infantry platoon commander in Europe during the final, vicious fighting World War II, had seen how inadequate equipment and poor decisions cost men their lives. The allegation that bad batteries were intentionally allowed to slip into the fleet rang untrue to Bowers, who nonetheless recognized that a bad battery might inadvertently enter the system. Navy desperation to obtain adequate stocks of Mk-46 batteries had prompted acceptance of batteries during the mid-1960s before testing was completed, said Bowers, who considered the arrangement less than ideal. Bowers was not familiar with any incident in which a Mk-46 battery created an uncontrolled fire inside a submarine.

There were incidents in which Mk-46 batteries became extremely hot within the Mk-37's torpedo casings, due either to a hot run or electrolyte leakage, but no one seems to know of a full or partial detonation of a Mk-37 torpedo due to a propulsion battery fire. The batteries that burned during testing were outside the heavy aluminum torpedo casings, where they could burn dramatically in the open air. A battery fire inside a warhead-equipped torpedo could heat the back of the high-explosive warhead adjacent to it, but the flames would be contained.

The Mk-46 torpedo battery was developed during the late 1940s and early 1950s to replace an older silver-zinc battery—a "secondary" battery that had to be removed and recharged every thirty days. This shortcoming threatened the combat-readiness of nuclear submarines capable of operating for months without returning to port. The answer was the Mk-46 silver-zinc "primary" battery, whose electrolyte was separated from its battery cells, giving it virtually unlimited shelf life. A primary battery can be stored for years until needed. The battery was activated by rapidly flooding its cells with the electrolyte mixture of 30 percent potassium hydroxide and 70 percent distilled water.

An electrolyte tank held $3\frac{1}{2}$ gallons of potassium hydroxide secured by a silver or gold foil seal. An electrically activated "squib," a tiny charge similar to a toy rocket motor, produced gas pressure that ruptured the seal and forced the nonflammable electrolyte around the silver and zinc battery plates. When this flooding system proved unreliable, a piston was employed that also was driven by gas pressure.

Should the electrolyte seal fail to open fully or leak, the hazardous result could be incomplete wetting of the silver and zinc battery cell plates. Partial wetting of the plates caused the generation of oxygen and explosive hydrogen along with electrical arcing—a bad combination. When exposed to moisture or partially wetted by electrolyte that was mostly water, the zinc-oxide plates had a tendency to undergo a violent exothermic—heat-producing—reaction. This heat then caused the silver-oxide plates to release large quantities of oxygen.

As the battery discharged, it also produced explosive hydrogen and additional oxygen, which were separated by electrolysis from the electrolyte's water. The overheating battery might combust spontaneously or it might arc, igniting the hydrogen or the battery's plastic components. Fed by pure oxygen and feeding on the plastic components of the battery, the resulting fire in an uncased battery could be both spectacular and dangerous. If the silver and zinc plates were completely immersed in the electrolyte, their chemical energy would instead be safely released as 450 amps of electricity.

Bowers was well aware of this phenomenon. "At elevated temperatures of 200 degrees Fahrenheit and above, the silver oxide decomposes," said Bowers. "What you have in effect is a conflagration of the zinc burning as well and this melts the plastic cases of the individual cells. I have seen fires that shot 50 to 100 feet in the air on an uncased Mk-46 battery."

One of the common problems encountered during the development and production of the Mk-46 battery was the premature failure of the foil seal holding back the electrolyte. This allowed the chemical to dribble into the cells and dampen—but not completely cover—the plates. Because of this complex set of issues, torpedomen who heard the propeller clacking against its prop lock in the torpedo room or whirring freely in the torpedo tube would have no idea if the weapon was activated by a stray electrical signal in a classic hot run, or the failure of the electrolyte tank seal.

The Mk-46 primary battery was nothing if not an individual example of the thousands of complex components that must be precisely engineered, fabricated, and maintained to ensure the safe operation of a submarine.

Lawsuit

The story of the Mk-46 battery is exceedingly strange.

Those that originally built the batteries were old-line battery producers for the military, including Exide Storage Battery and Yardney Electric Corporation. (Yardney pioneered silver-zinc battery design in America.) By the mid-1960s, a newcomer known as Whittaker Power Sources Division entered the game as well. The navy wanted multiple sources of supply and a competitive atmosphere, although, in the end, this competitive atmosphere would be less competitive for Exide and Yardney than it was for Whittaker. The individual manufacturers were allowed to maintain their proprietary trade secrets, so that each battery maker had to solve its technical problems independently while meeting navy specifications. This meant that any company designing the batteries had to reinvent the wheel to solve the challenges posed by the navy's specifications. On something as crucial as a volatile battery, it would seem that information sharing would be a prudent thing to do, even if licensing agreements had to be drawn up. Nevertheless, said Bowers, each battery company followed its own path.

Exide and Yardney were producing large numbers of batteries for the navy by 1960. The navy's high testing standards and the difficulty in manufacturing the batteries to specifications meant that a number of batteries failed to pass the performance tests. The batteries were subjected to temperatures ranging from −60 degrees Fahrenheit to 160 degrees Fahrenheit for extended periods and then shaken so violently that their internal components broke loose. To get Mk-37 torpedoes into the fleet, waivers were granted to both manufacturers if randomly selected sample batteries failed to produce the required current after the grueling testing.

Bowers considered the standards ridiculously high: "I was trying to get the upper temperature limit reduced to 120 degrees because the possibility of storing these batteries at 160 degrees Fahrenheit was highly unlikely—a figment of someone's imagination. And besides, there is variability here because storage doesn't occur at a single temperature."

When Whittaker Power Sources began producing Mk-46 batteries in 1965, it was strictly held to navy specifications, unlike its competitors that were given variances if their batteries did not measure up. As a result, Whittaker's batteries fared poorly, and the 1965 contract was canceled. One reason may be that the Whittaker batteries were being tested at Keyport by Thorne's group, which had better and newer test equipment and a philosophy that required a strict adherence to standards. (Whittaker's batteries were considered particularly prone to electrolyte seal malfunctions according to Keyport's testing personnel, though Whittaker would later prove in court that its batteries were no worse than Yardney's or Exide's.)

Eager to acquire the contract to produce the badly needed batteries, Whittaker negotiated a second production contract in 1967. It was this lot of silver-zinc batteries that Thorne believed was so problematical. The complicated story of Mk-46 battery production came to a head when Whittaker—which purchased Yardney in 1971—sued the navy before the Armed Services Board of Contract Appeals for its double standard on battery testing. Whittaker demonstrated that the navy's standards were so impossibly high that no manufacturer could meet them and that Exide and Yardney previously obtained acceptance of its Mk-46 batteries because neither had to meet the standards imposed on Whittaker. The Board of Contract Appeals ruled in favor of Whittaker and awarded the firm compensation. An important legal concept known as "commercial impracticability"—now studied in law schools across America—was established by this lawsuit, which was not resolved until 1979. The concept held that a manufacturer is not liable for failing to comply with a manufacturing contract whose standards are impossible to meet.

Few if any submarine force personnel were aware of the story behind Mk-46 battery. Despite its problems, the battery was used in the Mk-37 torpedoes sold to navies around the world. None is known to have destroyed its host submarine. Although bulletins were issued and training was conducted to teach torpedomen how to deal with hot-running torpedoes—a recognized though relatively rare problem—it appears that hot runs attributed to stray electrical signals or crew mistakes may have been caused by faulty electrolyte seals.

In Craven's autobiography, *Silent War*, published in 2001, he claims that the submarine force was ordered to remove this bad group of torpedo propulsion batteries while the *Scorpion* was at sea. This alleged recall notice was not mentioned during inquiry testimony given by SUBLANT or SUBRON 6 weapons officers, although it would seem to be the sort of bulletin they would have reported to the court even if they were not specifically asked about it.

Despite claims of a cover-up regarding the instability of the torpedo battery, the possibility of a Mk-46 battery fire was discussed in considerable detail during the inquiry into the *Scorpion*'s loss.

Craven has also expressed outrage that the navy withheld information about Mk-46 battery fires during testing. Despite his claim that the navy hid this fact, detailed testimony about the problems posed by the inadvertent activation of Mk-46 batteries *was* presented during the inquiry by Cmdr. George R. Langford, SUBLANT's tactical weapons officer.

When asked by the Court of Inquiry about problems with the Mk-37 torpedo, Langford described the "severe overheating" that could occur when the torpedo's Mk-46 battery was accidentally activated. He described a 1961 incident at the submarine base in New London when he was called to the diesel-electric submarine *Jallao* to inspect a badly charred Mk-37 torpedo. The battery had activated while in its rack and created so much heat that it melted some of the warhead's HBX-3 explosive, though no detonation occurred. This incident may have to suffice as the only field test of the effect a burning Mk-46 battery would have on a Mk-37 torpedo warhead. Langford testified that he had the torpedo offloaded so he could disassemble and inspect the weapon.

It's also notable that the intense, oxygen-fed fire in the *Sargo's* stern torpedo room in 1960 melted but failed to trigger a high-order detonation of the HBX-3 explosive in two Mk-37 torpedo warheads. The Findings of Fact from the *Sargo* inquiry concluded there had been a "low-order detonation" of the warheads, although the *Sargo's* commanding officer, John Nicholson, said there was no blast damage inside the compartment.

A Mk-46 battery fire may have occurred aboard the ballistic missile boat *Thomas A. Edison* in 1963. *Edison* weapons officer J. Denver McCune and his torpedo gang noticed the propeller of a rack-stored Mk-37 clacking against its propeller lock after running electronics tests on the torpedo. McCune had the weapon loaded into a torpedo tube. "It was so hot that when you put your hand on it, it hissed the way your mother's did when she placed it against a hot iron," recalled McCune, who ordered the weapon impulsed into the ocean.

Craven's persuasive description of an errant torpedo as the cause of the *Scorpion's* loss in newspaper and television interviews since the mid-1980s has led many to believe that the mystery surrounding the *Scorpion's* loss was long ago resolved. This has been a surprise to other scientists deeply involved in the investigation of the *Scorpion's* loss who believed that the cause of the disaster remained an open question.

Findings of Fact

After ending its first session on July 25, 1968, the Court of Inquiry prepared its Findings of Fact, laying out all the factual determinations made during the inquiry, with an Opinion section stating the court's conclusions. An amended Findings of Fact was developed after the inquiry reconvened in November 6, 1968, with the acquisition of the *Scorpion's* wreck photographs. In both documents, the court infers that a torpedo blast is the most likely culprit.

The court originally believed that the *Scorpion's* pressure hull, fully flooded by a torpedo explosion, would be unmarked by damage due to hydrostatic collapse. Since the four internal bulkheads were only capable of withstanding a maximum of 500 feet of depth, they would collapse in rapid succession before reaching the *Scorpion's* estimated crush depth of 1,400 feet.

When photographs of the *Scorpion* wreck were obtained and reviewed, it was plain that the submarine was in three separate sections. The torpedo room was lying some distance from the operations compartment, and the tall fairwater was sheared from the submarine's back. It was also seen that the engine room plunged forward into the auxiliary machine space ahead of it due to hydrostatic collapse of the hull. Based on this evidence, the court altered its scenario. The court reasoned that the torpedo room and fairwater had sheared off upon impact with the seafloor, and the collapse of the bulkhead between the engine room and the auxiliary machine space had drawn the engine room inside the compartment ahead of it—a somewhat contradictory observation. This scenario would later be roundly disputed by navy structural experts. The court also provided a detailed analysis of what caused the remaining fourteen of the fifteen acoustic events following the supposed "explosion" that some believed triggered the disaster. The court based its speculation on an acoustic analysis that would also be criticized by other navy physicists.

The incorrect assessment that the operations compartment was not damaged by hydrostatic collapse was inadvertently and erroneously encouraged during the *Scorpion* inquiry by Peter Palermo, director of the Submarine Structures Section of the Naval Ship Engineering Center. Palermo actually believed the opposite was the case.

"Nowhere in any of the pictures could we see any damage of the type that we would normally associate with a hydrostatic collapse of a submarine pressure hull," Palermo told the court on November 14 in his heavy Brooklyn accent. Palermo would clarify his testimony December 10 after conducting a closer examination of the wreck photographs. When asked by the president of the court, Bernard Austin, if his testimony still stood, Palermo told the court, "Yes, sir. There's *no* evidence that we could see in the pictures that would indicate hull rupture [implosion] but I don't think we could rule it out as a possibility at this stage."

Palermo's answer stumped Austin, who believed that implosion damage had been ruled out weeks ago. "By hull rupture you mean from something like a piston effect and telescoping?" asked Austin, referring to a cylinder of incompressible water driven through the submarine by the collapse of the engine room.

"No," replied Palermo matter-of-factly, "the collapse of the control room due to hydrostatic pressure." Palermo, a structural engineer who spoke in precise scientific shorthand, had subtly qualified his initial description of the *Scorpion*'s unusual hull damage as nothing "we could *normally* associate" with the hydrostatic collapse of a pressure hull. Palermo always suspected it was implosion damage, but it was like nothing he had seen before.

Austin was taken aback by this and asked Palermo if hydrostatic collapse was the "initial event" that caused the loss of the *Scorpion*.

"Basically [implosion] was the primary cause of failure and we haven't seen anything to cause us to change our opinion," Palermo stated resolutely. A year later Palermo would examine an even clearer set of wreckage photographs that further reinforced his belief that the *Scorpion* had imploded upon reaching crush depth.

Palermo had little real-world data to draw on regarding what implosion damage to a *Skipjack*-class hull would look like. Although obsolete submarines were sunk to observe the effects of hydrostatic pressure, only scale models of *Skipjack*-class hulls were brought to failure in pressurized tanks. Even these tests failed to implode the models realistically, since the pressure within the test tank was instantly reduced at the moment of collapse.

The *Thresher* and the *Scorpion* were the only two submarine hulls constructed of HY-80 steel accidentally subjected to implosion forces. Although most remain classified, images of the *Thresher* are said to show a submarine torn apart more completely by implosion forces than was the *Scorpion*. In addition, the *Thresher*'s stern had not telescoped into the compartment ahead of it—a fascinating and somewhat unnerving sight on the *Scorpion*'s wreck. This mystery may have been resolved by Robert S. Price, a physicist at the Naval Ordnance Laboratory and a witness who testified during both sessions of the Court of Inquiry.

Price understood that the *Scorpion*'s cone cylinder juncture, which allowed the larger-diameter auxiliary machine space to join the engine room's narrower hull segment, was slightly different than the juncture on the *Thresher*. This difference allowed the *Scorpion*'s engine room to drive 50 feet forward into, and around, the auxiliary machine space in a millisecond. To convince skeptics, Price made a paper model and provided a demonstration of the collapse mechanism.

Schade's Theory: The Trash Disposal Unit

COMSUBLANT Arnold F. Schade was nothing if not the perfect example of a submarine force officer. Dapper and dedicated, Schade was imbued with great military bearing and had seen combat during the ruthlessly efficient World War II submarine campaign against the Japanese.

Among the issues worrying Schade was that the terrific speed of the nuclear-powered boats placed them at the mercy of their hydraulically operated control surfaces. A sudden failure could put the stern planes in "full dive," meaning a high-speed plunge toward crush depth. So concerned was Schade about the reliability of these control plane systems that he submitted an unsolicited letter to the *Scorpion* Court of Inquiry expressing his worries on the subject to underscore the urgency of the issue.

Schade, however, knew that the one drill practiced constantly by every submarine crew was how to counteract a stern plane mishap. The procedure was simple, but its execution had to be immediate and flawless: the order was given for "emergency back," putting the propeller in reverse while blowing ballast to create buoyancy. Aside from the rapidity of its execution, the recovery procedure's success depended on the boat's buoyancy, speed, and depth at the time of the failure.

Although the *Scorpion* had experienced severe plane failures and executed successful recoveries, the court determined that the boat's control plane system was so reliable that such a failure was not considered a likely cause of the submarine's loss.

Inquiry testimony also revealed that Slattery may have decided to operate the *Scorpion* no deeper than 350 feet—150 feet shallower than its ordinary depth restriction imposed because it lacked SUBSAFE certification. Underwood testified that Slattery imposed the depth restriction near the end of the Mediterranean deployment, although the limit was not necessarily a "rigid restriction," but one based on recovery calculations performed by Slattery and Lloyd. This, however, was disputed: Elrod testified that no depth restriction shallower than the 500-foot limit already imposed by Naval Ship Systems Command was in effect.

What really concerned Schade was the trash disposal unit, the worrisome TDU. It was a component that could threaten the submarine if its 10-inch outer ball valve and the galley's inner access hatch were opened simultaneously. This type of mishap was a flooding casualty from which the submarine might not recover. For this reason, the TDU was operated only at periscope depth, or generally no deeper than 50 feet to reduce the hydrostatic pressure.

After viewing the photographs taken by the *Mizar's* camera sleds, Schade noted that the number two periscope was partially extended, as well as two communications antennas—a trio of masts that experts testified could only be raised intentionally. This told Schade that the *Scorpion* was at or near periscope depth at the time of the fatal mishap. The most dangerous process executed at that depth, reasoned Schade, was use of the TDU. Schade pushed his theory hard, but found himself shut out

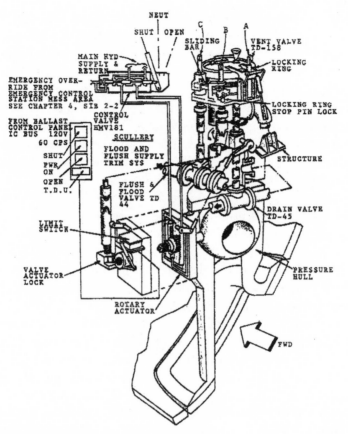

The *Scorpion's* trash disposal unit with its muzzle ball valve facing the sea and its breech hatch inside the submarine above.

by the court, which had chosen to accept that the *Scorpion* was most likely destroyed by one of its own torpedoes.

"We can only speculate—but since we are convinced that the initial casualty was a flooding casualty at some depth near periscope depth or less than [classified] feet—that such flooding could have been associated with the kind of evolution that is not unusual at periscope depth," Schade insistently told the court. "For example, the trash disposal unit is operated at shallow depth, and this could have jammed and caused internal flooding. Again, this is pure speculation. We do believe that it was an uncontrolled flooding situation which occurred forward which prevented them from surfacing." When Schade was asked by the court which component he suspected more in the mishap, the snorkel—which also could provide a path for water—or the TDU, Schade's reply was immediate: "I would say that the trash disposal unit would have priority over the snorkel simply from the viewpoint that there should be three ways that you could correct a snorkel casualty."

Schade believed that if the interlock linkage system failed and the ball valve and the inner hatch were simultaneously opened, a stream of seawater could burst into the galley. The problem with flooding in the galley is that it is a contiguous part of the operations compartment, one of the boat's largest compartments besides the engine room.

The seawater could run unimpeded down the decks of the multistory operations compartment entering the main storage battery, where a massive discharge or battery fire might occur. This type of casualty would be difficult to control unless the crew reacted quickly.

Schade believed that the *Scorpion*'s crew should have been able to recover from a TDU mishap. However, realizing that failures often travel in pairs on a submarine, with the first problem often triggering a second, Schade warned, "There might have been additional material failures, flooding which caused fires, loss of propulsion, or there might have been personnel failures, a lack of appreciation of what was going on, and the ability to counter it in time, but I think it would have to have been something else at the same time."

The court would disregard Schade's theory, derived from his experience and the research efforts of his staff. Within the Opinion section of the Findings of Fact, the court would address Schade's theory succinctly: "while the sequence of events postulated by the Commander, Submarine Force U.S. Atlantic Fleet is considered possible, the weight of the evidence leads to the conclusion that such a sequence of events was not probable."

12

The Inquiry

When the Court of Inquiry was established and ordered to "inquire into the circumstances surrounding the loss of USS *Scorpion*," an investigative staff was assembled at Norfolk's CINCLANTFLT headquarters, and evidence was impounded. As this was happening, typewriters clattered away, generating orders to uniformed and civilian naval personnel to appear as witnesses.

Though the Court of Inquiry failed to interview Radioman Chief Daniel Pettey and other sailors who had served on the submarine, the court stringently interrogated ninety witnesses, including other former members of the crew. The court also reviewed thousands of documents in two separate sessions during the last half of 1968. The resultant transcript of the proceedings, which also included evidentiary exhibits, totaled more than two thousand pages. Many thousands of pages of official documents, memoranda, and reports were available to the court as well.

A steady parade of officers, enlisted men, engineers, and physicists was questioned. The expertise of the witnesses ran the gamut from torpedo safety devices and submarine structural design to a navy physician who reviewed the medical records of the crew. When photographs of the *Scorpion*'s wreckage arrived in Norfolk on November 6, 1968, more than three months after the last session adjourned, the court immediately reconvened for a second session of study and testimony. Additional witnesses were called and attempts were made to understand what had happened to the submarine based on expert analysis of the images. The investigative activities of the court's members were not strictly confined to a conference room in the CINCLANTFLT headquarters building at Naval Station Norfolk, particularly after the arrival of the wreckage photographs. Not only did the seven members of the Court of Inquiry hear testimony and confer with one another, they also involved themselves in studies and discussion outside the court.

Court member Harold Rich, a naval aviator and chief of staff to the commander of Fleet Air Wing 3, and the other members of the court inspected the *Shark*, the *Scorpion*'s sister ship. Another member of the court was Capt. Dean Horn, a World War II submariner with a master's degree in naval engineering who had also served as a technical adviser to the court on submarine construction.

Court member Rear Adm. Charles D. Nace, who reported aboard his first submarine eight months before the Japanese attack on Pearl Harbor, was free to ask any questions he thought necessary during the inquiry and did so. He also chose to obtain information in an extracurricular manner. After receiving the hefty sheaf of camera sled images of the shattered *Scorpion*, Nace, the commander of Submarine Flotilla 2 in New London, sought the help of Cmdr. Thomas W. Evans, who had departed the *Scorpion* just more than a year before its loss.

Evans served on the *Scorpion* from 1964 to 1967, first as communications officer and later as weapons officer. Evans was a good choice for Nace to turn to. As a graduate of Rice University—the same prestigious institution that had educated deep-sound-channel discoverer William Maurice Ewing—Evans had a background in metallurgy and physics.

Nace asked Evans to sift through the black-and-white photographs of the *Scorpion*'s debris and provide an analysis. Evans was stunned by what he saw. "You could tell the ship had exceeded its crush depth before being completely flooded. I observed yielding of the hull between the pressure ribs [reinforcing frames] near the operations compartment and the catastrophic implosion of the engine room into the auxiliary machinery space."

Nace and Evans worked together studying the images and obtained photographs of a quarter-scale test model of the *Thresher*'s hull to study how it failed in lab tests when it passed crush depth. Both men deduced that the *Scorpion* had failed in much the same way as had the *Thresher* model—by the collapse of the stern cone cylinder juncture, a rigid segment less capable of absorbing stresses, making it the weakest point on the hull. One thing that confused Evans was the massive amount of main storage battery debris, including battery plates, on the ocean floor. "It appeared to me that if this had happened due to [implosion] the battery

This model shows the stern engine room driven 50 feet into the submarine's hull when the cone cylinder juncture collapsed at frame 67.

plates would not have been scattered all over the ocean floor, but squished inside their cells."

The only two officers on the court who had commanded nuclear-powered submarines were A. J. Martin Atkins and Ernest R. Barrett. By 1968 both Atkins and Barrett were captains.

Atkins commanded four nuclear-powered boats between 1962 and 1968, including the *Scamp*, a sister ship of the *Scorpion*. Barrett entered the nuclear program at thirty-eight years of age in 1960 and in 1961 became the prospective commanding officer of the fast attack boat *Permit*.

The president of the board was Vice Adm. Bernard Lige Austin from Wagener, South Carolina. The 1924 graduate of the Naval Academy served on two diesel submarines and commanded a third between 1927 and 1937. During World War II, Austin commanded the destroyer *Woolsey* when it sank a German U-boat during the American invasion of North Africa. Soon after, he transferred to the Pacific as commander of Destroyer Division 46, where he was twice awarded the Navy Cross. In the culture of the navy, Austin was the paragon of a naval officer—he had sterling combat experience marked by personal heroism, a technical background (he had been an instructor in the Electrical Engineering and Physics Department at the Naval Academy), and he became president of the Naval War College.

His credentials—combined with his approaching retirement, which made him immune to influence—resulted in Austin being ordered to assume the role of president of the inquiry that investigated the 1963 loss of the *Thresher*. When asked to perform the same task when the *Scorpion* was lost, the retired sixty-five-year-old officer dutifully reported to Norfolk.

Although he had not served aboard a submarine for thirty-one years— a period during which submarine technology had radically changed— Austin led some of the toughest and most insightful grilling of the inquiry's witnesses. Austin's interrogations revealed a healthy skepticism.

The court was rounded out by Capt. Thomas John Moriarty, a 1939 graduate of the College of the Holy Cross who was commissioned in 1940. A year after completing his duty as a member of the inquiry, Moriarty was directing the NROTC program at Harvard University in the face of student and administration opposition fed by antiwar sentiment. The transcript of the inquiry indicated that Moriarty asked few questions in open court.

Rickover

No matter how oblivious the American public was to the *Scorpion*'s loss or the navy's investigation into the tragedy, those who knew anything about America's submarine force had likely heard of the legendary Vice Adm. Hyman G. Rickover, the so-called "Father of the Nuclear Navy." Those who knew of Rickover would naturally assume that the outspoken officer, who was something of a celebrity, would eagerly testify before the *Scorpion*'s Court of Inquiry about the demise of one of his undersea "offspring."

He was a superstar of the technology-worshiping 1950s and early 1960s who—like a crafty politician—gained the limelight by pretending to gruffly shun it. He was a self-styled loner, championing excellence in a world of mediocrity, at least from his own viewpoint. The public generally saw the Russian-born Rickover as imbued with quintessentially American traits—he was outspoken, devoted to logic, and abhorrent of unprogressive tradition. Rickover was pleased to present himself as a necessary but irksome burr beneath the saddle of a lethargic bureaucracy embodied by the navy.

When no one else would tell the truth, Rickover would cast light on a problem and make the case for his own philosophy of excellence. On the other hand, some saw him as the ultimate power broker who craftily gained control over the navy's nuclear power program and held it for decades.

Rickover's reputation for forthrightness would seem somewhat overstated when he successfully resisted testifying about the loss of the *Scorpion*. His affront to the court was unprecedented, but it was quintessential Rickover. He would appear regularly before Congress—his arena of choice, where he groomed powerful allies—but he was loath to being hauled before any inquiry where he would be grilled by lesser beings than senators or congressmen. When asked to report to CINCLANTFLT's headquarters in Norfolk regarding the *Scorpion*, an unhappy Rickover immediately left word for Austin to call him.

Fully aware of Rickover's thorny attitude, Austin returned Rickover's call and was immediately nonplussed when he found himself bargaining with Rickover as to how the head of Naval Reactors would answer the court's questions. Had the matter not been so serious, the conversation between the two vice admirals would have been comical. Austin felt obliged to include his version of their June 28, 1968, telephone conversation in the inquiry's record:

> Rickover said, "Rickover is here."
>
> Austin replied, "This is Austin. Go ahead."
>
> Rickover then said, "Well, you called me." (Austin's response was to coolly remind Rickover that it was Rickover who wanted to speak with him.) Rickover immediately began questioning the court's need of his testimony, a somewhat strange reaction considering that most officers were eager to assist the investigation.

"He [Rickover] said he did not see what he could tell us [about] where the *Scorpion* was or what caused it to sink, because he didn't know," Austin reported to the court. (Rickover's reasons were sarcastically disingenuous, since he knew the court didn't expect him to know such details.) "Then he wondered why we wanted to have him as a witness. I told him we simply wanted the most authoritative source of information on any dangers from radiation which might result from a submarine . . . sunk in approximately 2,000 fathoms of water. I also told him that we wished to have authoritative information on effects of great pressure on the reactor itself."

Rickover then began seeking a way to avoid the witness chair while still cooperating with the court. "He wanted to know if it wouldn't be all right if we sent him these questions in writing," said Austin. "I told him we could not conduct the court's business in this manner. If a witness were, in fact, available to testify before the court [it was necessary] because [answers] often generate other questions . . . I informed Admiral Rickover that it would be perfectly satisfactory to the court for him to choose anyone able to speak to the questions. This is what he finally agreed to."

Austin began telling Rickover which questions he wanted the Reactor Branch witness to address: "I told him that we would want to know whether or not the reactor would be crushed at such a depth and we would also like to know [of] any radioactivity danger to sea life or human habitation and he didn't like the wording of that." After Rickover had gotten what he wanted—which was not being forced to testify—he went a step farther by attempting to reshape the questions his representative would face. Rickover asked, "Can I reword that?"

"Reword it any way you want," shot back Austin. "I am just trying to convey what we are after." The international political nature of these questions became apparent when Austin told Rickover he needed "real answers to the questions regarding the effect of the reactor . . . rather than the false information being put out by Moscow."

The witness eventually sent by Rickover was civilian Souren Hanessian, associate director for submarines at the Division of Naval Reactors. Hanessian deftly answered the court's questions and assured its members that the Scorpion's S5W reactor could not detonate like a bomb or release radiation for an "indefinite period of time." He also explained how the reactor automatically lost criticality the moment electrical power was lost. (The loss of electrical power would scram the reactor by dropping the control rods into the shutdown position, halting further neutron collisions. In addition, the reactor's pressure vessel would probably not be crushed by hydrostatic pressure, since it was already filled with water.)

Any heat that might be generated by residual nuclear fission would be drawn away by the surrounding seawater, thereby preventing a destructive, radiation-spreading meltdown, said Hanessian. (The heat generated by a continuing fission process may have been the target of the thermal photography mission by the U.S. Air Force during the initial search.) The cladding on the rods containing the U-235 nuclear fuel would deteriorate at the rate of a few millionths of an inch per year, ensuring that the fuel would remain enclosed for many decades if not centuries. Furthermore, said Hanessian, "The maximum rate of release

Then rear admiral Hyman G.
Rickover faces the wind on
the *Scorpion*'s fairwater bridge
during acceptance trials in
1960.

and dispersal of the radioactivity in the ocean, even if the protective
cladding on the fuel were destroyed, would be so low as to be harmless."

What has not been officially stated is whether the S5W reactor still
resides within the *Scorpion*'s hull. Color video images taken by the navy
in 1986 do not appear to show the reactor inside the reactor compartment, and sizable depressions seen in the seafloor of the debris field ooze
indicate that unidentified heavy objects from the submarine buried themselves where they fell. However, a naval officer who observed the *Scorpion*'s wreckage insists that the reactor remains inside the submarine. On
the other hand, marine geologist Robert Ballard told *Fathoms* magazine
in 2003 that his navy-sponsored surveys of the *Thresher* and the *Scorpion*
wreck sites during the 1980s were for finding the S5W reactors that spilled
from both submarines. His team was to measure any radiation leakage and
assess its effects on the deep ocean because the navy was considering ben-
thic dumping of old naval reactors.

At the end of his testimony, Hanessian handed the court a memorandum from Rickover with additional information about the presumed
condition of the reactor, which Austin accepted.

As Austin began to express his appreciation to Hanessian for Rickover's cooperation—such as it was—Hanessian began dutifully taking
verbatim notes to carry back to his superior. When his note-taking could
not keep up with Austin's words, Hanessian halted the court's president
in midsentence: "Admiral, could you go a little slower please?" Austin, at

the end of his patience, answered Hanessian by reiterating the court's unwillingness to "interrogate Admiral Rickover by mail," and delivered a warning: "To clear the record, the court did not agree to limit itself to the questions which I indicated over the phone were our areas of major concern."

Despite the bureaucratic dance between Rickover and Austin, the testimony of Hanessian has held true. A radiological monitor on Buck Buchanan's towed sled showed no indications of abnormally high radiation readings at the *Scorpion* wreck site in October 1968. Radiation levels were normal during a second navy visit to the site, in 1969. A third visit to the site, reportedly made in 1979, also failed to detect any radiation. The most thorough radiological survey of the debris field by the navy took place in 1986, when sea life and soil samples failed to reveal abnormal radiation levels. If other radiological surveys have been conducted by the navy since 1986, they remain undisclosed.

Despite Rickover's contentiousness over appearing before the court regarding the *Scorpion*, the tiny, white-haired admiral was not always unyielding or harsh on the subject of the *Scorpion*.

Still shattered over the loss of their son, *Scorpion* machinist's mate David Stone, his parents, Vernon and Sybil, dashed off a letter to Rickover just days after the *Scorpion* failed to return. Enclosed with the letter was a copy of her son's comments about the *Scorpion's* mechanical problems during its time in the Mediterranean. If anyone could get to the bottom of the problem, believed the Stones and other families, it was Rickover.

Rickover wasted no time in drafting a return note, with a tone far different than the one he ordinarily took when dealing with his brother officers. On June 7, 1968, Rickover wrote:

> I wish to express sympathy for the loss of your son. His performance in the nuclear program reflects credit on himself, his family and the naval service.
>
> I appreciate your thoughtfulness and interest in sending me a partial copy of David's letter. It's obvious from his words that he was proud to be a part of the Navy and the nuclear program.
>
> Although there is nothing one can do at a time like this, I hope you will find some comfort in the knowledge that he served his country well.
>
> H. G. Rickover

13

Trial Horse for a New Overhaul Concept

In 1963 the *Thresher* was the lead ship in the newest class of nuclear-powered attack submarines, and to many it was an affirmation that America's undersea warships had reached a new level of sophistication and maturity. Tragically, just twenty months after being commissioned, this symbol of technical prowess imploded after helplessly sinking below its hull's collapse depth.

The April 10, 1963, disaster that killed 129 men off Cape Cod was the first involving an American nuclear-powered submarine, and it took place following a full shipyard overhaul. It was the navy's worst submarine disaster, and it screamed across the front pages.

The *Thresher* inquiry uncovered poor quality control in nuclear submarine construction and revealed submarine operating practices that bordered on the idiotic. A risk-taking culture had developed that tolerated, if not encouraged, perilous operating practices that defied common sense. The picture wasn't pretty in the shipyards, either. The most modern method of inspecting hull integrity and seawater piping welds—ultrasound technology—had not been used on the *Thresher* to locate structural voids. The means of testing the brazing of seawater piping joints was to whack them with a rubber mallet or pressurize them and watch for leaks. It was revealed that 13.8 percent of the *Thresher*'s seawater piping connections failed to meet minimum bond specifications following its overhaul.

The court speculated that the failure of a flexible seawater hose or a silver-brazed joint connecting the copper-nickel seawater piping was the most likely cause of flooding aboard the *Thresher* that perhaps triggered a scram of its S5W reactor.

The lethal beauty of the *Thresher's* modern nuclear submarine design belied fatal flaws that killed 129 men on April 10, 1963.

Robbed of its propulsion, negatively buoyant, and with no residual speed to drive it to the surface—examples of the foolhardy operating practices of the period—the *Thresher* continued to sink. The crew may have attempted to propel themselves to a shallower depth using the submarine's TLX-53A main storage battery—the same one carried aboard the *Scorpion*—but this was regarded as too anemic to drive a submarine to safety. (The crew may have husbanded the stored electrical power in an effort to restart the nuclear reactor, a process also governed by ridiculous rules that slowed the effort.)

A final strike was assessed against the submarine when it attempted to activate its main ballast tank blow system, which may have lacked adequate pressure to expel water at the boat's 1,300-foot test depth, itself an outrageous shortcoming. The court also speculated that moisture inside the high-pressure air bank flasks may have frozen due to the drastic drop in temperature that occurs when compressed air expands. This clogging may have prevented the air from purging the ballast tanks of water.

Without propulsion, buoyancy, or any forward motion, the *Thresher* continued to sink. Since its crush depth was 50 percent greater than its test depth, the *Thresher* probably reached 1,900 feet or slightly deeper when the cold grip of the Atlantic began undulating the thick HY-80 steel like hands pushing against taut canvas. The *Thresher*'s hull then collapsed with the finality of a thunderclap.

After the loss of the *Thresher*, it became glaringly obvious that much had to be done to make submarine operations safer.

The navy had to increase safety on its submarines no matter the cost or the effort. A program created to make submarines safer would, ironically, open a Pandora's box of difficulties for the navy.

SUBSAFE

In the aftermath of the *Thresher* inquiry, the navy's nuclear-powered submarines appeared to be expensive undersea accidents waiting to happen. Something had to be done, and the navy turned to Capt. Donald Hamblett Kern to tell them precisely what.

In 1963 Kern was the submarine project manager for what was then the Bureau of Ships. As an engineering duty officer he was well aware of the safety issues facing submarines. In December, just eight months after the loss of the *Thresher*, Kern submitted what has become known within the navy as the "SUBSAFE Letter," outlining how the Submarine Safety Program would make the navy's undersea fleet safer. His brief letter kicked off one of the navy's most expensive projects. It was an ambitious and necessary effort to make the navy's submarines safer, but it also would have unforeseen and wide-ranging implications for submarine maintenance and construction.

When called to testify before the inquiry into the loss of the *Scorpion*, five years later, Kern ticked off the four areas that SUBSAFE was designed to address: integrity of the pressure hull and the valve closures where seawater piping met the pressure hull; improved recovery procedures from flooding; greater reliability of the stern plane control surfaces; and a massive record-keeping effort to ensure that all safety-related materials and work met stringent specifications.

Submarines were also to receive a series of safety features, including an emergency main ballast tank blow system, the EMBT. Also known as "the super blow," the system could force water from the ballast tanks far faster and at greater depth than the submarine's ordinary blow system.

The number of hull penetrations—locations where seawater piping or other types of fittings entered the pressure hull—was also to be reduced. Those that remained as part of the main seawater system would be guarded by hydraulically operated emergency shutoff ball valves with remote switches. The ball valve, as effective as it was simple, provided a fast-operating pressure boundary of immense strength. Should an internal pipe or pipe joint fail, the ball valves could be remotely activated to shut off the flow of water.

Once a submarine met all the criteria of the program, including installation of an EMBT system, the navy would grant it SUBSAFE certification. "The purpose of SUBSAFE was to prevent flooding and increase recoverability," Kern told the *Scorpion* inquiry.

Even to the uninitiated, SUBSAFE seemed like a long-overdue, common sense solution. This begged the question of why it had not been initiated long before. The answer, of course, was that for the most part, the same safety systems and procedures employed on diesel-electric submarines, with their shallower diving depths and slower submerged speeds, were simply transferred to the nuclear-powered boats with little alteration when they entered service during the mid-1950s.

Although it held the promise of greater safety for sailors operating in a severe and hazardous environment, implementing the SUBSAFE program would be devilishly complicated to engineer and execute. The demands of the program would also generate subtle but wide-ranging problems that hampered maintenance on existing submarines and thwarted construction of new ones. Eventually the SUBSAFE program became its own worst enemy as the submarine force sought ways to defer the safety work in an effort to expedite overhauls and return submarines to duty sooner.

As Kern's "SUBSAFE Letter" was being distributed, an order halted construction of the *Flasher*, the *Greenling*, and the *Gato* at Electric Boat Company in late 1963. At the height of the Cold War, as the Soviets were building submarines at an alarming rate, American attack submarine construction came to a halt while the three fast attack boats were redesigned to receive SUBSAFE improvements. The *Flasher*, the *Greenling*, and the *Gato* would also be fitted with 14-foot extensions to their pressure hulls to provide greater reserve buoyancy.

Essentially, all submarines in "new construction" would receive SUBSAFE work packages, while existing submarines would be retrofitted at the earliest opportunity. The hard lesson soon learned by the submarine force was that adding safety systems to a completed boat was doubly hard, since existing equipment had to be removed to make way for the modifications.

It's been claimed that the navy had to give up an aircraft carrier to pay for the $500 million SUBSAFE program, an amount equal to $3 billion in present-day dollars. Even if the navy did delay construction of a flattop, the SUBSAFE expenditure was essential to ensure the safety of not only the attack boats but ballistic missile submarines as well.

Funding, however, turned out to be the smallest problem SUBSAFE posed to the navy's construction and maintenance program. As the astronomically high standards for components referred to as "SUBSAFE items" were developed, manufacturers began balking at the expense of meeting the tougher specifications yoked to the equally expensive paperwork required to ensure quality control. Items that fell under SUBSAFE's unyielding requirements were as varied as trash disposal unit components and piping for carrying seawater at ambient pressure within the submarine. The number of vendors who made copper-nickel piping for the navy dropped from "a half-dozen to two when additional government requirements drove [them] to sell to the private sector for the same cost [with] fewer headaches," Kern told the Scorpion's Court of Inquiry. This resulted in lead-time problems in which submarines under construction, or those receiving SUBSAFE work, were waiting three times as long for certain components. "Six months would turn into sixteen months lead time," said Kern. "The navy turned to its own shops [to manufacture components] but they too were soon overwhelmed."

When attack boats lacking SUBSAFE certification entered the shipyards for overhauls and nuclear refueling, the navy attempted to give them the work necessary to become certified. Submarine overhauls were difficult enough—the proverbial rebuilding of a watch through its stem hole—but safety improvements added an additional layer of complexity that was almost overwhelming. By the mid-1960s the terms "complex submarine overhaul" and "SUBSAFE overhaul" entered the navy's lexicon. The terms described the labyrinthine effort of an ordinary overhaul combined with nuclear refueling and SUBSAFE work.

Aside from the delays in constructing new submarines soon after the Thresher's loss, SUBSAFE had an immediate impact on the Scorpion. Stung by the Thresher's loss and mortified by a growing realization of quality control problems in submarine construction and maintenance, the navy decided that the Scorpion would receive not only its overhaul scheduled to begin in June 1963, but also intensified inspections of hull welds and piping joints and an effort to provide nascent SUBSAFE improvements, all of which extended the *Scorpion*'s time in the shipyard by four months.

Shipyard workers swarmed over the *Scorpion* as it received what may have been the most careful and thorough overhaul ever conducted on a submarine. Inspectors pored over 23,000 inches of hull welds using ultrasonic systems and found cracking in only 0.25 percent. (This hull inspection program was destined to become an element of SUBSAFE.) Many of the cracks originally believed to be problems were merely blemishes known as "surface indications" and required only minor grinding. This was good news, since it indicated a high degree of skill in the welding of the pressure hull.

The *Scorpion*'s seawater piping joints—leading suspects in the *Thresher*'s demise—were a different story. Using ultrasonic testing on all joints measuring $1/2$ inch or larger, an average of only 40 percent of the main seawater and auxiliary seawater connections met the inspection standard. Just 68 percent of the piping joints in all systems passed inspection, including those in the hydraulic system. While it could be argued that the ultrasonic testing was in the hands of inexperienced personnel at the time and that the conclusions were often subjective, the results were sobering nonetheless. What followed was a massive effort to repair all inadequate piping connections. The larger seawater piping joints that were brazed with silver solder were welded to provide far greater strength and reliability.

This effort to upgrade the piping connections and the extensive hull inspection added significantly to the safety of the *Scorpion*. However, not everything could be accomplished. Although studies regarding the installation of remotely controlled actuators for existing main seawater shutoff valves were made, there was not enough time to do the work. Should a piping connection fail, allowing seawater into the boat at ambient sea pressure, it would take a sailor with strong arms spinning a wheel as rapidly as possible to manually close a valve.

Super Blow

After Kern and his staff formulated the first twenty recommendations for SUBSAFE improvements, the CNO also decided that one of them—an emergency main ballast tank blow system—should also be installed on the *Scorpion* while it was in Charleston Naval Shipyard during the 1963–1964 period.

The emergency blow system bypassed the normal blow system that piped air from the high-pressure flasks to the boat's ballast tanks through a manifold. The ordinary blow system involved a greater amount of piping, meaning a reduction in air pressure. The EMBT system worked with less finesse, since it was only designed to be used in dire situations. When activated, it simply blew simultaneously through an abbreviated piping system that ran directly into the ballast tanks. When activated by switches on the ballast control panel, 2-inch ball valves snapped open in the blink of an eye, releasing air at 2,800 pounds per square inch directly from the high-pressure air flasks. The super blow didn't increase the volume or pressure of the air in the storage flasks; it simply allowed more of the available air to enter the ballast tanks closer to the original pressure.

Unworkable

Unfortunately, the emergency blow system installed on the *Scorpion* at Charleston could not be made workable. During one dockside test blow, the forward ballast tank valves did not open for sixty seconds, and those aft never opened. The valves that did open had trouble snapping back and reseating. The problem was the ball valves themselves. A dispute arose between SUBLANT and Charleston Naval Shipyard over whether the system worked, but SUBLANT successfully argued that the system was dangerously unreliable.

A different make of valves would have solved the problem, but time had run out for the *Scorpion*'s overhaul period, and the submarine was needed at sea. Ordering the new valves, waiting for their fabrication, and then tearing into the boat to install them would have delayed the *Scorpion*'s return to duty even longer. On May 20, 1964, SUBLANT ordered that the *Scorpion*'s emergency main ballast tank blow switches be "tagged out," with red cards indicating the system was disconnected and inoperable. The boat's ordinary blow system would have to suffice. Although forty-eight months would pass between when the EMBT system was judged faulty and the *Scorpion* was lost, there always seemed to be reasons why there was not enough time to make the system operable. When the *Scorpion* was lost four years and two days after the untrustworthy system was ordered disconnected, the tags would still be affixed to the emergency blow system switches.

Instead of making the EMBT system usable, the navy had a bureaucratic means of making *Scorpion* safer: it ruled that any fast attack submarine lacking SUBSAFE certification would operate no deeper than 500 feet, shaving 200 feet from its normal operating depth. This gave the submarine a greater margin of safety in case of flooding or stern plane failure, and theoretically meant the ballast tank blow system would have to push water out against less hydrostatic pressure.

This decision was somewhat disingenuous, since an endangered submarine suffering flooding or experiencing an uncontrolled dive might unexpectedly find itself well below its "restricted" operating depth. The order to place the *Scorpion* on a growing list of "limited in depth" or "LID" boats, as they became known among engineering duty officers, was a commonsense move, but the bureaucratic directive by the Bureau of Ships could not prevent the submarine from accidentally descending below its officially mandated depth restriction.

Making the *Scorpion* safer with an emergency blow system had not been forgotten. On May 27, 1965, nearly a year after completion of its first overhaul, SUBLANT sought guidance from the Bureau of Ships on how it could obtain SUBSAFE certification for the *Scorpion* that winter. The letter also asked the Bureau of Ships to specify the "corrective action that would certify the *Scorpion*'s emergency main ballast tank blow system." When the Bureau of Ships belatedly responded, it did not provide the information sought. Needless to say, the *Scorpion* did not receive repairs to its EMBT system or any other safety system work that winter.

Although the navy intended to SUBSAFE all its submarines by 1969, this was stymied by shortages of components and skilled workers. Almost immediately after the SUBSAFE program began, submarines entering the shipyard for overhauls were having their safety work "deferred." The mantra of "deferred but not canceled" was repeated many times during the Court of Inquiry proceedings into the loss of the *Scorpion* as officers explained that the *Scorpion*'s safety work was frequently delayed but never permanently shelved. In the case of the *Scorpion*—which was lost before it received SUBSAFE certification—it could be argued that unforeseen events had metamorphosed the "deferral" of its SUBSAFE work into a permanent cancellation.

When Slattery took command of the *Scorpion* from Lewis on October 17, 1967, the departing skipper presented him with a standard letter enumerating shortcomings in the submarine's condition. In it Lewis wrote that the "super blow . . . was defective in design . . . and restricted from use." Unlike some hard-core submarine officers unimpressed with pantywaist safety systems, Slattery was concerned that the EMBT system could not be utilized.

Slattery's interest in this flaw emerged on his third day in command of the *Scorpion*, when the boat was visited by the executive officer of the Submarine Safety Center, an organization established in response to the *Thresher* disaster. Slattery quizzed the officer about why the faulty emergency blow system failed and why it remained unrepaired for more than three years. Slattery was undoubtedly puzzled that the *Scorpion* had departed the shipyard—yet again—without the emergency blow system being made operable.

Overhaul Duration

As a general rule, fast-attack-boat overhauls prior to the SUBSAFE program took seven to ten months. With the advent of SUBSAFE this rule of thumb no longer applied. When the *Nautilus*—America's first nuclear submarine—entered Portsmouth Naval Shipyard on January 2, 1964, it was to receive a major refit, including its SUBSAFE work. Among the safety items installed was a working emergency blow system and remotely operated seawater shutoff valves. The *Nautilus* did not emerge from the shipyard until 27½ months later.

Worse, however, was yet to come.

The fast attack submarine *Skate* became something of a poster child for the growing problem of increasingly long overhauls. Norfolk Naval Shipyard, a political constituency unto itself with its sizable labor force, successfully lobbied for a role in nuclear-powered submarine maintenance. In 1965 the shipyard was given the task of performing a reactor refueling, an overhaul, and SUBSAFE work on the *Skate* that would keep shipyard employment levels high.

This plum came to the shipyard even though it had never before performed an overhaul on a nuclear submarine, much less one of the notoriously complex SUBSAFE overhauls. The *Skate*'s 1961 refueling-overhaul had taken just over seven months. Its SUBSAFE overhaul that began on April 28, 1965, would take nearly thirty months. "It was nothing short of a scandal," said an officer who helped oversee the effort.

Norfolk Naval Shipyard naval architect Clyde A. Decker was the coordinator on the non-nuclear portion of the *Skate*'s overhaul. "The effort got off to a bad start when Mare Island Naval Shipyard, which had not done any SUBSAFE work at the time, developed the overhaul plans," said Decker. "We had to redo the plans and find ways of cutting the hull to get the equipment out and it was our first nuclear submarine overhaul. The *Skate* also had equipment we had no experience with and we didn't even know the best way to get it out of the boat. There was pretty poor preparation for the overhaul and there was no system for keeping a proper sequence for taking things out and putting them back."

Decker also noted a deep and abiding fear of Hyman Rickover—the untouchable power before whom higher-ranking admirals, and even elected officials, trembled. What Decker saw were navy officers immobilized out of fear that Rickover would retaliate against them for violating his standards. "With Rickover looming over everything, all the submarine officers were scared to make a decision."

A submarine overhaul is manifestly difficult because equipment, piping, and electronics are often hidden behind other components in tight spaces. Because of this, components must be removed in a carefully planned sequence. Repairing one piece of equipment often meant removing other equipment and then reinstalling it. Sailors recall the maddening frustration of seeing the shipyard complete a difficult modification on the *Skate*, only to tear it out days later because other components behind it should have been overhauled first.

Not even additional money could solve the problem of delays. It was difficult for the navy to hire and retain highly skilled workers in competition with the private sector during the late 1960s, when unemployment was low and American industry was operating at capacity. Furthermore, SUBSAFE's high standards required that only the most capable shipyard workers be tasked to work on systems that fell within its purview, creating a shortage of specially qualified workers needed for other maintenance tasks.

The *Skate* overhaul became an open wound, defying all efforts to heal it. The moving target of SUBSAFE requirements, difficulty in obtaining spare parts, poor sequence planning on the repair process, and Norfolk Naval Shipyard's growing workload resulting from the Vietnam War conspired to trap the *Skate* in dry dock. The problem was an epidemic. By the late 1960s nearly 40 percent of the navy's nuclear attack submarines were in overhaul.

Alarmed at this drastic situation, Naval Ship Systems Command (formerly the Bureau of Ships) sent a letter to SUBLANT in November 1966 announcing that it was "actively pursuing new and revised methods for . . . complex ship overhauls." NAVSHIPS announced that "Major overhaul problem areas have been subjected to a systematic plan of attack." A study conducted in early 1966 and titled "Staff Study of Improvements in Complex Submarine Overhauls" called for sweeping changes. This NAVSHIPS study recognized that the failures to adequately preplan the overhauls, obtain repair materials on time, and provide enough skilled workers elongated submarine overhauls. Despite these revelations, the length of attack submarine overhauls continued to spiral out of control. The *Seadragon*, a *Skate*-class boat, entered Pearl Harbor Naval Shipyard on July 19, 1968, to set an infamous record for the longest overhaul of a nuclear attack submarine during the 1960s. It would not emerge from the shipyard for thirty-four months and ten days. Maintenance woes created by SUBSAFE also delayed its own implementation. By 1968—five years after the loss of the *Thresher*—only 35 percent of the navy's submarines had received SUBSAFE certification. Kern said that the navy had hoped to have all its submarines so certified by 1969, but admitted during the *Scorpion*'s Court of Inquiry proceedings that it might be 1974 or later before all of the safety work was completed.

The SUBSAFE program, the navy's most important response to the *Thresher* disaster, had fallen victim to its complexity, its appetite for scarce components, and its demand for skilled workers. Not only was it impossible to complete SUBSAFE refits on existing submarines in a timely fashion, the new construction of attack boats and missile boats continued to be delayed as well. In 1967, Secretary of Defense Robert McNamara revealed that the navy lacked seven of the thirty-one nuclear-powered attack submarines it had hoped to construct by that time.

Planned Availability Concept

As the shipyard struggled to free the *Skate* from dry dock, worries mounted about the upcoming overhaul of the *Scorpion* scheduled to begin on February 1, 1967.

By early 1966, skippers and their superiors were increasingly anxious about putting their fast attack submarines in overhaul. Submarine skippers preferred commanding a ship at sea to shepherding a submarine through an endless refit. Everyone was looking for a better and faster way of overhauling submarines.

By 1966, SUBLANT was actively working to reign in the duration of attack submarine overhauls. A March 2, 1966, letter from SUBLANT, then under the command of Vice Adm. Vernon L. Lowrance, designated the *Scorpion* as the subject of a new maintenance program designed to reduce the now normal overhaul periods of two or three years. It was not unusual for SUBPAC or SUBLANT—referred to as the "type command-ers"—to organize their own overhaul methods during the 1960s, accord-ing to Vice Adm. Joe Williams, who commanded Norfolk Naval Shipyard from 1973 until he took command of SUBLANT in 1974. "Everybody had their own damn ways of getting submarines scheduled and trying to get a handle on things," said Williams. "Each hand has five fingers and every finger wanted to do its own thing. There was never any one program."

The "new" program proposed by SUBLANT would be known by half a dozen names. It was variously referred to as the "major-minor overhaul concept," the "*Scorpion* planned overhaul concept," the "controlled dura-tion overhaul," or most often as the "planned availability concept." This program intended to shrink the duration of submarine overhauls by in-sisting on detailed planning, the advance procurement of parts, and elimination of nonessential work. The program also aimed to refurbish submarines during shipyard visits that were more frequent but of shorter duration. Not surprisingly, the nettlesome SUBSAFE program would be viewed as an obstacle to this new overhaul concept.

"Acute Political Embarrassment"

A March 24, 1966, letter to SUBLANT written by the Submarine Squad-ron 6 commander, Capt. Philip P. Cole, encapsulated the prevailing opin-ions and concerns regarding SUBSAFE-induced maintenance delays: "The inordinate amount of time currently involved in the routine over-hauls of nuclear submarines is a recognized source of major concern to the navy as a whole and the submarine force in particular and stands as a potential source of acute political embarrassment," wrote Cole. "Aside from any comments on the management of the naval shipyards, the causes of these prolonged periods of operational inactivity lie in three areas." Cole identified the old suspects of worker shortages, poor plan-ning, and difficult-to-obtain materials. He also blamed the "overall mag-nitude" of conducting an overhaul in tandem with SUBSAFE alterations among the reasons for the lengthy overhauls.

Cole's recommendation was to "sacrifice portions of the SUBSAFE certification program" while embracing depth restrictions on the *Scor-pion*, because, as Cole pointed out, "Of the three factors cited . . . the present SUBSAFE program features heavily in all. Cole suggested that "the elimination, for the present—of the most trying elements of [SUB-SAFE]—may conceivably reduce the overhaul time by an important amount."

"The USS *Scorpion* is a case in point," wrote Cole of the submarine's approaching overhaul. "It can be contemplated," Cole ominously wrote, "that the *Scorpion* will establish a new record in overhaul duration [and] the prospect is sufficiently disturbing to warrant serious consideration of the sacrifice in operational depth for the next overhaul cycle. It is not suggested that . . . design depth of these ships be abandoned but that this approach be taken until such a time as conditions permit a more orderly accomplishment [of the SUBSAFE work]." Cole could not have waved a more frightening flag to SUBLANT than suggesting that the duration of the *Scorpion*'s overhaul would exceed that of the *Skate*'s. If the "time savings" gained by eliminating SUBSAFE work were "attractive" to SUBLANT, Cole recommended that the *Scorpion*'s SUBSAFE work be deferred for its upcoming overhaul. The concept of "deferred but not canceled" was at work. Performing SUBSAFE work on the *Scorpion* during its 1967 maintenance would take two full years, officers estimated, as opposed to the eight months a "controlled" overhaul would require. SUBLANT was faced with the possibility of losing use of the *Scorpion* for a minimum of twenty-four months.

"I think at the time the submarine force was very concerned about the time off the line," Kern told the Court of Inquiry regarding hesitation over completing the *Scorpion*'s SUBSAFE work. "*Scorpion* was an effective operating unit of the fleet. I think they were hesitant about having it out [of service]. My understanding was . . . they would not get the ship back in a time frame that would be acceptable to them in consideration of the fleet requirements."

As SUBLANT moved the planned availability concept forward, it entered into discussions with NAVSHIPS and the CNO to obtain permission to deviate from the full SUBSAFE overhaul plan. Seeking deferment of SUBSAFE work along with a reduction in general maintenance work was a touchy subject barely three years after loss of the *Thresher*. Nonetheless, on June 16, 1966, SUBLANT sent a letter to CINCLANT-FLT warning that if the CNO ordered the full implementation of the *Scorpion*'s SUBSAFE improvements, the *Scorpion*'s time in the shipyard "will automatically be of very, very long duration."

On June 17, approval arrived from both NAVSHIPs and the CNO granting SUBLANT permission to employ the planned availability concept on the *Scorpion* during its upcoming overhaul. The *Scorpion* was to be the program's guinea pig. As Young noted in his March 25, 1966, memo, "The success of the 'major-minor' overhaul concept depends, essentially, on the results of our first case at hand: <u>SCORPION</u>." (The emphasis is Young's.) "The *USS Scorpion* is a 'trial horse' and all shipyard efforts should be slanted in this vein to make it work," Young wrote in a memo to his own files on September 2, 1966.

Although the submarine's work package was to be reduced, it appeared that some SUBSAFE work could be accomplished along with nuclear refueling and basic maintenance. The *Scorpion* would not, however, receive hull painting, nonessential work, and unessential alterations known as "ShipAlts."

In July 1966 the *Scorpion* underwent an inspection by the Board of Inspection and Survey, an organization established soon after the Civil War to ascertain the condition of the navy's ships. The inspection was a penetrating examination of the submarine's innards by experts. The *Scorpion* fared well and was graded "above average," thanks in no small part to the tough standards of XO Robert Fountain and the hardworking crew.

Deferral of SUBSAFE

What emerged during 1966 was a plan to bring sanity back into the submarine overhaul effort by determining, with greater precision, when submarine machinery and components needed to be repaired. If successful, this maintenance concept—known as "predictive maintenance"—could reduce a submarine's time in the shipyard while making it more reliable and safe. This was one of the basic tenets of the planned availability concept.

To assist in this effort, the J. J. Henry Company, a naval architect and marine engineering firm, began cataloging every component on the *Scorpion*, an effort that included taking five thousand photographs of the submarine's machinery. This unique effort was designed to help J. J. Henry engineers build a computerized database of the submarine's components. Every *Scorpion* component would be carefully studied in an attempt to predict when each was likely to fail.

"The *Scorpion* was to be the first effort but it [the submarine] was lost," said Welton G. Barnes, an engineer at Norfolk Naval Shipyard who was the program manager for the project and who oversaw the work of the J. J. Henry Company. "We were using computers to predict when a component or a piece of machinery would fail so we could tell a captain if it was going to fail during his next patrol or the patrol after next. This was advanced thinking for the time. I sometimes wondered if we were getting ahead of ourselves in this matter, but we wanted to gain control of these overhauls and the way to do it was to predict with some accuracy how long machinery would function before failure, and then design operating cycles around the components instead of just bringing the entire boat in. We were then going to put everything together and present it to NAVSHIPS to show if it was workable, and if so, how it was done." When the *Scorpion* was lost, the images taken by J. J. Henry workers of the *Scorpion*'s machinery were used to identify the submarine's debris that was eventually photographed on the seafloor. (Barnes never again had contact with the project, which disappeared with the *Scorpion*.)

After adoption of the planned availability concept in lieu of a full overhaul, the submarine's maintenance was about to be abbreviated even more. On September 21, 1966, Norfolk Naval Shipyard representatives informed SUBLANT that the shipyard would be unable to provide the requested ten thousand man-days per month for the *Scorpion*'s planned overhaul. The shipyard, faced with numerous repair and overhaul demands, warned that it could only throw additional manpower into the *Scorpion*'s planned availability concept overhaul if the work requests were designated "emergency repairs." This priority would not be granted. With the shipyard unable to provide adequate manpower, the efficiencies of the experimental overhaul would be lost, tainting assessments of the planned availability concept's effectiveness while threatening to turn the *Scorpion*'s shipyard visit into an endless struggle akin to the *Skate*'s. SUBLANT bowed to reality and issued an October 26, 1966, message advising, "heavy workload NAVSHIPYD NORVA this period gives every indication that an OVHL of extended duration required even with curtailment of overall work [package]. In view of . . . the critical need to maximize time on-line during this period, consider *Scorpion* [overhaul] be changed to a [restricted availability] for (1) Refueling (2) Interim Docking (3) Voyage Repairs." A "restricted availability" was a step well below a full overhaul. Items considered crucial for safety would be repaired—although the message indicates that no SUBSAFE work would be accomplished.

The *Scorpion*'s SUBSAFE work had apparently been eliminated. The authority for this materialized three weeks later, when the CNO issued a November 15, 1966, letter granting permission to defer SUBSAFE work. To further streamline the *Scorpion*'s maintenance, Capt. Clarence Russell Bryan, SUBLANT's assistant chief of staff for material, issued a November 29, 1966, letter ordering that no "extensive dismantling of operating gear and sea valves for examination shall be undertaken unless defects are known to exist."

When the *Scorpion* was officially released from Norfolk Naval Shipyard on October 6, 1967, after eight months, it had received 48,496 man-days of work for a total cost of $3,326,500. Of this dollar amount, 75 percent was devoted to the nuclear propulsion system, including the nuclear refueling. The remaining 25 percent, or $833,057, was spent on the boat's other systems. By comparison, the *Scorpion*'s sister ship the *Snook* received a $19.6 million SUBSAFE overhaul and refueling at Puget Sound Naval Shipyard at about the same time. Of this, $3.5 million was spent on SUBSAFE certification work. The *Snook*'s maintenance required 247,000 man-days and fifteen months to complete.

The *Scorpion*'s refit period, while obviously considered something far less extensive than a full overhaul by the standards of the day, remains officially listed as an "overhaul" by the navy.

Hot Potato

During the Court of Inquiry proceedings, court president Bernard L. Austin endeavored to unravel the complicated story of the *Scorpion*'s maintenance history.

Two of the key witnesses during the inquiry were Capt. Clarence Russell Bryan and his subordinate Cmdr. Harold L. Young, who were squarely in the glare of the inquiry's spotlight when both testified in June 1968. Bryan later became commander of Naval Sea Systems Command and retired as a vice admiral. Young also rose through the ranks and retired as a rear admiral.

Court of Inquiry president Austin struggled to understand the complex tale of maintenance, parts shortages, and the unfamiliar program known as the "planned availability concept." However, what interested Austin most was why the emergency main ballast tank blow system—one of the fundamental elements of the SUBSAFE effort—was not made operable between its 1964 installation and the loss of the *Scorpion* four

years later. Bryan told the court that SUBLANT did seek repairs to the
emergency main ballast tank blow system during a November–December
1965 maintenance period at Charleston Naval Shipyard. Unfortunately,
said Bryan, it was realized the work was too complex to be accomplished
during the two months the *Scorpion* was to be in the shipyard.

Bryan then attempted to describe the heavy impact the SUBSAFE
program had on the navy's maintenance efforts, but Austin interrupted
his testimony with a rebuke: "Don't turn me off too short, Captain."

"No, sir, this is the same trail," assured Bryan as he tried to explain
that the *Scorpion* was to receive an emergency blow system during its
1967 overhaul but, once again, did not.

"I hope we can find a better reason than we have thus far," growled
Austin, impatient with the convoluted story of the emergency blow system. "Thus far it's been everybody tossing a hot potato from his hands to
somebody else's." The frustrated Austin resumed his probe into why the
Scorpion did not have an emergency blow system: "Captain Bryan, may I
ask you a few simple questions? You have given us a very detailed high-
light of the ups and downs of why we don't have a satisfactory EMBT
blow system on the *Scorpion*, but at this point I am slightly confused; the
Scorpion was under overhaul in Charleston Naval Shipyard in 1963 at
the time the *Thresher* was lost?"

"[The] *Scorpion* had yet to enter [Charleston Naval Shipyard]," corrected
Bryan. (The submarine entered the shipyard two months later.)

An exasperated Austin then restated his question, "Is there available
to the submarine service today a satisfactory [emergency] high-pressure
blow system for the main ballast tanks?"

"Yes, sir."

"Why then did the *Scorpion* go to sea without such?"

"In my opinion the reason why it was not done rests with the fact
that [the] *Scorpion* was operating at the restricted depth of [500] feet,
[and] it was intended that she would stay at that depth until she got the
complete SUBSAFE certification package," Bryan explained.

Austin then moved in to deride the notion that a directive on a
scrap of paper would magically keep the *Scorpion* from descending beyond
500 feet: "There isn't any guarantee that if you get a stuck stern plane
. . . you aren't going to go below test depth [and] that [the] ship . . . could
be brought back in a safe condition."

"I really believe that today when someone says to a commanding
officer of a ship, 'Don't exceed a certain depth unless thus and so,' that
there is a greater assurance that he won't than there was five or six years

ago," said Bryan, hinting that daredevil submarine commanders had not been disposed to obey safe operating procedures until the terrible lesson of the *Thresher* disaster. "We have given the skippers of ships more information and knowledge on how to run their ship."

Austin's response glistened with ice: "This is most gratifying, and I'm sure it has prevented many accidents since *Thresher*, but with the best training, with the greatest cognizance of the curve of increase of depth and hazard, and decrease in time available to do something about that hazard, no commanding officer, no matter how well trained, how well oriented, how well motivated, can guarantee against such things as a stern plane jamming on full dive except by never allowing full dive to get on them. He cannot, by his own degree of expertise and know-how, guarantee against a failure of equipment which will cause his ship to take an excursion."

"Now," added Austin condescendingly, "isn't that an obvious statement?"

"Yes, sir," responded Bryan.

Austin then turned from interrogating Bryan to editorialize on the odd logic of delaying the installation of an important safety system such as the emergency blow system for four years: "I still think there is some question [about] the wisdom of putting off something just because there was . . . a logical-sounding reason for so doing—if it could have been done."

Although coincidence counts for little in a technical investigation, Bryan then revealed to the court a substantially ironic disclosure: the *Scorpion*, the second nuclear-powered submarine lost by the navy, was also the only fast attack submarine in SUBLANT's stable of boats that lacked a fully certified SUBSAFE system. Despite the agony of instituting the SUBSAFE program, all of the navy's nuclear-powered submarines were certified by the 1970s. Although the navy lost twenty-two submarines in noncombat mishaps between 1900 and 1968—an average of nearly one submarine every three years—the loss of the *Scorpion* marked a sharp break in that deadly cycle.

Although accidents, fires, fatalities, and battery mishaps still occur, the U.S. Navy did not lose a single submarine between 1968 and 2004. By any measure, this is a remarkable achievement in safety, although it was preceded by decades of tragedy and the destruction of two nuclear-powered attack submarines with all hands within a five-year period.

14

Ishmael

S oon after the *Mizar*'s camera sleds photographed the wreckage of the *Scorpion*, a call came to the fast attack submarine *Lapon*, moored at Norfolk's Destroyer and Submarine Piers. The disembodied voice of an officer commanded that Electrician's Mate Second Class Daniel Lee Rogers be brought to the phone.

Rogers, surprised by the call, quickly made his way through the 292-foot boat to the control room. After the officer confirmed that Rogers served aboard the *Scorpion* between February 1967 and January 1968, he asked the electrician's mate to describe the floor tiles in the submarine's control room. Rogers, with a superb memory for small details, told the officer what he remembered, realizing that investigators must have finally located the *Scorpion*.

Considering the circumstances under which Rogers departed the *Scorpion*, it's remarkable that this phone call would be his only contribution to the investigation.

Rogers was one of five *Scorpion* sailors who sidestepped death aboard the boat. Rogers had warned of dangerous circumstances due to leadership problems and was concerned about the boat's mechanical condition.

Learning that the *Scorpion*'s remains had been discovered reopened still-fresh emotional scars for Rogers. Like the demoralized radioman Pettey, Rogers hated serving on the submarine, where he viewed the morale as atrocious. Rogers escaped the *Scorpion* by submitting a letter disqualifying him from submarine duty.

Rogers burned with a desire to serve on submarines when he joined the navy in the early 1960s and qualified for the nuclear propulsion program but was erroneously told he was medically unqualified for submarine duty. After serving a year on the nuclear-powered cruiser *Bainbridge*, Rogers learned he could qualify for submarine duty. He was soon assigned to Submarine School, and reported to the *Scorpion* in February 1967 as it entered Norfolk Naval Shipyard.

Rogers was surprised at how difficult it was to get things accomplished. Spare parts seemed unobtainable, and when machinist's mates or electrician's mates requested shipyard assistance for tasks beyond their ability, it never seemed to be available.

Although a submarine neophyte, Rogers became concerned about what he perceived as the haphazard nature of the repairs. Rogers became leery when ordered to weld an aluminum bookshelf to a pressure hull reinforcing ring of HY-80 steel in the operations compartment. Rogers complied despite the fact that the shelf's aluminum was metallurgically incompatible with the steel of the frame. After trial and error, Rogers got the shelf fastened, but later worried about diminishing the strength of the hull. "It just seemed that no one should be welding on the pressure hull without special permission," Rogers recalled.

Rogers, gaining a better understanding of the *Scorpion*—and eager to do the best possible job—began to point out items that needed replacement or repair to superiors who seemed uninterested in his opinion. He found that some of the *Scorpion's* officers were distrustful of his advice and that of his fellow sailors. By September, Rogers had become depressed, feeling there was no sense of mutual respect on the boat, at least in the engineering spaces. From Rogers's perspective, the crew—particularly those serving aft of the control room in the engineering spaces—were badly dispirited. While Rogers may have perceived slights when none existed, his estimation of morale aboard the *Scorpion* was strikingly close to the dour view held by Pettey.

When the *Scorpion* began sea trials on October 2, 1967, Rogers experienced submerged operations for the first time and found the experience thrilling. He actually loved submarine duty, but had come to hate the negative atmosphere and the unrelenting repair workload aboard the *Scorpion*. He would soon come to distrust the boat's condition.

During the high-speed dash to St. Croix, U.S. Virgin Islands, during the Weapon System Accuracy Trials on November 15, Rogers experienced the potent oscillation of the *Scorpion* as it corkscrewed through the water at high speed. "Goddamn, it was so bad the shaft was flopping back and forth in the rear shaft seal," said Rogers. "One of the guys in the auxiliary machine space claimed the motor generators were swaying six inches in both directions." The problem reappeared two days later, further cementing Rogers's mistrust of the boat.

The problem that so unnerved Rogers was the same one that also had vexed SUBRON 6 commander Jared E. Clarke III, prompting Clarke's request for high-level engineering assistance during the fall of 1967. Although the vibration may have disappeared after air pockets were bled from the hydraulic system, Rogers's concerns could not be mollified. "That was pretty much the final straw. There were so many instances when something had gone awry. The equipment was used up and we were trying to get more out of it. I had a very uneasy feeling about it [the *Scorpion*]. The stuff on the *Scorpion* was crashing right and left. You were constantly repairing, jury-rigging, getting it back together, and getting it on line."

Disqualification

Despite his love of submarine duty, Rogers decided that the crew's morale, coupled with the *Scorpion*'s seemingly unending mechanical problems, were unendurable. His only way off was to void his agreement to volunteer for the submarine duty he once craved. "I didn't realize how depressed I was until I made that decision," Rogers said. "The moment I turned that request in, I had a spring in my step. I was relieved even though I knew I was committing career suicide. I didn't care, I wanted off. I didn't want to see that boat again."

Rogers, with the help of Machinist's Mate Second Class Cecil Mobley, researched the *Atlantic Submarine Fleet Personnel Manual* and studied COMSUBLANT instruction 1306.12: "Disqualification from submarine duty; Request for." Mobley, who shared Rogers's views, believed the letter might alert others that morale aboard the submarine was seriously low. Mobley suggested changes and did the typing. Rogers recalled his naïveté in believing he was about to notify the navy of a great problem: "I really thought I was doing something, at least from the worm's-eye view." The twenty-two-year-old Mobley, who encouraged Rogers during the drafting of the letter, would die aboard the *Scorpion*.

Although he didn't want to leave the submarine service, Rogers saw no other means of escaping the *Scorpion* other than withdrawing his agreement to volunteer for submarine duty. His letter claimed he was unable to adapt to submarine life. The remainder of the letter was filled with complaints about circumstances on the boat. Rogers turned his request for disqualification in to Slattery on December 29, 1967:

I find I am unable to adapt to the submarine environment as found on the USS *Scorpion*.

The reasons for my inability to adapt are partially due to working conditions and partially due to officer-enlisted relations on board this ship.

It has been stated that submarine duty pay and proficiency pay are just compensation for long hours spent on board. No amount of money, however, can compensate for the marital problems caused by this type of life and the loss of time needed to conduct personal affairs.

Nor does any facet of duty aboard *Scorpion* compensate for the personal humiliation experienced as a result of not being trusted by certain officers on board. These same officers have no respect for professional pride which is found in almost every petty officer and disregard their petty officer's [sic] opinions even when solicited.

My personal opinion is that such a lack of leadership on a vessel places all personnel in danger, but even disregarding that, it is still necessary for the crew to work and live together under closer than normal conditions and a lack of moral [sic] makes this extremely difficult.

For the above reasons I do not feel that I am able to serve to the very best of my abilities aboard *Scorpion* and believe I would be of greater service to the navy elsewhere.

The incendiary accusation "My personal opinion is that such a lack of leadership on a vessel places all personnel in danger . . ." would not endear Rogers to Slattery. Though he didn't say it, a lot of Rogers's frustration was directed at Lt. William Harwi, the engineer officer, whose resignation was pending, and who disregarded the electrician's mate concerns.

Slattery, like all fast-attack-submarine commanders, was faced with the constant struggle of retaining trained personnel in the demanding submarine service, and Rogers's angry letter posed a dilemma. Although Rogers had not yet qualified as a submariner, he was a nuclear-trained electrician's mate with a year of service on a surface ship and was still too valuable to lose. Despite Slattery's unhappiness at receiving Rogers's highly critical letter, an attempt, albeit a heavy-handed one, would be made to keep Rogers aboard.

Rogers recalled being subjected to a "good-guy, bad-guy routine," with Harwi launching a "scathing attack" against him for attempting to leave the *Scorpion*. Rogers, warned Harwi, would be stripped of permission to serve in the nuclear program, even on a surface ship if he departed the

Scorpion. Rogers stood his ground and refused to withdraw his letter. On the heels of this confrontation Lt. John Sweet, the submarine's electronics officer, took a softer approach, extolling the benefits of staying aboard. Neither tactic worked: Rogers still intended to disqualify himself from submarine duty.

Like Pettey, Rogers considered Fountain a martinet, though he found Slattery completely approachable. Although Rogers had only served under Slattery for a little over two months, the commanding officer's rapport with the crew prompted Rogers to incorrectly assume that Slattery was a "mustang," an ordinary sailor who had risen through the ranks.

While it was true that Slattery had a common touch, he was a true believer, with respect only for those who successfully met the challenge of submarine duty. Lives were at stake, and Slattery needed achievers who could stay motivated in the face of the dismal and the difficult. Rogers had broken ranks and played the "sea lawyer" to escape a situation he didn't like.

Slattery was in no mood for the whining of a young sailor weary of demanding work and long hours. Rogers would pay a price for his impertinence. Slattery cut Rogers's angry, six-paragraph letter to two paragraphs and eliminated the reference to "danger." Slattery left in Rogers's claim of being "unable to adapt to the submarine environment" and "marital strain" (Slattery's term) as reasons for disqualifying himself from submarine duty.

In his own letter approving Rogers's request to depart submarine duty, Slattery admitted that the electrician's mate reported aboard while the boat was faced "with an abnormally heavy maintenance and training requirement" that may have "colored his initial impression of submarine duty." Slattery also wrote that Rogers had been "encouraged to defer this decision." In the face of this persuasion (the lobbying efforts by Harwi and Sweet), Slattery noted that Rogers remained "unwilling or unable to exert the extra effort required to meet nuclear submarine standards. It is considered that he not be accorded the privilege of earning dolphins." Slattery was not through with Rogers. He also recommended that he not even be "assigned duty involving nuclear reactor operation[s] in the surface program." It appeared that Harwi's threat was not a bluff: stay aboard or see your nuclear propulsion career ruined.

Unshaken by these threats, Rogers signed the heavily edited version of his disqualification letter on January 2, 1968. He was banished to the submarine barracks as a janitor, something that didn't perturb him in the least. "When I walked off the submarine for the last time, I felt as if 200 pounds had been lifted off of me," recalled Rogers.

Rogers was soon ordered to report to Submarine Squadron 6 commander Jared E. Clarke III. When he was finally admitted to the squadron commander's office, the sailor realized he had failed to put on his neckerchief. Clarke ignored the missing kerchief as he tapped the papers on his desk that included Rogers's truncated disqualification letter and Slattery's stern recommendations. Clarke, who had seen his share of unhappy sailors and bad blood on submarines, asked Rogers for his side of the story: "Why do you want to get off submarines?"

"I told him I didn't really want to get off submarines, I just wanted to get off *Scorpion*," said Rogers, who stammered out his complaints, telling Clarke he was demoralized by conditions on the boat. Rogers noticed that Clarke seemed disinterested: "Clarke sat there and acted like he'd heard it all before, like he wasn't even paying attention."

After Rogers had exhausted his complaints about duty aboard the *Scorpion*, Clarke lifted Rogers's paperwork with a dramatic flourish and dropped it into the trash can next to his desk. "Which boat do you want to go to?" Clarke inquired. Stunned by this sudden change of fortune, Rogers didn't have a ready answer. Within days, Rogers was assigned to the fast attack boat *Lapon*. Although it's not known why Clarke gave Rogers another chance, the navy's difficulty reenlisting nuclear-trained submarine sailors during the 1960s may have given Clarke reason enough.

Rogers found that the *Sturgeon*-class boat "was more like a submarine ought to be." What impressed him most was that strict formality had been discarded. (It was the custom on the *Lapon* for enlisted men to call the officers by their last name without "mister.") When Rogers reported aboard in early 1968, the spanking new submarine had been in service for two months. Aside from its newness, it also differed from the *Scorpion* in that it was 44 feet longer—to provide additional inherent buoyancy deemed necessary after the *Thresher* disaster—and was built with all the Submarine Safety Program improvements also prompted by the tragedy.

On February 15, 1968, the day the *Scorpion* departed, Rogers went to Pier 22 to say farewell to his former shipmates. As the boat backed away, Rogers helped heave its mooring line to the deck gang. One sailor coiling the line inside its locker saw Rogers and began to curse him. Rogers was stung by this unexpected disdain, but waved good-bye anyway as the water widened between the submarine and the pier.

Dispirited by bad morale and poor conditions on the *Scorpion*, Electrician's Mate Daniel Rogers left the submarine a month before its fatal voyage.

Rogers spent the next fourteen weeks working successfully on his submarine qualification on the magnificent new *Lapon*. When his former submarine failed to return on May 27, 1968, the *Lapon* was one of the first boats to dash into the raging weather to hunt for the *Scorpion*. During the search, Rogers agonized at the loss of friends with whom he had served for a year. He was racked with guilt for allowing his complaint letter to be whittled to virtually nothing to smooth his escape when he should have raised a louder alarm. During the search, nightmares began to plague Rogers, who dreamed he was in the maneuvering room as the *Scorpion* flooded. In this dream, lights are flickering and men are yelling and neither Rogers nor his shipmates can find the source of the water. When he awoke, Rogers invariably found himself clawing at the underside of the bunk above. The dream persisted for years, and survivor's guilt became Rogers's uncomfortable companion for life.

He was also consumed with anger. Rogers had always believed something had gone off track on the *Scorpion*. To him it was apparent that the morale was bad and that the submarine was in such poor shape it required more frequent attention than others he later served on.

When the Court of Inquiry was convened to investigate the *Scorpion*'s loss, Rogers braced for a summons to testify, but it was a call that never came. Rogers's telephone interview with navy investigators regarding the *Scorpion*'s floor tiles indicated that the court was well aware of his service on the *Scorpion*. Following the call, he again prepared to be called before the court, which reconvened in November 1968. To Rogers's surprise, his testimony was never requested.

In 1987, Rogers was enraged to see John Craven on television explaining his controversial theory about how a hot-run torpedo destroyed the *Scorpion*. Rogers, who long believed that an ordinary malfunction led to the loss of the submarine, was appalled at the theatrically dramatic theory. (Like COMSUBLANT Schade, Rogers had long suspected the trash disposal unit or a stern plane failure as the culprit.)

Rogers—who had been ignored by the navy's Court of Inquiry—gained notoriety as an interview subject regarding the *Scorpion*, appearing on several television documentaries. On Memorial Day weekend in 1998, Rogers was in Washington, D.C., to be interviewed for yet another documentary about the mysterious demise of the *Scorpion*. Rogers, who was a chain smoker and a heavy drinker, decided to leave his hotel and walk to the Vietnam Veterans Memorial wall, only to collapse in the oppressive heat. Immobilized by a stroke and the effects of congestive heart failure, he was rushed to Georgetown University Hospital. He would recover, but additional strokes would seriously affect his ability to speak.

Embittered by his experience on the *Scorpion*, Rogers's self-destructive behavior continued. The former electrician's mate died July 1, 2002, in Ames, Iowa, at sixty-one. "He was never the same after he served on that boat," observed his mother, Betty Himes. "He never cared about living after he lost his friends on the *Scorpion*. I believe the whole experience killed him as well."

Rogers has been labeled a "deserter" by submariners who believed he should have perished on the boat with his shipmates—as if the act of pointlessly dying had intrinsic value. Career submarine officers see Rogers as a vocal know-it-all. "You've always got one of those guys on a submarine," was the loathing observation of one attack submarine skipper who commanded submarines during the 1960s.

Rogers was cognizant that others had died in his place. In a sense, Rogers was Herman Melville's Ishmael in *Moby Dick*, the alienated sailor who alone survived disaster by clinging to the empty, floating coffin of a shipmate. Ultimately, none can dispute the fact that six months after Rogers warned of a "lack of leadership" that "places all personnel in danger" on the *Scorpion*, the attack submarine spiraled into the depths.

Had he not persisted in gaining his release from the *Scorpion*, the body of Dan Rogers would be cradled as well inside the crumbling chalice of an ancient undersea caldera.

15

Scorpion Phase II Operations

As the *Scorpion* inquiry's second session began, Naval Ordnance Laboratory scientist Robert S. Price was summoned to the Naval Research Laboratory. When he arrived and took his seat, he heard John Craven discuss his theory of how a torpedo launched by the *Scorpion* may have turned back and destroyed the submarine. As he listened, Price grew increasingly skeptical.

What Craven said ran counter to everything Price knew about underwater explosions and the acoustic signals they generated. Price was a research physicist whose specialty was the effects of explosions on submarine hulls. Because of this he was appointed to the *Scorpion* evaluation group to analyze the 750 images of the *Scorpion*'s wreckage obtained by the *Mizar*. Underwater acoustics and blast damage photographs were the tools Price had used for a quarter century to analyze and assess the effects of undersea weapons on submarine hulls.

What Price saw in the *Scorpion* photographs immediately told him there had not been an internal or an external explosion. Although some were mystified by the telescoping of the stern forward into the hull, Price moved quickly to solve this enigma. For those confused by this phenomenon, Price made a scale model of the *Scorpion*'s hull using stiff paper and demonstrated how the hydrostatic collapse of its uniquely shaped cone cylinder juncture would draw the stern forward. He then used another model to show why the *Thresher*'s hull, of somewhat different design, did not behave the same way at collapse depth. (Price would later use a paper model to demonstrate, somewhat conclusively, that the battleship *Maine* had not been destroyed by the Spanish.)

Price was singularly unconvinced that a torpedo struck the *Scorpion*, noting that a segment of the operations compartment's hull was pushed noticeably outward, the opposite sort of damage Price expected to see in a torpedo explosion.

Price, whose secret work was little known outside the communities of naval ordnance and hydroacoustic science, had powerful company in his doubts about Craven's torpedo theory.

Schade, the COMSUBLANT, was also adamantly opposed to the theory that the *Scorpion* was lost to one of its own torpedoes, as was Ephraim P. Holmes, the commander in chief of the Atlantic Fleet. And—perhaps predictably—witnesses from various organizations within the Naval Ordnance Systems Command had pooh-poohed the notion of an accidental torpedo blast, a self-serving position to be sure. (Craven has glibly tarred the entire ordnance organization for resisting the torpedo theory because of collective "denial.")

One witness, however, had spoken against his own self-interest with his assessment that implosion and not a torpedo blast had caused the *Scorpion's* loss. That witness was Peter Palermo, who, as head of the Submarine Structures Section at the Naval Ship Engineering Center, ran the office that originally validated the *Scorpion's* pressure hull design. While Palermo believed the *Scorpion's* hull had admirably exceeded its design limits before failing under immense pressure, the *Mizar's* photographs led him that believe that implosion rather than explosion was the deathblow, due to some unknown problem that dragged the boat to collapse depth.

When Holmes reviewed the Court of Inquiry's proceedings and conclusions—including the opinion of Schade—he determined that "total commitment to any of the scenarios contained in the record is not warranted" and forwarded this recommendation to CNO Thomas H. Moorer, who concurred. Officially, despite the strong opinions of a variety of experts, nothing had been resolved   at least in the view of admirals such as Schade and Holmes—regarding the reasons behind the *Scorpion's* loss.

Trieste II: Another Look

Craven, despite his enthusiasm for his torpedo theory, realized that more information was needed to prove any theory with finality and sought approval for an additional photographic survey of the *Scorpion's* wreckage using the newest version of the manned *Trieste II* bathyscaphe. The chief of naval operations acted quickly, granting his permission on December 24, 1968.

This project would be known as "USS *Scorpion* Phase II On-Site Operations," and it would be under the long-distance auspices of Craven, who, as head of the Deep Submergence Systems Project (DSSP), oversaw Submarine Development Group 1, which possessed the newest *Trieste II* deep submergence vehicle.

The most visual symbol of DSSP during the late 1960s was the third of the *Trieste* series of deep-submergence vehicles invented by Swiss scientist and balloonist August Piccard. To make the *Trieste* heavy enough to sink, it carried discardable steel shot ballast, with buoyancy provided by a "balloon"—a steel tank filled with incompressible gasoline. A pressure-resistant sphere served as an undersea gondola for the crew.

Although it was actually the *Trieste III*, secrecy dictated that it would be referred to as the *Trieste II*, like its predecessor, to camouflage its heightened capabilities. It was not only more maneuverable but also capable of recovering objects from the seafloor weighing more than 2 tons.

Although the navy would say nothing about the *Trieste II*'s real mission, the public was encouraged to believe it was little more than a sightseeing conveyance for scientists. The latest *Trieste*, however, was on the verge of entering the Cold War in a most serious way. By 1967, the second *Trieste II* was preparing to participate in a secret effort code-named Operation Sand Dollar, to retrieve Soviet missile components from the Pacific seafloor. This mission would be interrupted when the CNO's orders landed on the desk of Lt. Cmdr. Robert F. Nevin, the commander of *Trieste II*.

Nevin and his team were ordered to dive to the *Scorpion*'s wreck site to obtain clearer photographs of the wreckage, retrieve artifacts, and provide eyewitness accounts of the damage. The *Trieste II* was well equipped for this reconnaissance effort, since it was equipped with satellite still cameras and video cameras. The bathyscaphe also carried a sonar system to help it navigate and locate objects on the seafloor.

Despite the *Trieste II*'s improvements, it was still an 85-ton craft even before 66,000 gallons of high-octane aviation gasoline filled its massive float, and it remained hard to wrestle even in modest currents. If the ungainly vehicle became tangled on the *Scorpion*'s wreckage, its three-man crew could share eternity with the *Scorpion*.

To avoid this danger while enabling close-up photography of the wreckage, the navy funded a crash program to design and build the world's first video camera–equipped, remotely operated vehicle. It took only forty days for the HydroProducts firm in San Diego to complete a pair of barrel-shaped swimming vehicles known as the Tortugas that could be deployed from the *Trieste II*. Unfortunately, the $100,000 effort failed, since cables carrying commands to the vehicles could not withstand the sea pressure.

On February 23, 1969, the *Trieste II* departed San Diego within the *White Sands*, a specially configured floating dry dock. The *Trieste II* and the *White Sands* then passed through the Panama Canal on the way to Mayport, Florida. After arriving in Mayport, another twenty-six days were spent installing new equipment on both the *Trieste II* and the *White Sands*. One item essential for the operation was a reliable satellite navigation system to position deep ocean sonar transponders so the *Trieste II* could accurately navigate the debris field. The best system then available was an experimental model known as the Magnavox 70 HP Satellite Navigation System, a forerunner of today's global positioning system. The navigation system was aboard the battleship *New Jersey* that was off the coast of South Vietnam belching 2,000-pound shells toward the enemy. The *New Jersey*'s enterprising skipper, J. Edward Snyder, had craftily obtained the navigation system from Magnavox using personal connections but found it too accurate to correlate with military maps of the period. When asked to relinquish the refrigerator-sized system, Snyder gladly shipped it to the *White Sands*.

The *White Sands*, the fleet tug *Apache*, and the destroyer *Ruchamkin* formed the small flotilla that would conduct the Phase II operations and arrived at the *Scorpion*'s wreck site on June 1. The on-site boss of the effort was Capt. Robert Gautier, the commander of Submarine Development Group 1, to which the *Trieste II* belonged. Also aboard was a team of experts to assess any evidence that was gathered. This group included Capt. Harry A. Jackson, a naval architect and submarine designer; Lt. Cmdr. Clark David Sachse, another expert on submarine design; and Lt. Cmdr. J. A. Youse, an authority on undersea weapons. The only civilian among the group was Richard K. Sibley, a photographic interpretation expert from the Naval Reconnaissance and Technical Support Center.

On June 11, the bathyscaphe was allowed to float from the dock of the *White Sands*. On June 22, after two test dives to check equipment, the *Trieste II* descended, with Lt. John Field, Lt. William "Stretch" Leonard, and Chief Warrant Officer Larry Hawks. As the vehicle came to within 600 feet of the seafloor, one of the men spotted the *Scorpion*'s propeller, which had been expelled several hundred feet from the stern

The *Trieste II* bathyscaphe is pictured inside the *White Sands*.
Its secret undersea espionage mission was interrupted so it could
investigate the *Scorpion* disaster.

when the engine room collapsed forward into the auxiliary machine space. The propeller's steel shaft already exhibited a rusty orange color.

As the balky *Trieste II* closed the distance to the bottom, it landed atop the *Scorpion*'s ejected propeller shaft, placing the propeller's blades between the bathyscaphe's landing struts. All three men realized they were on the verge of being trapped. A heavy trail ball that was dragged beneath the vehicle to keep it near the seafloor also threatened to catch on the propeller's blades if the bathyscaphe moved forward. Moving sideways was impossible because one of the struts was blocked by a propeller blade. This forced them to release shot ballast and ascend vertically to

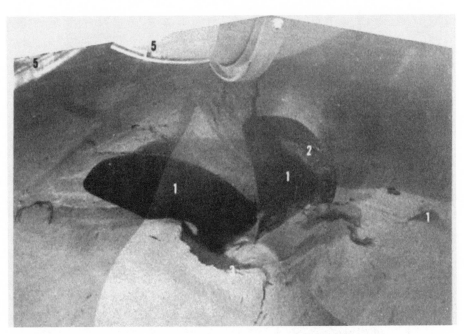

This image shows blades of the *Scorpion*'s ejected propeller jutting from the seafloor ooze, with one blade—numbered "2"—bearing an unidentified gouge.

500 feet. During this maneuver, the *Trieste II* drifted from the debris field and was unable to reacquire it. After an unproductive fourteen-hour dive, the team returned to the surface.

Electrical problems also endangered the crew. The silver-zinc batteries used by the bathyscaphe to power its systems and lights were being infiltrated by seawater because they had been loaded with the wrong compensating oil. To counter seawater infiltration, green packing material known as "monkey shit" was continuously pumped into external electrical connections. When one of the silver-zinc batteries failed, the *Trieste II* was brought back aboard the *White Sands* for a four-day battery replacement. Blown fuses, electrical shorts, and the serious burn-through of one exterior electrical cable plagued the remaining dives. If these problems weren't enough, one morning the cantankerous *Trieste II* was discovered missing. Its tow cable snapped in darkness, prompting a desperate search that eventually located the 85-ton vehicle.

On July 10, during the fourth dive, the *Trieste II* and its three-man crew would have success. With all of its systems working, Lt. Anthony

Dunn, Leonard, and Lt. Ross Saxon made the slow descent into the volcanic caldera 2 miles below. The vehicle arrived atop the debris field, and photographs were made of small items. It was then that Dunn looked up to see the severed bow of the *Scorpion* looming in his view port. "The first time we saw it we had a head-on view and it was a big surprise," he recalled.

What Dunn and his companions saw was the forward fourth of the submarine, which had wrenched loose at the bulkhead between it and the operations compartment before it impacted with enough velocity to dig itself into a massive trench of globigerina ooze. The fine silt, composed of the calcareous shells of foraminiferans, billowed into suspension like a cloud at the time of the impact and settled upon the nose of the bow like snow. This incredibly fine silt created problems for Dunn as well when stirred by the movement of the bathyscaphe's propellers or skids. As clouds of silt obscured their view, the lighting systems failed, making visibility too poor for additional photographs. The decision was made to return to the surface.

While just a few feet away from the submarine's wreckage, Dunn was mesmerized by what he saw. It seemed obvious that the submarine's hull had been crushed by hydrostatic pressure. "When she imploded it created such a hammer effect it blew the [forward] hatch off," recalled Dunn. (While the forward hatch is off its hinges, the stern hatch was also pushed open, though it remains attached to the submarine.)

On July 12, the day after the sixth dive, Craven came aboard the *White Sands* to discuss how the operation was progressing. Gautier and Jackson were photographed on the floating dry dock speaking amiably with Craven, although the two naval officers were becoming convinced by the photographic evidence—and the observations of the *Trieste II* crews—that Craven's torpedo theory was off-base.

No matter the resistance he encountered, Craven remained intrigued by his torpedo scenario and was unmoved by the doubts of Gautier, Jackson, or Sachse. Unshaken by criticism, the massively confident Craven— a poker player extraordinaire—relieved his victims of $500 during nightly poker games aboard the floating dry dock. Just prior to his departure, the scientist made a munificent gesture by donating the money as a party fund for those who remained.

By the seventh dive, the hazardous descents were becoming slightly more relaxed. Dunn, Leonard, and Hawks made another agonizingly slow dive, with only blackness visible through their viewing ports. In this dark,

From left are John Craven, Capt. Harry Jackson, and Capt. Robert Gautier. Jackson and Gautier disagreed with Craven's theory of how the *Scorpion* died.

cramped, threatening environment, Stretch Leonard fractured the silence with a comically loud bout of flatulence. "He tried to deny it," said Dunn like a suspicious detective who couldn't be fooled. "We were all laughing. I told him we were going to have to let the charcoal [air] filters take over."

With the tension broken, the three men continued their descent to the debris field, where they obtained excellent photographs of damaged main storage battery cells, and clear images of the bow torpedo shutters—of which several appeared to have been jarred slightly open on impact. Dunn, who was piloting the bathyscaphe to the whir of its electrical propulsion motors, moved in for even closer shots of the bow section. "We fell into the hole with it while taking pictures," said Dunn nonchalantly of this potentially dangerous mishap.

As the uncooperative *Trieste II* was wrestled to a position behind the disembodied bow section, the crew trained a spotlight on the torpedo room bulkhead, which was videotaped. The destruction they saw was immense: 2-inch-thick pressure hull steel was folded and torn like thin sheets of soft wax. The dive crew initially believed they could see an open watertight door in the mangled bulkhead, and for years this discovery intrigued the navy, which was desperate to peek inside the torpedo room.

The Corpse

On the eighth dive, conducted during July 21–22, something was seen by the bathyscaphe's crew that the navy would keep secret for twenty-nine years. Saxon was piloting the vehicle as Lt. David Byrnes handled the camera systems. Lt. John Field was serving as the copilot when the *Trieste II* glided east across the front of the bow before turning north for the stern section several hundred feet away.

At this moment the three men spotted the only human remains seen during the nine dives of the Phase II operations. The bathyscaphe was traveling at half a knot, 2 to 3 feet from the bottom, when Field spotted a body 20 feet ahead. The sighting lasted forty-five seconds as Saxon vainly attempted to slow the clumsy vehicle. Because the uncooperative *Trieste II* could not be maneuvered to bring the cameras to bear, no images of the corpse were captured.

Although the three submariners had steeled themselves for just such a sight, what was completely unexpected was that Saxon and Byrnes were convinced the sailor was wearing a standard-issue orange life preserver, something none of the men expected to see. Both recalled that the man's legs were askew, while Byrnes more specifically recalls that one of his pants legs seemed to be floating upward. While Byrnes recalls the man wearing blue, standard-issue dungarees, Saxon recalls that the body was lying facedown and wearing "nuclear power type" coveralls.

Field's account recalls the body as lying face up: "Although it doesn't seem scientifically possible, it appeared to me that the flesh was still on the face, and the hair—dark and about 3 inches long—was still on the head. The corpse was wearing dark (possibly blue) coverall-type clothes. The clothes seemed to be 'puffed' out, as if filled with a gas. The trousers appeared to have a 'tight' elastic type of cuff. The corpse also had on what appeared to be a light-colored . . . yellow vest." Field wrote that only later did he realize the body may have been wearing a life jacket.

The *Trieste II* soon glided past the body in the current. The body would never again be seen. It was the only sighting of human remains during the operation, but it raised profound questions about what happened to the *Scorpion* during the final minutes of life. The two most important questions were why was a *Scorpion* sailor wearing a life preserver, and why was his body intact if exposed to the monumental force of a pressure hull's hydrostatic collapse?

The puzzling ramifications of this discovery range from meaningless to immense.

Submariners generally agree that no sailor would put on a life preserver unless he was ordered to the weather deck of a surfaced submarine. Had the *Scorpion* lost its struggle while on the surface and the sailor was not inescapably tethered to the boat by a safety harness, his life preserver could have carried him dozens, if not hundreds of miles away. Schade and others wondered if the submarine surfaced or at least neared the surface during its final moments of distress. After all, its number two periscope and two of its antennas were in an extended position, as they would be while near the surface.

Although a sailor inside a dying submarine might put on a life preserver as his final, desperate act, its buoyancy would be squeezed out by sea pressure even at a relatively minor depth. If the sailor's body were expelled upon the submarine's impact with the bottom, he would certainly not float to the surface. If expelled from the submarine following an implosion at its crush depth of roughly 1,400 to 2,000 feet, it's unclear if the sailor's body would have landed just a few dozen feet from the main wreckage after a descent of nearly 9,000 feet. The main segments of the hull, which weighed hundreds of tons, would have far different velocities and trajectories than a human body.

If a sailor was tethered to the deck of the surfaced submarine by a safety line and dragged downward when it sank, he may have been pulled to the bottom at speeds estimated at 20 to 35 miles per hour. Whether a human body or the safety harness would remain intact under these conditions is uncertain, although if either did, it might also account for why a body wearing a life preserver was found so close to the wreckage.

The sailor wearing the life preserver could have just reentered the submarine or been preparing to go on deck when the boat took its fatal plunge. The possibility also exists that some malfunction brought the *Scorpion* to the surface long enough for one or more sailors to go on deck. Of note is the fact that the stern line locker is open and a hawser is spilling out, though this could have been caused by shock of the cone cylinder juncture failure that drew the engine room into the hull.

A serious failure that came close to sinking a submarine a decade later provides an interesting comparison. On June 16, 1978, the fast attack boat *Tullibee* was conducting operations 120 feet below the Mediterranean when sailors noticed white sand in the bilge beneath the propeller shaft. Although it matched the color of the sound-dampening Wausau quartz sand packed inside the hollow propeller shaft, the concerns of the sailors were dismissed by superiors, who identified it as sand sucked aboard during a recent visit to Naples Harbor. Even after the enlisted men correctly pointed out that the sand near Naples was of the dark, volcanic type, their warnings were shrugged off.

"We prepared ourselves for what we thought was coming," said Electrician's Mate First Class David Heckman, who was convinced that the *Tullibee's* shaft was fractured. Heckman's fears were substantiated when the call went out on the 1MC system, "Flooding in the engine room!" The propeller shaft had indeed suffered a crack that extended around its circumference at the stern tube seal, allowing water to gush into the engine room. Fortunately, the shaft was still inside the stern seal, reducing the amount of flooding. As flooding added weight to the stern of the boat, the situation went from bad to worse, and the emergency main ballast tank blow system was activated, sending the *Tullibee* to the surface that was roiled by hideously rough weather. Despite making it to the surface, the boat was still in serious trouble as it continued to take on water that caused it to ride low at the stern. As the submarine struggled to stay afloat, crew members tightened the backup seal to reduce the rate of flooding, only to discover that this secondary seal did little to stanch the flow.

The effort to remove water from the *Tullibee's* engine room was also hampered by a poorly working drain pump—an example of the notorious "second casualty" Schade suspected in the loss of the *Scorpion*. *Tullibee* executive officer Steven Jay Loucks shouldered the sailors aside and stepped in to overhaul the drain pump.

A gang of *Tullibee* sailors donned life preservers and clambered topside, where they threw open the stern line locker so they could loop a hawser around the propeller to hold the aft end of the fractured shaft in place. As sailors bloodied their hands to hold the *Tullibee's* propeller, massive swells washed over the submarine's deck, knocking them off their feet or shoving them overboard, to dangle from their safety lines. The *Tullibee* was later towed to Rota, where it spent two months receiving repairs.

Although a main propulsion shaft breakage might have generated the initial, unexplained sound recorded twenty-two minutes before the main collapse of the *Scorpion*—while also explaining why various masts were raised as the crew prepared to surface—this theory, like so many others, cannot be verified. There are many reasons why a submarine might surface in midocean and put life-jacketed sailors on the deck.

What was most curious about the sighting of the body by Saxon, Byrnes, and Field was that it was not initially considered a high-priority observation. The mission was tightly focused on gathering photographic evidence to resolve the *Scorpion* mystery, which had already become a hotly disputed enigma within the navy. It was only six months later, in February 1970, that the three officers were asked to provide a written report to Gautier about the body they had seen. "There were no photographs of the body so we initially didn't give it much thought," said Gautier, who was devoted to keeping the investigation focused on factual data rather than opinion and speculation.

Artifacts

Harry Jackson, the chief analyst among the experts on the *White Sands*, was eager to visit the *Scorpion*'s wreck, although he was warned that observations made through the small view ports were of poor quality. Nonetheless, Jackson believed it might help him better understand what happened to the smashed submarine. Craven remembers the subject coming up and gladly gave his blessing to Jackson's making the trip. Dunn recalls Jackson as a gentlemanly officer who effectively solved several of the *Trieste II*'s numerous mechanical problems with his engineering acumen: "We liked him and we wanted him to go along. We were all for it."

On the ninth and final dive to the wreck site, on July 30–31, the *Trieste II* was piloted by Nevin, accompanied by Jackson and Byrnes. Nevin pinged a signal to the deep-ocean transponders, but the navigational devices were beginning to fail after nearly two months on the seafloor. He was able to obtain a response from only one, which he used to guide him to a spot several hundred feet north of the disembodied bow. As the trail ball thumped into the ooze, the *Trieste II*'s descent halted. Nevin then reeled in the trail ball's cable to draw the *Trieste II* closer to the seafloor. Nevin applied propulsion and skimmed just above the ooze at a speed equal to that of a walking man. As Jackson looked through his view port, he observed the debris on the seafloor slowly passing by.

A chunk of the *Scorpion*'s main battery is held by the *Trieste II*'s manipulator arm. Analysis of the piece revealed the possibility of a battery explosion.

On this trip, Nevin had decided to use the manipulator arm—a device similar to those used when handling nuclear materials—to retrieve artifacts.

"I saw a wallet lying on the seafloor with money sticking out of it," said Nevin. "I could have picked it up but it just didn't seem like the right thing to do. We then saw fish and some type of crab." Nevin had also been amazed at the sight of so much paper in the debris field: "There were a lot of books strewn on the bottom. It appeared to have been ejected when the wreckage landed. If it had spilled out at a shallower depth, it would have fallen in a more dispersed pattern." Nevin remembers seeing fabric tablecloths, an item unique to the officers' wardroom, since enlisted men ate on uncovered steel tables.

The sight of so much main storage battery debris was intriguing, and Nevin glided toward a chunk of red plastic—a segment of main storage battery cell cover still attached to a copper connector. Activating the manipulator arm's controls, Nevin extended the large pincers around the debris, lifted it gingerly from the seafloor in a swirl of silt, and held it aloft so it could be photographed by the 70mm satellite camera and the video camera. Nevin then dropped it into a basket and went on the prowl for more artifacts.

What caught Nevin's eye next was the frame of a standard navy-issue micrometer drum sextant lying near a piece of mangled piping 25 yards north of the stern. As the arm lifted the sextant it was also photographed and videotaped. Stripped of its micrometer drum, mirror, and scope, the bronze frame was dinged and scratched following its violent expulsion from the operations compartment where it had been stored.

When the *Trieste II* finally surfaced, the recovered items were kept in seawater until they could be transferred to the Naval Research Laboratory in Washington for detailed analysis. Nevin had no idea that the unremarkable chunk of battery casing contained intriguing clues that would raise even more questions about the *Scorpion*'s demise.

16

The Last Investigation

As they were brought to the surface and processed, submarine designer Capt. Harry A. Jackson immediately began studying the photographs revealing the bizarre scene of destruction 2 miles beneath the *White Sands*.

Jackson and the four-person group he led were known as the "on-scene analysis team," whose job was to unravel whatever story was encoded in the *Scorpion*'s damage. Along with Submarine Development Group 1 commander Gautier, the team pored over photographs and dozens of hours of videotape. They also debriefed the dive crew members—all experienced submariners—about their observations and impressions.

While he was not a submarine officer, few knew submarine construction better than Jackson, widely considered an officer of great integrity. A 1940 graduate of the University of Michigan's Department of Naval Architecture and Marine Engineering, Jackson entered the navy as an engineering duty officer overseeing the repair of submarines during World War II. At war's end he moved into submarine design and construction, became the fourth graduate of the navy's nuclear propulsion program, and helped design the experimental *Albacore* and later the ill-fated *Thresher*. While his contributions on the *Thresher*-class design were not considered at fault in its loss, Jackson profoundly impressed submarine officers with his outspoken concern over the tragedy while others preferred a lower profile.

Implosion

It became apparent to Jackson that the *Scorpion* suffered implosion damage after it had gone below its crush depth. As to precisely how the *Scorpion* ended up in this fatal predicament, Jackson could only speculate.

A Mk-37 torpedo blast breaks the keel of a decommissioned diesel-electric submarine, demonstrating the obvious damage the torpedo could inflict.

The superb photographs brought back by Robert Nevin and his *Trieste II* pilots seemed to be self-explanatory: the stern cone cylinder juncture collapsed, sending the engine room inside the hull, and the operations compartment suffered massive implosion damage, severing the torpedo room. There was no sign of an internal or an external explosion on the hull, and not a scrap of debris from a detonated torpedo was located in the debris field.

Before seeing the *Trieste II* images, Jackson reviewed Buck Buchanan's camera sled images taken the previous fall and realized that there was no evidence of the external torpedo explosion that John Craven postulated. Jackson and Gautier were well aware of the percolating dispute between those beguiled by Craven's torpedo theory and those, such as themselves, who saw little or nothing to substantiate Craven's hypothesis.

This second camp of experts, which also included Robert Price at the Naval Ordnance Laboratory and Peter Palermo at the Submarine Structures Section, was at a disadvantage in marketing their case against a torpedo explosion. Those who believed that hydrostatic collapse rather than an explosion had smashed the *Scorpion* were like detectives at the scene of a crime: they could determine that a victim had been shot, but they could only guess about the events that led to the fatal wound. Given the seriousness with which they viewed their responsibilities—influenced in no small part by Gautier's insistence on adhering to evidence—the on-scene analysis team was unwilling to speculate beyond what was supported by the facts.

"Craven talked about that torpedo theory at the time and Bob [Gautier] and I took him to task at the time," said Jackson. "It [the torpedo theory] was a possibility, but it was highly unlikely, we told him." Jackson said there was no changing Craven's mind. "You've got to know John; when he goes on record of saying something, it's the gospel truth and there's no reason for him to change his story. Since he said it, he'd have to defend it."

The Wreck

Although much has been made of how the *Scorpion*'s wreckage is arrayed on the seafloor—with some erroneously claiming its bow is pointed back toward Europe—the way its main pieces fell actually tells very little about how the submarine died. The bow, sheared from the operations compartment at frame 26, is pointing 345 degrees north-northwest, and not east, away from Norfolk, as some have speculated.

It may have glided to the bottom at a substantial velocity, since it plowed a trench that extends to the rear of the shattered compartment. Seen from above, the bow is bent like a banana to port, perhaps due to its collision with the seabed—as speculated by the Phase II analysis. The possibility also exists that the hull deformed as massive hydrostatic pressure built against the hull, bending it on the fulcrum of its internal framing. The steel plating at the top and along the port side is severely wrinkled by this compression: the 2-inch-thick, blast-resistant steel is twisted and ripped, as if it had been no more substantial than tinfoil.

The aft section of the hull lies on an east–west axis, with the forward end pointing toward the United States. The forward portion is lying on its starboard side, but the stern engine room section that telescoped into it is horizontal to the seafloor, as if it were still moving. The stern planes are in a 5-degree rise position, and the rudder shows only a modest shift of 15 degrees to the left. Considering that the baseball-bat-thick, plane-operating rams and the hydraulic lines were undoubtedly bent—if not sheared by implosion and impact forces—the angle of these surfaces, no

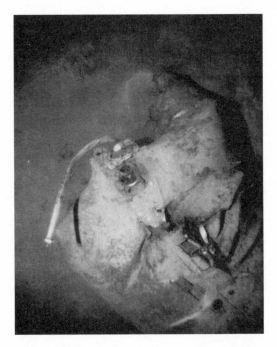

This image of the aft portion of the *Scorpion*'s torpedo room indicates to some that it was sheared from the submarine by hydrostatic collapse.

matter how dramatic, might reveal little. The same is true for the fairwater planes, which appear configured for a shallow dive. All the control surfaces have slight scalloping because their steel skin has been pushed against their internal framing by hydrostatic pressure.

Several hundred feet from the stern, the propeller and its shaft lay partially buried in the silt. The forward end of the shaft is protruding upward from the muck at a 45-degree angle, and at least two of the blades are plainly visible jutting from the ooze, with the tip of a third barely visible. Jackson and his colleagues speculated that the shaft broke away from its thrust bearing and was expelled during the implosion of the engine room. What is curious about the propeller is a sizable abrasion visible on the aft face of one blade that could not be explained. This gouge appears considerably larger than the palm-sized scar discovered the previous fall.

What stunned experts was the sight of the stern driven 50 feet inside the hull, with only the control surfaces protruding from the auxiliary machine space. All the navy experts agreed that the cone cylinder juncture was a complicated hard point that might be the first to fail once the

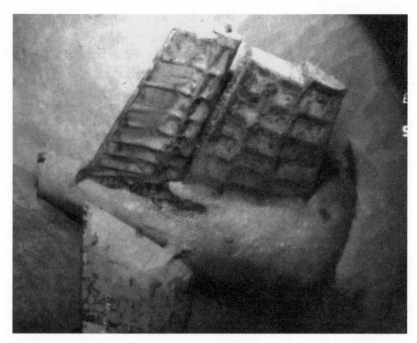

Dusted by silt from its initial seafloor impact, the rudder and a stern plane protrude from the *Scorpion*'s hull in this 1986 image.

Scorpion exceeded its maximum depth, although it had been reinforced. It was at this juncture that a clean, annular break occurred, propelling the engine room into and around the equipment of the auxiliary machine space. In effect, the engine room became a 2-inch-thick HY-80 steel cookie cutter moving at incredible velocity into the compartment ahead of it.

The operations compartment, which was a massive interior space on the *Scorpion*, suffered terrible damage. A sizable portion of the compartment's pressure hull appears to be missing—imploded by unlimited force at the moment of collapse, according to the Phase II analysis report— and most of the debris seen on the seafloor originated from this space, which contained the control room. Although some have characterized the operations compartment as being obliterated and missing, Palermo has long believed that much of its hull plating may be bent back like the top edge of a paper bag folded inside itself.

It was apparent to Jackson that the implosion of the operations compartment at the point where the fairwater met the hull resulted in the finlike structure being torn free from its disintegrating perch. The fairwater, which was not located during the Phase II dives, had been photographed earlier by the *Mizar*'s camera sled, which revealed that a sizable notch had been torn from the lower aft portion of the fairwater. At that point on the fairwater the diesel exhaust manifold cover or "turtleback" began and extended along the spine of the hull. The fairwater is also missing its lower, deck access door.

Curiously, the starboard running light on the fairwater is pushed out and in the locked position, a configuration employed only when the submarine was operating on the surface. The possibility exists that it was inadvertently left in the open position after surfacing near Rota on the night of May 16–17, or that it popped open due to the force of the implosion and the violent detachment of the fairwater.

The massive jolt experienced by the fairwater must have been immense; although the starboard fairwater door remains attached, its port counterpart was photographed by the *Mizar* in the debris field. It's hardly surprising that the deck-level fairwater door is missing as well, since the fairwater sail is torn along its bottom edge where it was ripped from the hull. A bolted fairwater access plate was also photographed on the seafloor, indicative of a "water hammer" caused by a shock wave of high-pressure water when the hull imploded.

Another possible example of the water hammer effect is the forward escape access hatch, which was forced open and sheared from its hinges like the port fairwater door, according to the Phase II analysis. Jackson believed that hydrostatic pressure unseated the lower trunk hatches, filling the escape trunks with high-pressure seawater that then sprang the deck access hatches. Some argue that external sea pressure would hold the hatches in place against the intrusion of seawater at equal pressure and that only an internal explosion could force them open. However, it's highly unlikely that simultaneous explosions occurred in both the torpedo room and the engine room that would spring hatches on opposite ends of the boat.

The belief that the *Scorpion* was at or near the surface at some point during its final moments, and the presence of a sailor in a life preserver, prompt speculation that perhaps the stern access hatch was opened from the inside before the *Scorpion* made its fatal plunge. This, however, seems

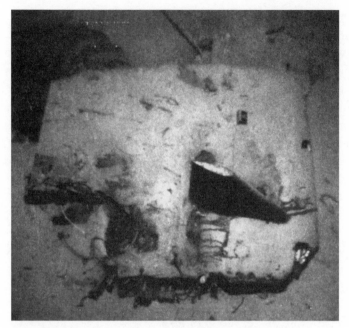

This 1986 image shows the *Scorpion*'s starboard running light deployed on the violently detached fairwater.

extremely unlikely, since the last thing a crewman would do, or be allowed to do, is open a weather deck hatch on a submarine fighting to remain buoyant.

It seems obvious to investigators such as Price, Jackson, and Gautier that neither an external torpedo explosion nor a high-order internal detonation seems to have occurred. While some have attempted to compare the *Scorpion* disaster to the August 12, 2000, sinking of the Russian submarine *Kursk*—which was indeed destroyed by a pair of internal weapon explosions—there are actually no similarities.

Although the *Scorpion*'s bow/torpedo room is sheared from the disintegrated operations compartment, it is relatively unscathed. By comparison, the bow of the *Kursk* suffered devastating damage when it was indisputably rocked by a pair of high-energy explosions. The first blast represented the force of 550 pounds of high explosive, with the second equivalent to 10,000 pounds of high explosive, according to geologists who studied the seismograph recordings of the detonations.

By most accounts, the explosions tore through the *Kursk*'s double hull, obliterating the forward escape trunk and hatch—along with much of the bow—with the greatest damage occurring during the sympathetic detonation of other warheads in the second blast. The aft escape hatch, which was some distance from the torpedo room, remained secured and operable. Unlike the *Scorpion*, the deep-diving *Kursk* sank in water 350 feet deep—far above its crush depth—precluding implosion damage. There is simply no similar, catastrophic damage to the *Scorpion*'s torpedo room. As for theories that a torpedo battery fire led to the loss of the *Scorpion*, the navy has no evidence of fire in the debris field.

The Structural Analysis Group

With the *Scorpion* Phase II operations completed, the ships of the flotilla headed for their respective ports. Despite the success of the Phase II operations in gathering photographs and accumulating *Trieste II* crew observations, the information still failed to substantiate any theory regarding the *Scorpion*'s loss, lamented Gautier.

The CINCLANTFT Ephraim Holmes reviewed the findings of the Phase II operations and on October 14, 1969, reported to Moorer that "no new evidence has been developed which will materially affect the conclusions of the original and supplementary Courts of Inquiry." Holmes told Moorer that there were two options the navy could pursue regarding the results of the Phase II operations: reconvene the original Court of Inquiry, or convene a new inquiry. Neither of these options was considered worthwhile, given that a wide cross section of witnesses had already been interviewed. It was decided that the Court of Inquiry, whose second session ended on December 19, 1968, would be the last public hearing at which the *Scorpion*'s loss would be investigated. It would not, however, be the last scientific investigation.

It was decided that an additional, formal analysis of all the physical evidence in hand regarding the loss of the *Scorpion* would be conducted as an extension of the Phase II operations. The evidence to be reviewed would include the *Mizar* and *Trieste II* still and video images as well as the SOFAR signals intercepted by Gordon Hamilton's La Palma SOFAR station. The main storage battery debris would also be subjected to intensive scientific analysis.

The team conducting this technical investigation was dubbed the Structural Analysis Group or SAG and would be chaired by Peter Palermo, head of the navy's Submarine Structures Section. It would also include Kenneth Hom, a physicist with the Naval Ship Research Development Center, and scientist Richard Swim of the Naval Research Laboratory. Logically enough, key members of the Phase II operations analysis group would be on the SAG as well, including Jackson, Sibley, Youse, and Sachse.

Another group member would be Robert Price, the Naval Ordnance Laboratory research physicist who had been so leery of Craven's torpedo theory. Price was ordered in December to begin his study of the *Scorpion's* acoustic signals, and he selected fellow NOL research physicist Ermine America Christian to assist in the effort to analyze the *Scorpion's* final sounds. Their goal would be to ascertain the true nature of the fifteen signals and to determine if any—especially the first—possessed the acoustic characteristics of an explosion, as Craven suggested.

Price was never comfortable with the idea that any of the *Scorpion's* fifteen SOFAR signals indicated an explosion. He wanted to conduct an in-depth analysis of the La Palma recordings to see if his hunch was correct. Christian, a native of Macon, Georgia, had conducted underwater explosives research during World War II, like Price, and was a recognized authority on the bubble pulse phenomenon, the earmark of underwater explosions.

The hydroacoustic signals generated by the *Scorpion* were unusual in their tonal quality and had puzzled Price. To understand these sounds more precisely, Price needed to duplicate the *Scorpion's* sinking to compare the signals it generated as its compartments imploded. (Price had obtained British recordings of acoustic signals of submarine test sinkings, but quaintly enough, they arrived on scratched phonograph recordings instead of audiotape and were of poor quality.)

Price became euphoric in December 1968 when, by happenstance, he and Christian learned that the diesel-electric submarine *Sterlet* was to be sunk as a torpedo target off the California coast. The exercise would occur on January 31, 1969, and the weapon was to be a Mk-37 launched by the *Sargo*. Though not a perfect comparison—the pressure hull design was older and the *Sterlet* would be on the surface when struck—it was nonetheless an opportunity to monitor the acoustic events produced by a submarine sunk by a Mk-37. Price convinced his superiors to allow a scientist to record the explosion of the torpedo against the *Sterlet's* hull, and the sounds created by the submarine as it sank below its collapse depth.

Recording the sinking was not an easy task. The *Sterlet* was manned by four sailors who would set it on a circular course at 6 knots before they abandoned the boat. Peter Sherman, a fearless NOL scientist and former air force officer, jumped from a helicopter into the center of the submarine's orbit and set up a recording system floating inside a Styrofoam case. Sherman completed his daredevil act and was plucked from the water to observe the test. Minutes later, the *Sargo* launched the torpedo, which struck the *Sterlet* in the stern. A spout of water rushed skyward, and the submarine quickly sank.

Sherman's adventurous effort paid off, and by early February, Price, Christian, and Sherman were studying the sounds of not only the submarine's implosion noises but also a series of underwater signal charges that were also detonated at various depths as part of the test. (The daring Sherman and his wife would perish nine years later in the crash of his vintage P-38 warplane near Whitehouse, Ohio.)

Price and Christian analyzed an original recording of the *Scorpion*'s signals and compared them to the sounds generated by the *Sterlet*. What Price finally determined was diametrically opposed to what Craven believed happened to the *Scorpion*, and was more in line with the findings of the Phase II analysis team's conclusion that blamed implosion alone for the condition of the *Scorpion*'s wreckage. Like Craven, however, Price also had reached a controversial conclusion.

While initial analysis of the *Scorpion*'s destruction noises and the position of its periscope and fairwater masts indicated the submarine was at or near the surface, Price believed the submarine had not generated its death throes until it was at a great depth.

The *Scorpion*, stated a report written by Price and Christian, had imploded far deeper than its officially established collapse depth. The first of the fifteen acoustic signals conclusively identified as generated by the dying submarine was not generated by an explosion, but perhaps the implosion of the cone cylinder juncture segment of its hull if not the operations compartment. The other signals, said Price dismissively, "were just noise, just the sound of metal banging together." He also determined that the odd qualities of sounds produced by the *Scorpion* were not necessarily unique after studying the recorded sounds of three British submarines that were intentionally sunk below crush depth and then recovered.

What was puzzling was the large number of sounds created by the *Scorpion* during its death dive. The *Sterlet* had produced only three identifiable acoustic events during its sinking off the California coast, compared with the *Scorpion*'s fifteen sounds. Although additional signals can be generated by sound energy reflecting off undersea mountains or ridges, Price pointed out that test explosions near the *Scorpion* wreck site failed to generate any reflections or echoes. Price was convinced that the *Scorpion*'s hydroacoustic signals were all original sounds generated by the doomed submarine.

Price and Christian found no characteristics of an explosion in the La Palma signals associated with the loss of the *Scorpion*. The implosion sound generated by the *Sterlet*'s sinking had similar characteristics to the first *Scorpion* acoustic signal. Craven and Hamilton's demonstration that an underwater explosion's bubble pulse could be swallowed was confronted by Price, who stated that yes, no bubble pulse was recorded in the *Sterlet* sinking when struck on the surface by a Mk-37 torpedo. However, Price said that while a bubble pulse may vent into a submarine's hull or into the atmosphere during a shallow-water detonation, the identifiable shock wave generated by an underwater blast will still be radiated, and no such characteristic existed in the *Scorpion* signals.

In addition, Palermo—who later reviewed the images gathered by the *Trieste II*—could plainly see that the bulkhead between the torpedo room and the operations compartment was "loaded forward" toward the torpedo room by what he believed was the hydrostatic collapse of the operations compartment. A hypothesized torpedo explosion within the torpedo room, he said, would have tended to shove the bulkhead toward the control room. The depth at which the *Scorpion*'s hull failure occurred— according to Price's still-secret calculations—may have been as deep as 2,000 feet, nearly 600 feet below what is rumored to be its official collapse depth of 1,400 feet. Palermo said that hull-strength calculations used by the navy are intentionally conservative and that the failure of a submarine hull at a deeper-than-expected depth should not necessarily be surprising. Palermo also pointed out that modern design and fabrication techniques on the *Scorpion*'s hull may have resulted in not only a stronger-than-expected pressure envelope, but also one that would collapse somewhat uniformly in a single instant at several specific structural locations.

To answer those who would doubt that the *Scorpion*'s hull could survive as deeply as he believes it did, Price's report mentions a mishap involving the diesel-electric submarine *Chopper*, which was nearly lost with all hands on February 11, 1969. The *Chopper* episode also revealed the potentially disastrous hazards that a loss of depth control poses to a submarine.

The *Chopper*, a submarine augmented with increased battery power and hull streamlining as part of the GUPPY (Greater Underwater Propulsion Program) after World War II, had a test-depth rating of 400 feet (indicating a collapse depth of perhaps 600 feet). On the day of its harrowing mishap, the *Chopper* was operating off Andros Island, Bahamas, at a depth of 150 feet. Without warning, its two motor generators producing alternating current tripped offline, robbing the submarine of its control and instrument functions and sending the boat into a dive. With its twin propellers still pushing the submarine forward and downward—despite an all-back order from the control room—the boat took a 15-degree dive and eventually plunged it to a crushing 1,011 feet, or as many as 400 feet below its official crush depth. As the submarine's hull groaned and deformed under the immense hydrostatic pressure, the crew prepared for their deaths. At that moment, however, the *Chopper*'s fatal plunge abated and the submarine began to rise.

Since its ballast tanks had been blown during the uncontrolled dive, the *Chopper* was now fully buoyant and rose so rapidly that the crew could not slow the ascent. The submarine was soon shooting upward at an astounding 83-degree angle. Loose items began to fly toward the stern as men hung on to anything they could grip. When the *Chopper* reached the surface, sailors claim it shot out of the water for fully half its 311-foot length before plunging downward 200 feet and then bobbing back to the surface.

Had a single hull weld or an internal seawater piping joint failed at the great depth to which it plunged, the *Chopper* would have been doomed. It was considered somewhat of a miracle that the submarine's hull did not fail soon after exceeding 600 feet. Donald I.. Forbes, the skipper of the *Chopper*, said the 21-inch torpedo tubes were so compressed by hydrostatic pressure that they would never again accept torpedoes. The circular hull frames in the aft portion of the boat were deformed as well. The *Chopper* never again submerged.

The pressure hull of the *Chopper* was of high tensile steel (HTS), possessing roughly half the strength of the HY-80 steel used in the framing and the hull of the *Scorpion*, a boat whose pressure hull was of a more advanced design. Given the *Chopper*'s example, it's not hard to believe that the *Scorpion* may have endured an uncontrolled dive far deeper than its own estimated collapse depth.

As far as Price and Christian were concerned, an explosion had nothing to do with the sounds of the *Scorpion*'s loss. It was apparent to both that seawater had not fully filled the *Scorpion* at the time it passed its collapse depth, an event that would have equalized the pressure and precluded implosion of the pressure hull. If the boat had been the victim of flooding, it may have only been enough to make it lose buoyancy. The acoustic energy generated by the collapse of the *Scorpion's* hull at great depth, said Price, was the initial signal recorded by Gordon Hamilton's hydrophones at La Palma.

If the *Scorpion's* death groans made sense to Price and Christian—who believed that the submarine collapsed well below 1,400 feet—the telescoping of the submarine's stern into the hull was also being conclusively explained by Palermo's personnel, using a scale model in a pressurized tank. When taken to collapse depth, the stern of the model was drawn forward into the steel cylinder. This explanation of stern damage was accompanied by a better understanding what happened in the forward part of the hull. An examination of the damage to the British submarines *Stoic*, *Achates*, and *Supreme*—sunk to study pressure hull collapse—revealed damage similar to that observed in the operations compartment of the *Scorpion*. The mystery was now less of a mystery.

Main Storage Battery Explosion

Although the recovered sextant frame had little to reveal about the loss of the *Scorpion*, when the chunk of main storage battery cover was subjected to microscopic and spectrographic analysis, the seemingly insignificant lump of plastic had its own story to tell: it revealed that a battery explosion could have rocked the submarine before its hull imploded.

The analysis conducted at Portsmouth Naval Shipyard and the Naval Research Laboratory indicated that the piece of red plastic battery cover had been "violently, but locally torn, particularly at the location of the bus connection. . . . The deformation appears to have started on the inside, or the battery side of the cover." (The indication here is that the explosion occurred inside the battery.) An extremely small speck of steel with tungsten content also was discovered embedded in the outside of the cover fragment. (The presence of superhard tungsten is curious, since it's a specialized material used mostly on the cutting edges of tool steel.) In addition, twenty fragments of aluminum material identical to that used by the battery's flash arresters were embedded at high velocity into both sides of the plastic, indicating they collided with the battery cover material as the result of an explosion.

The analysis by the Portsmouth Naval Shipyard team was also swayed by the massive scattering of battery fragments in the *Scorpion*'s debris field, as revealed by photographs taken by the *Mizar* and the *Trieste II*. The Portsmouth group also speculated that the explosion probably occurred while the battery well was dry and not flooded, since water would have reduced the velocity of the fragments, keeping them from penetrating the plastic so deeply. Although a flood of seawater could trigger a massive discharge of the boat's 65-ton battery with horrific consequences, an outright blast could only be triggered by an accumulation of hydrogen gas not drawn off by the boat's ventilation system.

An intriguing piece of debris photographed by the *Trieste II* on the seafloor ooze was the negative tank flood valve operating gear, a contraption that opened and closed the valve for a small trim tank known as the "negative tank," positioned along the keel. Located inside the enlisted men's washroom, the device was lying amid a plethora of main storage battery debris. The negative tank—which could be quickly deballasted to provide emergency buoyancy for the submarine—was adjacent to and forward of the massive battery's compartment. The enlisted men's washroom was directly above the tank at the frame that separated the torpedo room from the operations compartment.

This again raised the prospect of a battery explosion, although experts testified during the Court of Inquiry proceedings that while a 30 percent concentration of hydrogen in the air was explosive, if ignited it would not generate enough blast pressure to rupture the *Scorpion*'s hull. Nonetheless, the 1955 hydrogen explosion aboard the surfaced diesel-electric submarine *Pomodon* bent internal deck plating, incinerated compartments, and proved fatal to five sailors. If a battery explosion could not shatter the *Scorpion*'s hull, it could certainly create a chain of events that might prove fatal to a submerged boat.

Nonetheless, the main storage battery—while not responsible for ripping the submarine apart—is a perennial suspect in unexplained submarine mishaps owing to the history of fatal and near-fatal battery problems on navy submarines during the previous century. One such mishap that reminded the navy it could never become complacent about main storage battery hazards occurred in a spectacular fashion just three days before the sixteenth anniversary of the *Scorpion*'s loss.

This occurred when the nuclear-powered attack submarine *Guitarro* suffered a life-threatening malfunction involving its main storage battery on May 19, 1984. This took place while a group of prospective commanding officers were undergoing torpedo training off the coast of Southern California.

As the officers demonstrated their abilities to command the submarine while launching exercise torpedoes, the complex torpedo tube system appeared to be operating normally. When a torpedo is launched and the torpedo tube muzzle door is closed, the water is rapidly drained to a water round torpedo (WRT) tank below the torpedo room adjacent to the battery well. Unfortunately for the *Guitarro*, a striker plate that deflected the incoming water before it struck the tank's internal wall had fallen away. For months, if not years, a high-pressure jet of seawater struck the same spot inside the twelve-year-old WRT tank. On that fateful day, the abrasive and corrosive jet of water finally penetrated the corroded tank and soaked the battery each time a torpedo was launched.

As the saltwater inundated the main storage battery, chlorine gas was produced by electrolysis, triggering automatic alarms that told the crew it was time to "suck rubber." Sailors and officers struggled into their emergency air breathing (EAB) masks, and the submarine neared the surface to send a distress signal. The battery, now shorted by saltwater, began to discharge, creating a massive amount of heat inside the battery well. Some sailors claimed that the soles of their shoes melted to the deck. In addition, a considerable amount of oxygen and explosive hydrogen were being generated, recalled Ken Sunahara, then a lieutenant on the *Guitarro*.

Things then went from bad to worse when the "toxic gas" alert was changed to "fire in the battery compartment," a type of fire that most submariners believe is nearly impossible to extinguish. Sunahara recalled that he and his men placed duct tape "over every kind of opening" to keep the gases out. "Some guys said they could see the duct tape bulging as the gases tried to push their way out of the battery well," said Sunahara.

Unaware that the defective WRT tank was allowing seawater into the battery each time a torpedo tube was drained for reloading, the decision was made to launch the remaining exercise torpedoes. This, of course, made things worse, by pumping more seawater into the battery well. Finally, after three hours, the heat died down and the toxic gases dissipated enough to allow the crew to take off their EABs. After repairs the *Guitarro* was eventually returned to service.

Although a main storage battery mishap was considered a somewhat remote possibility by the *Scorpion*'s Court of Inquiry, the condition of the recovered segment of plastic battery cover and the scattering of so much fragmented battery debris raise suspicions about this component.

Conclusions

On June 29, 1970, Palermo and the Structural Analysis Group he chaired issued their full report, titled "Evaluation of Data and Artifacts Related to USS *Scorpion*." The once-secret report was deemed so sensitive it was not released until 1998, just ahead of the thirtieth anniversary of the *Scorpion*'s loss.

Palermo, the submarine structural expert, had concentrated on the *Scorpion*'s hull design and the characteristics of its hull steel. For years there had been profound worries about the HY-80 hull steel of the *Skipjack*-class boats because the first boat of the class had immediately suffered cracking in its hull welds. The problem was identified as "hydrogen-assisted cracking" or "hydrogen-assisted corrosion" in which infinitesimal hydrogen molecules were freed from moisture in the hull steel and welding rods during welding. These molecules infested the welds like miniature ball bearings, where they engendered embrittlement that led to cracking. There was real concern that the boats built with the steel might be unsafe.

Developed during and after World War II as a superstrong armor to reduce the vulnerability of aircraft carriers to torpedo attack, the steel's chemical composition—combined with a complex formula for tempering—made it nearly twice as strong as steel used in submarine hulls of the 1940s. HY-80 steel could sustain blast pressures of up to 80,000 pounds per square inch, and its suitability as a pressure hull material was quickly recognized.

The cracking problem was identified before the *Scorpion* began to take shape at Electric Boat Company, and a crash program was instituted to ensure that the exotic HY-80 steel could be welded without hydrogen-related problems. The solution was to use electrical strip heaters where hull sections came together to raise the temperature of the steel to 250 degrees Fahrenheit. This drove moisture from the edges of the segments to be joined. The melting of a temperature crayon's mark would tell the welder when the steel was the right temperature. In addition, an improved welding rod was employed that was also heated before use. With this process carefully instituted during the *Scorpion*'s construction, the *Scorpion* was later found to have an extremely low incidence of weld cracks.

Despite a plethora of rumors to the contrary, by all official accounts, the *Scorpion's* hull was sound.

The *Scorpion's* hull had also been carefully checked for circularity during its 1963–1964 overhaul. (A perfectly symmetrical shape was a substantial aspect of a hull's strength.) While a segment of its hull was found to be slightly out of specification, it was considered within safe tolerances and granted a waiver. Furthermore, in 1965, the newly adopted procedure of ultrasonic testing was used on 23,000 inches of hull weld. While 3.14 percent of the welds showed "indications" of cracking, most were merely blemishes, and only 0.25 percent were actually cracks, an extremely low number. Interestingly enough, hull weld cracks have a tendency to cure themselves as a submarine sinks deeper, since the hydrostatic pressure pushes these cracks together, rather than apart.

However, no submarine's hull is perfect. Dennis Jaster, a machinist's mate second class on the *Scorpion's* sister ship *Scamp* in 1965, recalled watching in amazement as a shipyard worker repaired a hull weld on his submarine. Years before, a shipyard welder merely packed welding rods between two hull plates to fill the seam more quickly. Jaster said he wouldn't have believed it if he hadn't seen it. The dangerous trick was an old one, dating back to World War II, where this risky shortcut earned the nickname "slugging."

As for the *Scorpion*, however, Palermo's report stated, "All available evidence indicates that the material condition of the pressure hull was good, and that premature hull failure did not occur." His conclusion was bolstered, of course, by Price's acoustic assessment that the *Scorpion's* pressure hull failed much deeper than its 1,400-foot maximum depth.

Despite their efforts, the Structural Analysis Group and the "on-scene analysis group" together had been unable to solve the riddle of what precipitated the *Scorpion's* fatal plunge. Many of the old suspects in the *Scorpion's* demise were still there: stern plane failure, human error, or main storage battery explosion.

There was no physical evidence of a collision, and the detonation of a torpedo's high-explosive warhead did not seem to be a factor, according to a structural review of the wreck photographs and the acoustic analysis by Price and Christian. Even the stern plane failure—a somewhat common mishap—seemed like a doubtful suspect because of the added safety factor that the submarine's depth restriction allowed for recovery. Although physical evidence indicated that an explosion of the main storage battery may have taken place, one could only guess what triggered this event. In short, the Structural Analysis Group could find nothing to conclusively support any scenario.

The possibility exists that the battery explosion occurred after another fatal event doomed the submarine. As NSRDC research physicist George Chertock testified during the inquiry, virtually any scenario can be entertained: "We can do this by scratching our heads and coming up with our best guess."

Palermo, Price, and Jackson never believed they could prove precisely what caused the *Scorpion* to exceed its collapse depth. Although Craven became well known during the late 1980s for newspaper interviews and a television appearance on ABC's *Good Morning America* discussing his torpedo theory, Structural Analysis Group members such as Price and Palermo would say nothing until after the 1998 release of the group's report.

Eternal Patrol

Although the *Scorpion*'s story surfaced in the public's consciousness occasionally during the intervening years, the subject was mostly shrouded in rumor and speculation.

One enduring and unsettling result of the disaster was that a substantial amount of radioactive material remains on the seafloor, inside or very near the *Scorpion*'s fragmented hull. Within the contorted and disembodied torpedo room are two W-34 nuclear warheads and their plutonium cores. It's believed that the plutonium cores, if they had broken open, would simply lie inside the torpedo room or sink into the seafloor ooze. If undisturbed, they would pose little radiation hazard. Plutonium, for all its power as a bomb material, also is an insidiously subtle carcinogen. Its alpha particles cannot penetrate the skin externally, but if ingested or inhaled, sickness and death will follow.

Inside the *Scorpion*'s S5W pressurized water reactor remains a fuel assembly of enriched uranium 235, advertised by Rickover's representatives as safe and stable due to the reactor design. If exposed to fire and burned in the atmosphere, both plutonium and U-235 could have been widely dispersed. Buchanan employed a system for detecting radiation while the *Mizar* photographed the debris field in fall 1968 but found nothing other than normal background levels. Nor were unusual radiation levels detected during the Phase II operations the following summer. Knowing that it needed to monitor the *Scorpion*'s wreck to guard against tampering, and mindful of environmental concerns about radiation, the navy would keep an eye on the shattered submarine while keeping its precise location a secret.

In 1979, it's said, an operation again employing the *Trieste II* returned to examine the submarine and take radiation measurements, which revealed nothing other than normal background readings.

In 1984 the U.S. Navy gave deep ocean geologist Robert Ballard of Woods Hole Oceanographic Institution the task of performing a photographic survey of both the *Thresher* and the *Scorpion*, using a towed camera sled whose development it had financed at his urging. The sled was known as the *Argo*, and was equipped with low-light television cameras, 35mm still cameras, and sidescan sonar. The camera sled was a greatly updated version of Buchanan's "fish" pulled behind the *Mizar* during the 1960s. The second component of the Argo system was a swimming camera vehicle known as *Jason Jr.* During the summer of 1985 Ballard supervised the mission to the *Scorpion* wreck site, where he took photographs of the shattered submarine only with the towed *Argo*. The swimming camera vehicle *Jason Jr.*—the descendant of the Tortugas originally developed for the 1969 Phase II operation—was still being assembled.

The public would not be immediately informed of this secret effort. They might not have noticed anyway. Ballard, who had long craved the chance to find the RMS *Titanic*, which sank in the Atlantic on April 15, 1912, obtained permission to hunt for the ill-fated liner after completing his navy mission on the *Scorpion*. His discovery of the *Titanic* created a worldwide commotion. As a result, Ballard, a marine geologist, became the world's best-known shipwreck hunter. His *Scorpion* mission, a navy secret, was not made public for nearly seven years.

With *Jason Jr.* ready the following year, Ballard in July 1986 returned to the *Titanic* wreck site, where he gathered the astonishing images of the ocean liner using the *Jason Jr.* swimming vehicle deployed from the submersible vehicle *Alvin*. During this expedition Ballard obtained remarkable photographs of the *Titanic's* ghostly ballroom. After the excitement over the latest *Titanic* images died down, Ballard returned to the *Scorpion* in August and September 1986 to allow navy and Woods Hole Oceanographic Institution crews to make a dozen dives on the submarine's wreck site using the *Alvin–Jason Jr.* system.

Jason Jr. swam right up to and partially inside some compartments of the mangled *Scorpion*, obtaining extraordinary images at extremely close range. A design criterion for *Jason Jr.* was that it had to be small enough to enter the torpedo room through an open hatch or a torpedo tube. Unfortunately, no such pathway existed due to the jumbled nature of the wreckage. The navy dive officers were unable to maneuver *Jason Jr.* into the torpedo room through what was identified as an opening by the *Trieste II* crew seventeen years earlier. The *Trieste II* crews had been fooled by a dark, square area in the bulkhead that appeared to be an open passageway. It was instead a piece of twisted hull steel blocking the hatch.

An elaborate radiation monitoring effort near the *Scorpion's* wreckage was conducted in 1986 as well. Fish were captured and water samples were collected under the supervision of the Knolls Atomic Power Laboratory. Neither the two *Astor* torpedo warheads nor the U-235 core inside the reactor had released any radiation—a claim still regarded suspiciously by environmental groups. When the lights were switched off at the end of the last-known dive, on September 7, 1986, the *Scorpion* and the gray volcanic crater in which it lay returned to a state of utter darkness.

The extraordinarily clear video images and still photographs acquired by *Jason Jr.* were subsequently forwarded to Peter Palermo, the submarine structures expert who was still at Naval Sea Systems Command. Palermo reviewed the images but saw nothing to change his opinion that the *Scorpion* was most likely destroyed by hydrostatic collapse.

Ballard's 1985 and 1986 expeditions to the *Scorpion* site were not revealed until the navy suddenly decided in 1993 to release the Court of Inquiry's Findings of Fact completed nearly twenty-five years before, accompanied by a heavily edited videotape and still pictures of the shattered submarine taken by *Jason Jr.*

Despite the expenditure of millions of dollars and the earnest efforts of some of America's most talented scientists and naval personnel, the *Scorpion's* demise remains unexplained. Craven, despite the controversy he stirred, may eventually be proven right, or all, with their various theories, may be proven wrong. It seems almost fitting that the *Scorpion* has remained so curiously anonymous and its destruction continues to be so puzzling after nearly four decades. Like other fast attack submarines of the Cold War era, the *Scorpion's* life was cloaked with as much secrecy as its demise.

While opinions abound about what killed the *Scorpion* and its crew among experts and casual observers alike, it seems that the only chance for unraveling the mystery might be an inspection using a new generation of remotely operated vehicles, or even the complete recovery of the three major hull sections and other major pieces of debris such as the propeller and shaft for a full analysis.

The death of the submarine and its ninety-nine men remains confused not only by a lack of evidence but also by disagreements over the evidence. Spending money in large quantities to gather additional evidence while disturbing what the navy considers an officially protected gravesite may seem not only financially wasteful but also sacrilegious.

Although a secret 1974 effort known as Project Jennifer raised at least a portion of the Soviet submarine *K-129* that sank ten weeks before the *Scorpion*, no similar effort was made to retrieve America's own submarine. Even the Russian government—under immense public pressure—hired the Dutch firms Mammoet and Smit International to raise the gargantuan submarine *Kursk* from a less daunting depth of 350 feet below the Barents Sea. The U.S. Navy—for practical reasons—might want to avoid the risk of damaging the *Scorpion's* nuclear warheads or reactor should a risky recovery be attempted using a salvage ship floating 2 miles above.

An obvious question is whether similar technology should be used to recover the *Scorpion's* hull segments. This may be moot for some relatives who've decided they can live without an answer. Raking over these flickering emotional coals might provide little comfort to parents and siblings, though many still desire an answer to what caused the *Scorpion's* loss.

Understanding disasters involving complex machines when no witnesses survive is perhaps the most difficult challenge. That no final official answer has been arrived at regarding the reason for the *Scorpion* tragedy does not make it an insoluble mystery, only a puzzle whose solution is not yet known.

As swimming camera technology evolves into smaller and smaller devices, the chance that more of the nooks and crannies of the *Scorpion's* wreckage will be explored seems obvious—if the navy is willing to invest in such a project. While this might involve the touchy intrusion inside a wreck that is considered an honored burial site, it seems that such would not unduly bother the men of the *Scorpion*. If they could speak, they might ask that the explanation for their deaths be uncovered and revealed.

Insistent letters from loved ones pleading for an answer were sent to the navy by the hundreds in the first few years after the disaster. In the decades since, elderly parents and siblings still penned letters to the navy inquiring if any new information was available about the disaster. That correspondence has slowed to a trickle and will soon cease, though some family members of the crew—most notably the sisters of sailors—persist in writing gadfly letters to congressmen, or anyone else, who might help them find out why the *Scorpion* was lost.

As time has passed, the insistent clamor for an answer from the families of the *Scorpion*'s crew has receded to a murmur as age and death have taken their toll. Someday there will be only silence.

Epilogue

Not long after the *Scorpion* was lost, a small memorial was erected near Pier 22, where the submarine had docked at Naval Station Norfolk when not on patrol. The modest, waist-high monument containing the names of the crew and officers still stands on the waterfront alongside the Elizabeth River.

By 2005, almost all the submarines of the *Scorpion*'s era had fallen to the welding torches of the breakers at Puget Sound Naval Shipyard. The last sister ship of the *Scorpion* scrapped under the navy's Submarine Recycling Program was the *Sculpin*, which was cut to pieces in 2001. Its contaminated reactor was hauled away to be stored in Hanford, Washington. The pressure hulls that once sheltered submariners from the crushing depths went unceremoniously to smelters.

By 2000, even Pier 22—the *Scorpion*'s former pier—had become so decrepit it was demolished and replaced. The nearby memorial, however, was untouched. It stands as a curiosity, if not a warning, to young submariners who might pass by while embarking on their first undersea mission.

A larger and far more handsome memorial was erected at Huntington Park at Newport News in 1992. It was an impressive block of polished granite faced with the names of the *Scorpion*'s men on a bronze plaque. Theresa Bishop, the wife of Chief of the Boat Walter Bishop, dedicated the memorial with the help of other *Scorpion* widows and relatives. It was a source of great pride to Mrs. Bishop, who died eight years later following a long illness.

Another memorial to the *Thresher* and the *Scorpion* stands at the Naval Academy library in the form of a two-sided glass sculpture. Buildings at various naval installations have been named after members of the *Scorpion*'s crew, including Bishop, Slattery, and Cross.

As fine as these gestures are, it seems apparent that the most appropriate monuments to the men of the *Scorpion* will remain their shattered ship and the memories of those who knew them.

Officers and Crew of the USS *Scorpion* (SSN 589)

CMDR Francis Slattery, Commanding Officer
LCDR David Lloyd, Executive Officer
TMC Walter Bishop, Chief of the Boat

LCDR Daniel Stephens
LT John Burke
LT George Farrin
LT Robert Flesch
LT William Harwi
LT Charles Lamberth
LT Laughton Smith
LT John Sweet
LT(jg) James Forrester Jr.
LT(jg) Michael Odening
FTG2 Keith Allen
IC2 Thomas Amtower
MM2 George Annable
FN Joseph Baar Jr.
RM2 Michael Bailey
IC3 Michael Blake
MM1 Robert Blocker
MM2 Kenneth Brocker
MM1 James Brueggman
MMC Robert Bryan
RMSN Daniel Burns Jr.
IC2 Ronald Byers
MM2 Douglas Campbell
MM2 Samuel Cardullo
MM2 Francis Carey II
SN Gary Carpenter
MM1 Robert Chandler
MM2 Mark Christiansen

SD1 Romeo Constantino
MM1 Robert Cowan
SD1 Joseph Cross
RMC Garlin Denney
FN Michael Dunn
ETR2 Richard Englehart
FTGSN William Fennick
PO3 Vernon Foli
SN Ronald Frank
CSSN Michael Gibson
IC2 Steven Gleason
STS2 Michael Henry
SK2 Larry Hess
ET1 Richard Hogeland
MM1 John Houge
EM2 Ralph Huber
TN2 Harry Huckelberry
EM3 John Johnson
RMCS Robert Johnson
IC3 Steven Johnson
QM2 Julius Johnston III
FN Patrick Kahanek
TM2 Donald Karmasek
MMCS Richard Kerntke
ETR3 Rodney Kipp
MM3 Dennis Knapp
MM1 Max Lanier
ET1 John Livingston

ETN2 Kenneth Martin
QMCS Frank Mazzuchi
ET1 Michael McGuire
TM3 Steven Miksad
TM3 Joseph Miller Jr.
MM2 Cecil Mobley
QM1 Raymond Morrison
EMC Daniel Petersen
QM3 Dennis Pferrer
EM3 Gerald Pospisil
IC3 Donald Powell
MM1 Earl Ray
CS1 Jorge Santana
HMC Lynn Saville
ETN2 Richard Schaffer
SN William Schoonover
FN Phillip Seifert
ETC George Smith Jr.
MM2 Robert Smith
ST1 Harold Snapp Jr.

ETN2 Joel Stephens
MM2 David Stone
EM2 John Sturgill
YN3 Richard Summers
TMSN John Sweeney Jr.
ETN2 James Tindol III
CSSN Johnny Veerhusen
TM3 Robert Violetti
STS3 Ronald Voss
FTG1 John Wallace
MM1 Joel Watkins
MMFN Robert Watson
MM2 James Webb
YNC Leo Weinbeck
MMC James Wells
SN Ronald Williams
MM3 Robert Willis
IC1 Virgil Wright III
TM1 Donald Yarbrough
ETR2 Clarence Young Jr.

Bibliography

Books

Abelson, Philip H. "Ross Gunn." In *National Academy of Sciences of the United States of America: Biographical Memoirs*. Vol. 74. Washington, D.C.: National Academy Press, 1998.

Abrams, Dr. Herbert L. "Sources of Human Instability in the Handling of Nuclear Weapons." In *The Medical Implications of Nuclear War*. Washington, D.C.: National Academy Press, 1986.

Arkin, William M., and Joshua Handler. *Neptune Papers Number III: Naval Accidents, 1945–1988*. 1st ed. Washington, D.C.: Greenpeace International Press, 1988.

Ballard, Robert D., with Rick Archbold. *The Discovery of the* Titanic: *Exploring the Greatest of All Lost Ships*. New York: Warner/Madison Press, 1987.

Ballard, Robert D., with Will Hively. *The Eternal Darkness: A Personal History of Deep-Sea Exploration*. Princeton, N.J.: Princeton University Press, 2000.

Ballard, Robert D., with Malcolm McConnell. *Explorations: My Quest for Adventure and Discovery under the Sea*. New York: Hyperion, 1995.

Bentley, John. *The* Thresher *Disaster: The Most Tragic Dive in Submarine History*. Garden City, N.Y.: Doubleday, 1975.

Blackman, Raymond V. B. *Jane's Fighting Ships*. New York: McGraw-Hill, 1968–1969.

Bullard, Edward C. "William Maurice Ewing." In *Biographical Memoirs*. Washington, D.C.: National Academy Press, 1980.

Burcher, Roy, and Louis Rydill. *Concepts in Submarine Design*. Cambridge Ocean Technology Series, no. 2. Cambridge, Eng.: Cambridge University Press, 1994.

Burleson, Clyde W. *The Jennifer Project*. College Station: Texas A&M Press, 1997.

——— . *Kursk Down!: The Shocking True Story of the Sinking of a Russian Nuclear Submarine*. New York: Warner Books, 2002.

Burns, Thomas S. *The Secret War for the Ocean Depths: Soviet-American Rivalry for Mastery of the Seas*. New York: Rawson, 1978.

Cox, Albert W. *Sonar and Underwater Sound*. Lexington, Mass.: D. C. Heath, Lexington Books, 1974.

Craven, John Piña. *The Silent War: The Cold War Battle beneath the Sea*. New York: Simon & Schuster, 2001.

Edsall, Margaret Horton. *A Place Called the Yard: Guide to the United States Naval Academy*. Rev. 5th ed. Annapolis, Md.: Douglas W. Edsall, 1984.

Eller, Ernest McNeill. *The Soviet Sea Challenge: The Struggle for Control of the World's Oceans*. Chicago: Cowles, 1971.

Forman, Will. *The History of American Deep Submersible Operations, 1775–1995*. Flagstaff, Ariz.: Best, 1999.

Freeman, Gregory A. *Sailors to the End: The Deadly Fire on the USS Forrestal and the Heroes Who Fought It*. New York: William Morrow, 2002.

Friedman, Norman. *U.S. Naval Weapons: Every Gun, Missile, Mine, and Torpedo Used by the U.S. Navy from 1883 to the Present Day*. Annapolis, Md.: Naval Institute Press, 1982.

——— . *U.S. Submarines since 1945: An Illustrated Design History*. Annapolis, Md.: Naval Institute Press, 1994.

Gannon, Robert. *Hellions of the Deep: The Development of American Torpedoes in World War II*. University Park: Pennsylvania State University Press, 1996.

Gorshkov, S. G. *The Sea Power of the State*. Annapolis, Md.: Naval Institute Press, 1976.

Gray, Edwyn. *The Devil's Device: Robert Whitehead and the History of the Torpedo*. 1975. Rev. and updated ed., Annapolis, Md.: Naval Institute Press, 1991.

——— . *Few Survived: A Comprehensive Survey of Submarine Accidents and Disasters*. London: Leo Cooper, 1996.

Heezen, Bruce C., Marie Tharp, and Maurice Ewing. *The Floors of the Oceans: I. The North Atlantic; Text to Accompany the Physiographic Diagram of the North Atlantic*. Geological Society of America, Special Paper 65. New York: Geological Society of America, 1959.

Isenberg, Michael T. *Shield of the Republic: The United States Navy in an Era of Cold War and Violent Peace*. Vol. I, 1945–1962. New York: St. Martin's Press, 1993.

Laqueur, Walter. *The Struggle for the Middle East: The Soviet Union in the Mediterranean, 1958–1968*. New York: Macmillan, 1969.

Largess, Robert P., and James L. Mandelblatt. *USS Albacore: "Forerunner of the Future."* Portsmouth Marine Society, Publication 25. Portsmouth: Peter E. Randall, 1999.

Lederer, William J. *The Last Cruise: The Story of the Sinking of the Submarine USS Cochino*. New York: William Sloane, 1950.

Love, Robert W. Jr. *History of the U.S. Navy*. Vol. 2: 1942–1991. Harrisburg, Pa.: Stackpole Books, 1992.

Mateczun, John. "U.S. Naval Combat Psychiatry." In *War Psychiatry*, ed. Franklin D. Jones, Linette R. Sparacino, Victoria L. Wilcox, Joseph M. Roth-berg, and James W. Stokes. Washington, D.C.: TMM Publications, Office of the Surgeon General, 1989.

McGruther, Kenneth R. *The Evolving Soviet Navy*. Newport, R.I.: Naval War College Press, 1978.

Moore, John E. *Warships of the Soviet Navy*. London: Jane's, 1981.

Moore, Robert. *A Time to Die: The Untold Story of the* Kursk *Tragedy*. New York: Crown, 2002.

National Research Council, Committee on Undersea Warfare, Panel on Psychology and Physiology. *A Survey Report on Human Factors in Undersea Warfare*. Washington, D.C.: National Academy of Sciences, 1949.

Pennington, Howard. *The New Ocean Explorers: Into the Sea in the Space Age*. Boston: Little, Brown, 1972.

Polmar, Norman. *The American Submarine*. 2d ed. Annapolis, Md.: The Nautical & Aviation Publishing Company of America, 1983.

——— . *Atomic Submarines*. Princeton, N.J.: D. Van Nostrand, 1963.

——— . *The Death of the USS* Thresher: *The Story behind History's Deadliest Submarine Disaster*. Guilford, Conn.: Lyons Press, 1964.

——— . *Guide to the Soviet Navy*. 4th ed. Annapolis, Md.: Naval Institute Press, 1986.

——— . *Soviet Naval Power: Challenge for the 1970s*. New York: National Strategy Information Center, 1972.

Polmar, Norman, and Thomas B. Allen. *Rickover: Controversy and Genius; A Biography*. New York: Simon & Schuster, 1982.

Polmar, Norman, and K. J. Moore. *Cold War Submarines: The Design and Construction of U.S. and Soviet Submarines*. Washington, D.C.: Brassey's, 2004.

Polmar, Norman, and Jurrien Noot. *Submarines of the Russian and Soviet Navies, 1718–1990*. Annapolis, Md.: Naval Institute Press, 1991.

Rockwell, Theodore. *The Rickover Effect: How One Man Made a Difference*. Annapolis, Md.: Naval Institute Press, 1992.

Roscoe, Theodore. *United States Submarine Operations in World War II*. Annapolis, Md.: United States Naval Institute, 1949.

Sapolsky, Harvey M. *Science and the Navy: The History of the Office of Naval Research*. Princeton, N.J.: Princeton University Press, 1990.

Schwoebel, Richard L. *Explosion aboard the* Iowa. Annapolis, Md.: Naval Institute Press, 1999.

Scorpion *Operations Phase II: Cruise Book for USS* Apache, *USS* Whitesands, *and* Trieste II. Anaheim, Calif.: Allen, 1969.

Shenton, Edward H. *Diving for Science: The Story of the Deep Submersible*. New York: W. W. Norton, 1972.

Sontag, Sherry, and Christopher Drew, with Annette Lawrence Drew. *Blind Man's Bluff: The Untold Story of American Submarine Espionage*. New York: Public Affairs, 1998.

Tall, Jeffrey. *Submarines & Deep-Sea Vehicles: Early Submersibles, Diesel-Electric Submarines, Deep-Sea Roving Vehicles, and Rescue Vessels.* San Diego: Thunder Bay Press, 2002.

Thompson, Charles C. II. *A Glimpse of Hell: The Explosion on the USS* Iowa *and Its Cover-up.* New York: W. W. Norton, 1999.

United States Ship Scorpion *(SSN-589): In Memoriam.* Washington, D.C.: U.S. Government Printing Office, 1969.

Warner, Roy D., and Wayne R. Collier. *A Matter of Risk: The Incredible Inside Story of the CIA's Glomar Explorer Mission to Raise a Russian Submarine.* New York: Ballantine Books, 1980.

Watson, Bruce W. *Red Navy at Sea: Soviet Naval Operations on the High Seas, 1956–1980.* Boulder, Colo.: Westview Press, 1982.

Weir, Gary E. *Forged in War: The Naval-Industrial Complex and American Submarine Construction, 1940–1961.* Washington, D.C.: Brassey's, 1998.

———. *An Ocean in Common: American Naval Officers, Scientists, and the Ocean Environment.* College Station: Texas A&M University Press, 2001.

Weir, Gary E., and Walter J. Boyne. *Rising Tide: The Untold Story of the Russian Submarines That Fought the Cold War.* New York: Basic Books, 2003.

Wertenbaker, William. *The Floor of the Sea: Maurice Ewing and the Search to Understand the Earth.* Boston: Little, Brown, 1974.

Winkler, David F. *Cold War at Sea: High-Seas Confrontation between the United States and the Soviet Union.* Annapolis, Md.: Naval Institute Press, 2000.

Journals, Articles, and Papers

Abrams, Herbert L. "Human Reliability and Safety in the Handling of Nuclear Weapons." *Science & Global Security,* 1991, 325–349.

Allen, Timothy A. "U.S. Navy Analysis of Submarine Maintenance Data and the Development of Age and Reliability Profiles," n.d.

Andrews, Captain Frank A. (USN). "Searching for the *Thresher.*" *U.S. Naval Institute Proceedings,* May 1964, 69–77.

Avallone, Lieutenant Commander E. M. (USN). "Overhaul." *U.S. Naval Institute Proceedings,* May 1963, 75–83.

"Basic Information on the Fleets and Command Element of the Soviet Navy." *Navy Magazine,* January 1968, 15–19.

"Bethlehem Lukens Plate, Plate Steels for National Defense; Armor Plate for Military and Civilian Applications." Bethlehem Lukens Plate, Administrative Resources Center, October 2001.

"Bethlehem Lukens Plate, Spartan, A710, and HSLA-80/100 Steels; High Strength, Alloy Steels with Improved Weldability and Toughness." Bethlehem Lukens Plate, Administrative Resources Center. January 2002.

Bradley, Mark A. "Why They Called the *Scorpion* 'Scrapiron.'" *U.S. Naval Institute Proceedings*, July 1998, 30–37.

Brock, Captain C. C. (USN Ret.). "Comment and Discussion: Real Story of the *Scorpion?*" *U.S. Naval Institute Proceedings*, September 1999, 21–22.

Carlson, Major Verner R. (USA). "The Soviet Maritime Threat." *U.S. Naval Institute Proceedings*, May 1967, 39–48.

Cote, Dr. Owen R. Jr. "The Third Battle: Innovation in the U.S. Navy's Silent Cold War Struggle with Soviet Submarines." Center for Naval Warfare Studies (Newport, R.I.), Newport Paper 16, 2003, 1–100.

"Deep-Diving Miniature Research Sub to Be Built." *Naval Research Reviews*, October 1962.

Dudley, Commander H. G. Sr. (USN). "The Future Role of Soviet Sea Power." *U.S. Naval Institute Proceedings*, May 1966, 39–49.

Fountain, Rear Admiral Robert R. (USN Ret.). "Comment and Discussion: Why They Called the *Scorpion* 'Scrapiron.'" *U.S. Naval Institute Proceedings*, October 1998, 10.

Hansen, I. S., and D. M. Wegner. "Centenary of the Destruction of USS *Maine*: A Technical and Historical Review." *Naval Engineers Journal*, March 1998, 93–104.

Harrigan, Anthony. "Russia Tips the Scale: Report Published by House Armed Services Committee Shows USSR Has New Fleet, New Tactics, and New Appreciation of Sea Power." *Navy Magazine*, January 1969, 23–26.

Kelly, Orr. "Unexpected Soviet Advances in Submarines Stir Real Concern in Congress: Committees Press for New U.S. Attack Boats to Counter Red Threat." *Navy Magazine*, August 1968, 6–11.

Koper, Keith D., Terry C. Wallace, Steven R. Taylor, and Hans E. Hartse. "Forensic Seismology and the Sinking of the *Kursk*." *American Geophysical Union's Eos*, January 23, 2001, 37, 45–46.

Martin, Lieutenant George W. "*Trieste*: The First Ten Years." *U.S. Naval Institute Proceedings*, August 1964, 53–64.

McDonald, Captain C. A. K. (USN). "Real Story of *Scorpion?*" *U.S. Naval Institute Proceedings*, June 1999, 28–33.

"MIZAR Photographs *ALVIN*." *Naval Research Reviews*, July 1969.

Mooney, Rear Admiral John B. Jr. "Blind Hunt for the *Thresher*." *U.S. Naval Institute Proceedings*, April 1988.

Murphy, Captain F. M. (USN). "The Soviet Navy in the Mediterranean." *U.S. Naval Institute Proceedings*, March 1967, 38–44.

"NATO Documents the Soviet Sea Threat: SACLANT Report Tells Full Story of Russia's New Challenge on the Oceans." *Navy Magazine*, December 1968, 13–19.

Norris, John G. "Russia Builds and Boasts: Soviet Press Plays Up Vast USSR Maritime Buildup and Penetration of Farthest Reaches of the High Seas." *Navy Magazine*, December 1968, 20–23.

Price, Robert S. "USS *Scorpion*: An Account of Research into Causes, Effects, and Speculation." Privately printed, n.d.

Price, Robert S., and V. K. Shuler. "Sounds from the Implosions of Steel Cylinders under Water." Naval Ordnance Laboratory. Paper presented to Acoustical Society of America, April 3, 1973.

Rath, Bhatka B., and Don J. DeYoung. "The Naval Research Laboratory: 75 Years of Materials Innovation." *JOM: Journal of the Minerals, Metals, & Materials Society*, July 1998, 14–19.

"Recovery Operation of the Submarine *Kursk*." Mammoet-Smit International, no. 00.12.040-R-022, n.d.

Rogers, Commander Robert B. (USN). "Trends in Soviet Naval Strategy." *Naval War College Review*, February 1969, 13–29.

Satloff, Dr. Aaron. "Psychiatry and the Nuclear Submarine." *American Journal of Psychiatry*, October 1967, 547–551.

Serxner, Dr. Jonathan L. "An Experience in Submarine Psychiatry." *American Journal of Psychiatry*, July 1968, 25–30.

"Shipyards May Be Face-Lifted." *Marine Engineering/Log*, July 1967.

Smith, Captain T. J. (USN Ret.). "A Logical Explanation as to the Loss of USS *Scorpion* (SSN 589)." *Submarine Review*, October 1999, 107–116.

"Soviet Sea Power Shifts to Strategic Offensive: Secretary Ignatius Stresses Significance of Russia's Expansion of All Aspects of Its Naval Might, Indicating the Opening of a 'New Era of Global Maritime Importance.'" *Navy Magazine*, July 1968, 23–27.

Weir, Gary E. "Refining a Dialogue: The Project Hartwell Summer Study and Cold War Naval Ocean Surveillance, 1937–1961." *International Journal of Naval History*, April 2002.

Wells, Lieutenant Robert W. (USN Reserve). "The Soviet Black Sea Fleet." *U.S. Naval Institute Proceedings*, September 1967, 136–139.

Wertenbaker, William. "Rock Stars: William Maurice Ewing; Pioneer Explorer of the Ocean Floor and Architect of Lamont." *GSA Today*, October 2000, 28–29.

Newspaper Articles

American Geophysical Union News. "Forensic Seismology Provides Clues to *Kursk* Disaster," AGU Release 01-5, January 22, 2001.

AP/UPI dispatches. "Body Recovered in Flash Fire; Blazing Atomic Sub Is Flooded," June 15, 1960.

Baltimore Sun. "Data Point Up Soviet Sea Power," January 13, 1969.

Boston Globe. "A-Sub *Scorpion* Breaks Silence Ends Sea Scare," September 18, 1960.

————— . "Danger and Dissent on U.S. Sub," August 13, 1978.

Easton, MD *Star Democrat.* "Ermine 'Mari' America Christian," September 2, 1997.

Honolulu Advertiser. "Five Killed as Bomber Falls in Sea," March 31, 1938.

Houston Chronicle. "Rickover Says Russia May Take Lead in A-Subs," February 26, 1968.

New Orleans Times-Picayune. "Navy Shipyards Lack Workers: The Nation May Be Courting Another *Thresher* Disaster," December 2, 1966.

New York Times. "A Growing Threat from Russia's Submarines," April 21, 1968.

————— . "For the *Kursk,* a Risky Resurrection," September 4, 2001.

————— . "Navy Modernizes Shipyard Concept," January 3, 1967.

————— . "Radio Contact Is Lost with Atomic Submarine," September 16, 1960.

————— . "Rickover Charges Lag in Submarines," July 5, 1968.

————— . "Soviet Submarine Spurt Noted; U.S. Policy Is Hit," February 26, 1968.

Norfolk Ledger Star. "Analysis; Official *Scorpion* Report Disappointing," February 1, 1969.

————— . "Civilian Conjecture; *Scorpion* Posing Nuclear Question," June 11, 1968.

————— . "Court of Inquiry Opens in Norfolk; *Scorpion* Disappearance," June 5, 1968.

————— . "Divers Checking Unidentified Hull; Navy Doesn't Think It Is *Scorpion,*" May 31, 1968.

————— . "Embarrassing Claim; Pentagon Explains *Scorpion* Savings," December 17, 1968.

————— . "False Reports Plague *Scorpion* Crew's Kin," June 3, 1968.

————— . "Found during Sub Search; Sunken Hull Merchant Ship," November 20, 1968.

————— . "Hoax a Possibility; Wives Wait for News," May 30, 1968.

————— . "Hope of Finding *Scorpion* Ebbs as Hunt Goes on in Rough Seas: Unidentified Orange Object Seen in Area," May 29, 1968.

————— . "Hopes Dim if Sub below 300 Feet," May 28, 1968.

————— . "Hull of Sub Shown; Inquiry of *Scorpion* to Show Pictures," November 6, 1968.

————— . "Likely Cause of *Scorpion* Loss Still Being Kept Secret by Navy," March 26, 1975.

————— . "Long Probe of *Scorpion* Disaster Ends," December 20, 1968.

————— . "Navy Mum on *Scorpion* Crash Data," August 5, 1968.

————— . "New *Scorpion* Survey Due," February 1, 1969.

————— . "No Bathyscape Details; Navy Tight-Lipped on *Scorpion* Probe," April 16, 1969.

————— . "No Damage Done Sub by Bump," June 13, 1968.

————— . "No Possible Cause of Loss Cited; Ex-*Scorpion* Engineer Officer Testifies on 1964 Overhaul," June 25, 1968.

————— . "No Trace of Sub Found as Navy Presses Search," May 28, 1968.

————— . "Officer Testifies; Weather Not Seen Affecting *Scorpion*," June 19, 1968.

————— . "Photographs Scanned; *Scorpion* Inquiry Recesses for Study," November 8, 1968.

————— . "Photos of *Scorpion* Shed No New Light," January 26, 1970.

————— . "Photos Suggest Trouble inside *Scorpion*," January 3, 1969.

————— . "Prior to Sea Trials, *Scorpion* Rated as 'Outstanding,'" June 6, 1968.

————— . "Probe Acknowledged; Navy Denies Sub Steel Plate Defects," October 4, 1968.

————— . "Radio Fix Difficult to Obtain," May 30, 1968.

————— . "Resumes in Spring; Ship Halts Study of *Scorpion* Wreck," November 7, 1968.

————— . "*Scorpion* and Her Captain," May 28, 1968.

————— . "*Scorpion*, Buoy Not Connected, Pentagon Says," June 10, 1968.

————— . "*Scorpion* Hearing Closed," June 20, 1968.

————— . "*Scorpion* Inquiry in 12th Day; Sub's Crash into Seamount Theory Gains More Support," June 18, 1968.

————— . "*Scorpion*'s Mission Far from 'Routine,'" June 8, 1968.

————— . "*Scorpion* Search Centers at Hyeres Bank near Azores; 300,000 Miles Covered by Planes," June 4, 1968.

————— . "*Scorpion* Search to End Soon," October 9, 1968.

————— . "*Scorpion* Secrets Discussed," June 11, 1968.

————— . "*Scorpion*: The Probe Isn't Over," February 4, 1969.

————— . "*Scorpion* Wreckage Found," October 31, 1968.

————— . "*Scorpion* Wreckage; Sub Photos Flood Inquiry," November 3, 1968.

————— . "Search Pack Working Eastward; 2 Deep-Diving Rigs Flown to Azores as Hunt for Missing Sub Continues," June 1, 1968.

————— . "Search Unit Empty-Handed; Nothing Remotely Connected with *Scorpion* Found by Navy," June 8, 1968.

————— . "Small Piece of Metal Led Navy to Ill-Fated *Scorpion*," November 21, 1968.

————— . "Sub Found Near End of Search," November 1, 1968.

————— . "Sub Rescue Vessels Prepared," May 30, 1968.

————— . "Summary of *Scorpion* Report to Be Released This Week," January 27, 1969.

————— . "Testimony on Azores Area; *Scorpion* Mission Secret," June 7, 1968.

————— . "The Empty Sea; Splendid View of Nothing Filled *Scorpion* Hunters' Eyes," May 30, 1968.

————— . "Third Dive Finds *Scorpion*," July 10, 1969.

————— . "*Trieste II*'s Probes Successful; 9 Dives Made to *Scorpion*," August 7, 1969.

————— . "'Voice Message' from *Scorpion* Could Be a Hoax, Navy Warns; No Further Word Heard," May 30, 1968.

————— . "Witnesses Differ in Testimony; Two Debate *Scorpion's* Safety during Navy Court of Inquiry," June 10, 1968.

Norfolk Virginian-Pilot. "Despite Defects, Sub Was Safe, Officer Testifies," June 9, 1968.

————— . "A Few Facts, Logic, and a Computer; *Scorpion* Found by Deductive Reasoning," November 4, 1968.

————— . "'15,000 Inaccuracies' Estimated; Court Advised *Scorpion* Lacked Latest Charts," June 20, 1968.

————— . "Freon Leak on *Scorpion* 'No Danger,'" June 18, 1968.

————— . "Funds Taken from 1968 Budget; Long Search for *Scorpion* Cost $2 Million, Navy Estimates," December 21, 1968.

————— . "Hope for the *Scorpion*," May 29, 1968.

————— . "Inquiry Inconclusive; Secret of *Scorpion* Lies in the Depths," June 10, 1968.

————— . "'Intact' Report Denied; Navy Says *Scorpion* in Several Major Pieces," November 16, 1968.

————— . "Lab Ship to Hunt for Sub; Deep-Sea Cameras, Sound Gear Aboard," June 1, 1968.

————— . "Mission of Sub Secret; Deviations Expected," June 8, 1968.

————— . "Mystery Grows over Sub Loss," June 11, 1968.

————— . "Navy Denied Defective Steel in Submarines," October 4, 1968.

————— . "Navy Still Clings to Hope for Rescue of *Scorpion*," June 5, 1968.

————— . "New Probe of *Scorpion* Under Way," July 13, 1969.

————— . "No Flotsam Linked to *Scorpion*," July 3, 1968.

————— . "An Object, a Clanking, a Signal—and Then Nothing," May 31, 1968.

————— . "Patience Turned to Alarm," May 29, 1968.

————— . "Photographer of *Scorpion*; Mizar Held Back by Bad Weather," November 19, 1968.

————— . "Photos Reported Taken of Doomed Submarine," September 17, 1985.

————— . "Photos Studied; *Scorpion* Court Recesses Again," November 21, 1968.

——— . "Planes Widen Sub Hunt," June 2, 1968.

——— . "Probed *Thresher*; Adm. Austin Heads *Scorpion* Inquiry," June 4, 1968.

——— . "Record of Sound; *Scorpion* Cave-in Report Not Denied," August 5, 1968.

——— . "Reds Aimed Guns at *Scorpion*; Mystery off Crete," May 29, 1968.

——— . "*Scorpion* Carried Nuclear Arms," May 29, 1981.

——— . "*Scorpion* Debris Found at 10,000 Ft.; About 400 Miles from the Azores," November 1, 1968.

——— . "*Scorpion* Excellent: Ex-Exec," June 12, 1968.

——— . "*Scorpion* Families Shielded by Pension Programs," June 21, 1968.

——— . "*Scorpion's* Hull," November 1, 1968.

——— . "*Scorpion* Hunt Moves Eastward; Signal Believed a Hoax," May 31, 1968.

——— . "*Scorpion* Inquiry; Sub Faulty, Ex-Crewmen Tell Court," June 7, 1968.

——— . "*Scorpion* Photos Detailed," November 23, 1968.

——— . "*Scorpion* Repair List Investigated," June 13, 1968.

——— . "*Scorpion* Statement Clarified," June 16, 1968.

——— . "*Scorpion* Testimony Classified," June 27, 1968.

——— . "*Scorpion* Testimony; Seamounts Discounted by Search Supervisor," June 21, 1968.

——— . "Search Postponed; Court Views Pictures of *Scorpion* Debris," November 8, 1968.

——— . "Sub's Air-Conditioning 'Headaches,'" June 26, 1968.

——— . "Sub Lost, Navy Declares; Relatives Told Crewmen Dead," June 6, 1968.

——— . "Sub Probers Begin Study of Testimony," July 4, 1968.

——— . "Submarine Remains Shrouded in Secrets," May 27, 1988.

——— . "There's Hope for Crew, If . . . ," May 29, 1968.

——— . "3 Left *Scorpion* before Departure," May 29, 1968.

——— . "*Trieste* to Begin Study of *Scorpion* Wreckage," June 3, 1969.

Norfolk Virginian-Pilot and Ledger-Star. "M. Theresa Bishop, obituary," November 17, 2000.

——— . "Mystery of Sub's Sinking Unravels; *Scorpion* Tragedy Tied to Torpedo Accident," December 16, 1984.

Seattle Post-Intelligencer. "Navy Says Sinking of the *Scorpion* Was an Accident; Revelations Suggest a Darker Scenario," May 21, 1968.

——— . "Secrecy of Disappearance Compounded Families' Pain," May 21, 1998.

——— . "Spy Net May Have Doomed *Scorpion* before It Set Out," May 21, 1998.

——— . "Two Men Are Forever Linked by Tragedy of the *Scorpion*," May 21, 1998.

————— . "The USS *Scorpion*—Mystery of the Deep: The Navy Says the Submarine's Sinking Was an Accident; Revelations Suggest a Darker Scenario," May 21, 1998.

Stars and Stripes. "USS *Oklahoma City* Commander Relieved of Command after Collision," December 8, 2002.

U.S. Navy Chief of Information. "Comments by Chief of Naval Operations, Thomas H. Moorer," October 31, 1968.

Washington Post. "Rear Admiral J. R. Lewis, obituary," March 13, 1982.

Official Records and Reports

Atkins, Capt. A. J. Martin (USN). Officer Biography Sheet, May 17, 1973.

Austin, Vice Adm. Bernard L. (USN). Biography, Navy Office of Information, Internal Relations Division, December 23, 1968.

Barrett, Capt. Ernest R. (USN). Officer Biography Sheet, August 18, 1965.

Bryan, Rear Adm. C. R. (USN). Biography, Navy Office of Information, Biographies Branch, July 2, 1974.

Budding, Capt. W. A. Jr. (USN); Cmdr. E. T. Westfall (USN); Cmdr. F. F. Manganaro (USN); and Cmdr. J. E. Lenihan (USN). "Staff Study of Improvements in Complex Submarine Overhauls." Department of the Navy, Bureau of Ships, February 1966.

Holmes, Adm. E. P. (USN). Navy Office of Information, Internal Relations Division, June 30, 1971.

Horn, Capt. Dean A. (USN). Officer Biography Sheet, March 4, 1969.

Nace, Rear Adm. Charles D. (USN). Biography, Navy Office of Information, Biographies Branch, October 15, 1971.

Pellini, W. S., and P. P. Puzak. "Fracture Analysis Diagram Procedures for the Fracture-Safe Engineering Design of Steel Structures." NRL Report 5920. U.S. Naval Research Laboratory, Washington, D.C., March 15, 1963.

Price, Robert S., and Ermine A. Christian. "USS *Scorpion* (SSN 589) Results of NOL Data Analysis." NOLTR 69-160. U.S. Naval Ordnance Laboratory, White Oak, Md., January 20, 1970.

Rich, Rear Adm. Harold G. (USN). Biography, Navy Office of Information, Biographies Branch, September 13, 1974.

Schade, Vice Adm. Arnold Frederic (USN Ret.). Biography, Navy Office of Information, Biographies Branch, December 1, 1971.

Sheldon, Richard B., and John D. Michne. "Deep Sea Radiological Environmental Monitoring Conducted at the Site of the Nuclear-Powered Submarine *Scorpion* Sinking." (R/V Atlantis II Voyage 117, LEG 1, August 19–September 15, 1986). Schenectady, N.Y.: KAPL, Knolls Atomic Power Laboratory, October 1993.

Sheridan, Daniel, and G. L. Santore. "A Simulation Study to Evaluate Scenarios Postulated for *Scorpion* Tragedy." Hydromechanics Laboratory Test and Evaluation Report, Naval Ship Research and Development Center, Washington, D.C., October 1968.

U.S. Congress. Joint Committee on Atomic Energy. *Loss of the USS* Thresher. 88th Cong., 1st and 2nd sess., 1963 and 1964.

U.S. Department of Commerce, Environmental Science Services Administration. *Storm Data* 10, no. 5, May 1968.

Wohosky, R. C., R. L. Mash, and G. A. Edgley. "Defect Summary & Trouble History: TORPEDO Mark 37; 1959–1965." Report 619. Keyport, Wash.: U.S. Naval Torpedo Station, n.d.

Unpublished Materials

General

Ball, Captain George C. Jr. Papers. Joyner Library, East Carolina University, Greenville, N.C., n.d.

Boyne, Paul A. "*Scorpion*: The Final Chapters," n.d.

Buchanan, Chester L. "Down on the Farm," draft autobiography. Archives of the author, n.d.

Hamilton, Gordon R. "Summary of Underwater Acoustic's Research and Development at the Bermuda Sofar Station (Columbia University Geophysical Field Station, of Lamont-Doherty Geological Observatory), 1949–1970," January 3, 1998, modified November 20, 1998, and March 20, 1999.

Strickland, C. L. "Remote Controlled Underwater Vehicles," n.d.

Wells, Martin G. H., Eric B. Kula, and John H. Beatty, eds. "Metallic Materials for Lightweight Applications." Proceedings of the 40th Sagamore Army Materials Research Conference, August 30–September 2, 1993, Plymouth, Mass.

U.S. Navy Records

Price, Robert S., and Ermine A. Christian. "USS *Scorpion* (SSN 589) Results of NOL Data Analysis (U)," U.S. Naval Ordnance Laboratory, White Oak, Md., January 20, 1970.

Searle, Captain W. F. Jr. (USN). "Admiral Rickover and the *Scorpion*," November 17, 1999.

————. "Loss of the Submarines *Scorpion* and *Thresher*," July 13, 1999.

————. "Man's Deep Submergence Resources to the Turn of the Century," March 25, 1997.

————. "*Scorpion* Court of Inquiry," January 15, 1998.

Sheridan, Dan, and G. L. Santore. "A Simulation Study to Evaluate Scenarios Postulated for *Scorpion* Tragedy (U)," Hydromechanics Laboratory Test and

Evaluation Report, Naval Ship Research and Development Center, October 1968.

"Findings of Fact from the Record of Proceedings of a Court of Inquiry Convened by Commander in Chief U.S. Atlantic Fleet at Headquarters Commander in Chief U.S. Atlantic Fleet Norfolk Virginia to Inquire into the Loss of USS *Scorpion* (SSN-589) Which Occurred on or about 27 May 1968, Ordered on 4 June 1968."

"Findings of Fact from the Record of Proceedings of a Court of Inquiry Convened by Commander in Chief U.S. Atlantic Fleet at Headquarters Commander in Chief U.S. Atlantic Fleet Norfolk Virginia to Inquire into the Loss of USS *Sargo* (SSN-583) Which Occurred on or about 14 June 1960, Ordered on 4 June 1968."

"Findings of Fact from the Record of Proceedings of a Court of Inquiry Convened by Commander in Chief U.S. Atlantic Fleet at Headquarters Commander in Chief U.S. Atlantic Fleet Norfolk Virginia to Inquire into the Loss of USS *Thresher* (SSN-593) Which Occurred on or about 10 April 1963, Ordered on 4 June 1968."

"Findings of Fact from the Record of Proceedings of a Court of Inquiry Convened by Commander in Chief U.S. Atlantic Fleet at Headquarters Commander in Chief U.S. Atlantic Fleet Norfolk Virginia to Inquire into the Loss of USS *Chopper* (SS-342) Which Occurred on or about 11 February 1969, Ordered on 4 June 1968."

"Record of Proceedings of a Court of Inquiry Convened by Commander in Chief U.S. Atlantic Fleet at Headquarters Commander in Chief U.S. Atlantic Fleet Norfolk Virginia to Inquire into the Loss of USS *Scorpion* (SSN-589) Which Occurred on or about 27 May 1968, Ordered on 4 June 1968."

"The *Scorpion* Search 1968: An Analysis of the Operation for the CNO Technical Advisory Group." Prepared for chief of naval operations, November 5, 1969.

U.S. Navy Memoranda/Speedletters

1955

"Account of *Pomodon* Disaster" [incomplete document, no accompanying memorandum; enclosure only]; SUBPAC Notice 3040, July 18, 1955.

1962

"USS *Scorpion* (SSN589) Overhaul," from deputy commander, Submarine Force, U.S. Atlantic Fleet, to commander, Submarine Force, U.S. Atlantic Fleet, August 28, 1962.

"Confidential Report; forwarding of COMSUBLANT Operation Order No. 32-62; (1) Personnel; (2) Material," from commanding officer, USS *Scorpion* (SSN589), to commander, Submarine Force, U.S. Atlantic Fleet, November 28, 1962.

"USS *Scorpion* (SSN589), Confidential Report, forwarding of; CO USS *Scorpion* (SSN589), ltr 3000 ser 096 of 28 NOV 62 (with enclosure (1) and (2) thereto)," from commander, Submarine Force, U.S. Atlantic Fleet, to distribution list, December 12, 1962.

1963

"Report No. 9110–3, USS *Scorpion*, SS(N)589, Hull Integrity Surveillance Inspection, Inspected by Industrial Laboratory, Code 135; Charleston Naval Shipyard U.S. Naval Bank, Charleston, S.C.," December 20, 1963.

"USS *Scorpion* (SSN589), Critical Piping System Inspection and Repair," from chief, Bureau of Ships, to deputy commander, Submarine Force, U.S. Atlantic Fleet, and Commander, Charleston Naval Shipyard, August 20, 1963.

"USS *Scorpion* (SSN589), Emergency Main Ballast Tank Blow System, Interim Improved System For," from chief, Bureau of Ships, to deputy commander, Submarine Force, U.S. Atlantic Fleet, and commander, Charleston Naval Shipyard, November 20, 1963.

1963–1964

"Last Regular Overhaul and SubSafe Work *Scorpion*—handwritten notes regarding," June 14, 1963–April 28, 1964.

"Report—BUSHIPS—7303-4; Regular Overhaul; Charleston Naval Shipyard; USS *Scorpion* (SSN-589)," April 28, 1964.

"USS *Scorpion* Emerg Blow System Test," from commanding officer, USS *Scorpion* (SSN589), to commander, Submarine Force, U.S. Atlantic Fleet, April 28, 1964.

"USS *Shark* (SSN591) ARN SSN591-1 Provide Facility for Propeller Removal Installation while Waterborne," from commander, Submarine Force, U.S. Atlantic Fleet, to chief, Bureau of Ships, April 30, 1964.

1965

"Operational Readiness Inspection of USS *Scorpion* (SSN589), Report of," from commander, Submarine Division 62, to commander, Submarine Squadron 6, February 10, 1965.

"Time History of Stern Plane Jam and Recovery Actions, Information concerning," from commanding officer, USS *Scorpion* (SSN589), to commander, Submarine Force, U.S. Atlantic Fleet, March 23, 1965.

"SSNs under Construction; Alterations," from commander, Submarine Force, U.S. Atlantic Fleet, to chief, Bureau of Ships, April 5, 1965.

"USS *Scorpion* (SSN589) Interim Docking," from commander, Submarine Force, U.S. Atlantic Fleet, to chief, Bureau of Ships, May 27, 1965.

"USS *Scorpion* (SSN589) Removal of Torpedo Guide Wire from Shaft," from COMSUBRON SIC to GCNF/DEPCOMSUBLANT, July 27, 1965.

"Lead Hydraulic System Failure; Supplementary Report of," from commanding officer, USS *Scorpion* (SSN589), to chief, Bureau of Ships, August 28, 1965.

"Data for SSN588 Class, Flooding Effects," partial document, September 1, 1965.

"Lead Hydraulic System Failure, Supplemental Report of," from commander, Submarine Force, U.S. Atlantic Fleet, to distribution list, September 24, 1965.

"USS *Skipjack* (SSN585); Action as Result of Inspection of Hull Welds," from chief, Bureau of Ships, to deputy commander, Submarine Force, U.S. Atlantic Fleet, September 29, 1965.

"SSN588 Class; SubSafe Design," from chief, Bureau of Ships, to industrial manager, Groton, October 1, 1965.

"USS *Scorpion* (SSN589) O/H Start Dates; Change in," from 402 to 40—, N4—, October 10, 1965.

"USS *Skipjack* (SSN585); Action as Result of Inspection of Hull Welds," from commander, Submarine Force, U.S. Atlantic Fleet, to chief, Bureau of Ships, October 14, 1965.

"USS *Scorpion* (SSN 589)—Emergency MBT Blow System," from commander, Norfolk Naval Shipyard, to chief, Bureau of Ships, October 21, 1965.

"USS *Scorpion* (SSN589) Hull Inspection," from commander, Norfolk Naval Shipyard, to RUEGXC/DEPCOMSUBLANT, October 25, 1965.

"Supplemental Work Requests for Interim Docking, Submission of," from commanding officer, USS *Scorpion* (SSN589), to commander, Norfolk Naval Shipyard, October 26, 1965.

"USS *Scorpion* (SSN589); Submarine Safety Work Package," from chief, Bureau of Ships, to deputy commander, Submarine Force, U.S. Atlantic Fleet, October 26, 1965.

"Supplemental Work List 2," from commanding officer, USS *Scorpion* (SSN589), to commander, Norfolk Naval Shipyard, Portsmouth, Virginia, November 17, 1965.

"Submarine Pressure Hull Weld Defects," from chief, Bureau of Ships, to assistant secretary of the navy (I&L), November 24, 1965.

"FONECON LCDR Case P&E NORVA/402-11/30," from 402 to 40, November 30, 1965.

"FONECON Memo, LCDR Phil Case/Lt Duncan Staff," from 402 to *Scorpion* hull file, December 9, 1965.

"USS *Scorpion* (SSN589) PAV 6-1 for Interim Docking; Fixed Price," from commander, Submarine Force, U.S. Atlantic Fleet, to commander, Charleston Naval Shipyard, December 17, 1965.

1966

"USS *Scorpion* (SSN589), Submarine Safety Work Package Supplement," from chief, Bureau of Ships, to commander, Norfolk Naval Shipyard, January 10, 1966.

"Ultrasonic Inspection of HY-80 Hulls," from chief, Bureau of Ships, to commander, Submarine Force, U.S. Atlantic Fleet Submarines, January 28, 1966.

"Report—BUSHIPS—7303-4, Departure Summary—Repairs and Alterations; Interim Overhaul; Norfolk Naval Shipyard; USS *Scorpion* (SSN-589)," February 10, 1966.

"USS *Scorpion* (SSN589) PAV 4-11 Final Cost," from commander, Submarine Force, U.S. Atlantic Fleet, to industrial manager, U.S. Navy, Newport News, Virginia, February 21, 1966.

"SSN Overhaul Policy; Comments on," from commander, Submarine Squadron 6, to commander, Submarine Force, U.S. Atlantic Fleet, March 24, 1966.

"USS *Scorpion* (SSN589) Overhaul/Refueling Fact Sheet 1," from H. L. Young, to file, March 25, 1966.

"USS *Scorpion* (SSN589); Planning Letter of Alterations," from chief, Bureau of Ships, to commander, Norfolk Naval Shipyard; deputy commander, Submarine Force, U.S. Atlantic Fleet; and chief, Bureau of Naval Weapons, March 30, 1966.

"Submarine Safety Costs for USS *Scorpion* (SS(N)589)," from commander, Norfolk Naval Shipyard, to chief, Bureau of Ships, April 27, 1966.

"USS *Scorpion* (SSN589) Hull Status," from Admin/DepComsublant, to NAV-SHIPSYSCOMHQ, May 7, 1966.

"USS *Scorpion* (SSN589) Interim Docking," from commander, Submarine Force, U.S. Atlantic Fleet, to chief, Bureau of Ships, May 27, 1965.

"Overhaul Work List; Request for Delay in Submission," from commanding officer, USS *Scorpion* (SSN589), to deputy commander, Submarine Force, U.S. Atlantic Fleet, May 18, 1966.

"USS *Scorpion* (SSN 589) Preoverhaul Planning," from H. L. Young, DCSL/SSN/MATL CODE 402, to file, June 1, 1966.

"USS *Scorpion* (SSN589); Overhaul Planning," from commander, Naval Ship Systems Command, to commander, Norfolk Naval Shipyard, June 10, 1966.

"USS *Scorpion* (SSN589) Hull Status," from NAVSHIPSYSCOM HQ, to Dep-Comsublant, June 10, 1966.

"Overhaul of USS *Scorpion* SSN589," from COMSUBLANT to RUCKHC/CINCLANTFLT, June 16, 1966.

"SSN Overhaul and Maintenance Concepts; Comments and Recommendations on," from commander, Naval Ship Systems Command, to chief of naval operations, June 17, 1966.

"*Scorpion* Is Tentatively Scheduled for Overhaul and Recoring," from COMSUBLANT to RUCKHC/DEPCOMSUBLANT, June 22, 1966.

"*Scorpion* Core Life," from CINCLANTFLT to COMSUBLANT, June 24, 1966.

"Material inspection; personnel attending," from president, Board of Inspection and Survey, to commanding officer, USS *Scorpion* (SSN589), June 27, 1966.

"Equivalent Full Power Hours (EFPH) Remaining on USS *Scorpion* (SSN589); Request Schedule Change Due to [redacted]," from commander, Submarine Squadron 6, to commander, Submarine Force, Atlantic Fleet, June 1966.

"*Scorpion* Overhaul," from NAVSHIPSYSCOMHQ to RUECW/CNO, July 2, 1966.

"*Scorpion* Overhaul," from CINCLANTFWT to RUECW/CNO, July 8, 1966.

"*Scorpion* (SSN589) Preoverhaul Drydocking," from DEPCOMSUBLANT to COMSUBLANT, July 12, 1966.

"*Scorpion* (SSN589) M. I. Inspection 7/6–7/7/66," from 402 to 40B, July 12, 1966.

"USS *Scorpion* (SSN589) Hull Status," from ADMINO DEPCOMSUBLANT to DEPCOMSUBLANT, July 12, 1966.

"Submarine Regular Overhaul—Referral of Submarine Safety Certification," from chief of naval material, to chief of naval operations, August 17, 1966.

"Shipyard Work List Number SS-30/FY67 [for USS *Scorpion* (SSN589)]; Forwarding of," from commander, Submarine Force, U.S. Atlantic Fleet, to commander, Norfolk Naval Shipyard, August 24, 1966.

"*Scorpion* Overhaul Conference," from NAVSHIPYD NORVA to RUCKDR/COMSUBLANT, August 24, 1966.

"Ship's Force Work List," August 24, 1966.

"USS *Scorpion* (SSN589) Overhaul Planning," from commander, Submarine Force, U.S. Atlantic Fleet, to commander, Naval Ship Systems Command, August 30, 1966.

"USS *Scorpion* (SSN-589) Overhaul Planning Sheet 5," from H. L. Young, LCDR, USN, to file, September 2, 1966.

"*Scorpion* (SSN589) OVHL Planning," from COMSUBLANT to COMNAVSHIPSYSCOM HQ/RUECD, September 6, 1966.

"Submarine Regular Overhauls—Deferral of Submarine Safety Certification," from commander, Submarine Force, U.S. Atlantic Fleet, to commander in chief, U.S. Atlantic Fleet, September 29, 1966.

"*Scorpion* OVHL," from COMSUBLANT to CINCLANTFLT, October 1966.

"Submarine Regular Overhauls; Deferral of Submarine Safety Certification," from commander in chief, U.S. Pacific Fleet, to chief of naval operations, October 3, 1966.

"Productive Manning of SSN Overhauls," from commander, Norfolk Naval Shipyard, to commander, Naval Systems Command, and commander, Submarine Force, U.S. Atlantic Fleet, October 6, 1966.

"USS *Scorpion* (SSN589), 180-Day Letter for Authorized Alterations; Comments on," from commanding officer, USS *Scorpion* (SSN589), to commander, Norfolk Naval Shipyard, October 6, 1966.

"Submarine Regular Overhauls—Deferral of Submarine Safety Certification," from commander in chief, U.S. Atlantic Fleet, to chief of naval operations, October 19, 1966.

"*Scorpion* OVHL," from COMSUBLANT to NAVSHIPYD NORVA and NAVSHIPSYSCOMHQ, October 28, 1966.

"*Scorpion* (SSN589) Pre-OVHL Docking (RAV 6-17)," from COMSUBLANT to NAVSHIPYD NORVA, November 1, 1966.

"*Scorpion* OVHL," from COMSUBLANT to CINCLANTFLT, November 3, 1966.

"SSN Submarines; Installation of Automatic Submarine Control System (ASC)," from commander, Submarine Force, U.S. Atlantic Fleet, to commander, Naval Ship Systems Command, November 7, 1966.

"*Scorpion* OVHL," from CINCLANTFLT to RUECW/CNO, November 8, 1966.

"USS *Scorpion* (SSN589), Material Inspection—Report of," from commander, Naval Ship Systems Command, to chief of naval operations, November 8, 1966.

"Submarine Regular Overhauls—Deferral of Submarine Safety Certification," from chief of naval operations, to commander in chief, U.S. Atlantic Fleet; commander in chief, U.S. Pacific Fleet; and commander, Naval Ship Systems Command, November 15, 1966.

"Overhaul Planning; Improved Procedures for," from commander, Naval Ship Systems Command, to commander, Submarine Force, U.S. Atlantic Fleet, November 25, 1966.

"RAV Work List; Forwarding of," from commanding officer, USS *Scorpion* (SSN589), to commander, Norfolk Naval Shipyard, November 28, 1966.

"Shipyard Work List Number SS-30/FY67; Action on," from commander, Submarine Force, U.S. Atlantic Fleet, to commander, Norfolk Naval Shipyard, November 29, 1966.

"USS *Scorpion* (SSN589) Hull Status," from NAVSHIPSYSCOMHQ, to DEPCOMSUBLANT and NAVSHIPYD NORVA, December 6, 1966.

"Supplementary Report [USS *Scorpion* (SSN589)]; Forwarding of," from commander, Submarine Force, U.S. Atlantic Fleet, to distribution list, December 9, 1966.

"USS *Scorpion* (SSN589) RAV Work List; Forwarding of," from commander, Submarine Force, U.S. Atlantic Fleet, to commander, Norfolk Naval Shipyard, December 20, 1966.

"USS *Scorpion* (SSN589)—Authorization for Accomplishment of Reactor Plant Work During Restricted Availability," from commander, Naval Ship Systems Command, to commanding officer, USS *Scorpion* (SSN589), and commander, Norfolk Naval Shipyard, December 21, 1966.

"USS *Scorpion* (SS(N)-589)—Planned Overhaul Concept Meeting," from Code 215 to distribution list, December 28, 1966.

1967

"USS *Scorpion* (SSN589) Restricted Availability," from commander, Submarine Force, U.S. Atlantic Fleet, to commanding officer, USS *Scorpion* (SSN589), January 7, 1967.

"Planned Availability Concept for USS *Scorpion* (SSN589) Overhauls," from commander, Submarine Force, U.S. Atlantic Fleet, to commander, Naval Ship Systems Command, March 8, 1967.

"*Scorpion* Progress Report Number 2," from commanding officer, USS *Scorpion* (SSN589), to commander, Submarine Force, U.S. Atlantic Fleet, April 1, 1967.

"USS *Scorpion* (SSN589)—1800 KW SSTG Set Inspection and Overhaul Recommendations," from commander, Naval Ship Systems Command, to commander, Submarine Force, U.S. Atlantic Fleet, April 18, 1967.

"*Scorpion* Progress Report Number 3," from commanding officer, USS *Scorpion* (SSN589), to commander, Submarine Force, U.S. Atlantic Fleet, April 19, 1967.

"*Scorpion* Progress Report Number 7," from commanding officer, USS *Scorpion* (SSN589), to commander, Submarine Force, U.S. Atlantic Fleet, June 19, 1967.

"*Scorpion* Progress Report Number 8," from commanding officer, USS *Scorpion* (SSN589), to commander, Submarine Force, U.S. Atlantic Fleet, July 3, 1967.

"*Scorpion* Progress Report Number 9," from commanding officer, USS *Scorpion* (SSN589), to commander, Submarine Force, U.S. Atlantic Fleet, July 21, 1967.

"*Scorpion* Progress Report Number 10," from commanding officer, USS *Scorpion* (SSN589), to commander, Submarine Force, U.S. Atlantic Fleet, July 31, 1967.

"*Scorpion* Progress Report Number 12," from commanding officer, USS *Scorpion* (SSN589), to commander, Submarine Force, U.S. Atlantic Fleet, September 1, 1967.

"*Scorpion* Progress Report Number 13," from commanding officer, USS *Scorpion* (SSN589), to commander, Submarine Force, U.S. Atlantic Fleet, September 18, 1967.

"Admiralty Claims Report," from USS *Scorpion*, to COMSUBLANT, November 19, 1967.

"Preliminary Report on USS *Scorpion* (SSN589) WSAT," from NUWS NPT to RUEDBHB/NAVORDSYSCOMPQ, November 24, 1967.

"USS *Scorpion* (SSN589) High Speed Vibration; Request for Technical Assistance on," from commander, Submarine Squadron 6, to commander, Submarine Force, U.S. Atlantic Fleet, December 5, 1967.

"Underwater Hull Inspection on USS *Scorpion* (SSN589) to Determine Cause of Stern Vibration," from commanding officer, USS *Orion*, to commander, Submarine Squadron 6, December 5, 1967.

1968

"Disqualification from Submarine Duty, Request for," from EM2 (SU) Daniel Lee Rogers, USN, to commander, Submarine Division 62, January 2, 1968, and related correspondence.

"*Scorpion* Planned Availability Concept," from commanding officer, USS *Scorpion* (SSN589), to commander, Naval Ship Systems Command, January 27, 1968.

"*Scorpion* Planned Availability Concept (Second Endorsement)," from commander, Submarine Force, U.S. Atlantic Fleet, to commander, Naval Ship Systems Command, January 27, 1968.

"Shipyard Work Deficiencies," from commanding officer, USS *Scorpion* (SSN589), to commander, Norfolk Naval Shipyard, January 27, 1968.

"Analysis of Magnetic Tape Recordings; USS *Scorpion* (SSN589)," from commanding officer, Naval Submarine Base, New London, to commanding officer, USS *Scorpion* (SSN589), February 13, 1968.

"USS *Scorpion* (SSN589) Planned Availability Concept; Recurring Maintenance Items List," from commander, Norfolk Naval Shipyard, to commander, Submarine Force, U.S. Atlantic Fleet, February 16, 1968.

"USS *Scorpion* SSN589, P.A.C. Program, MK23 MOD GYRO COMPASS EQUIP.," from J. J. Henry Co., Inc., to Welton G. Barnes, Norfolk Naval Shipyard, March 6, 1968.

"USS *Scorpion* (SSN589) Planned Availability Concept; Recurring Maintenance Items List," from commander, Norfolk Naval Shipyard, to commanding officer, USS *Scorpion* (SSN589), March 12, 1968.

"Report—BUSHIPS—7303-4, Regular Overhaul for *Scorpion* (SSN589), Norfolk Naval Shipyard," March 19, 1968.

"Shipyard Work Deficiency," from commanding officer, USS *Scorpion* (SSN589), to commander, Norfolk Naval Shipyard, March 23, 1968.

"Interim Docking; Request for Scheduling of," from commanding officer, USS *Scorpion* (SSN589), to commander, Submarine Squadron 6, March 23, 1968.

"Standard Transfer Order of Pettey, Daniel K.," from USS *Scorpion* (SSN589) at Augusta, Sicily, to USS *Skipjack* (SSN585), March 28, 1968.

"*Scorpion* Planned Availability Concept," from commander, Submarine Squadron 6, to commander, Naval Ship Systems Command, April 4, 1968.

"Barge Sinking Incident," from USS *Tallahatchie County*, to CINCUSNAVEUR, April 19, 1968.

"Submarine Safetygram—Escape Trunk Flooding Casualty," from F. A. Slattery to COMSUBLANT, April 20, 1968.

"Interim Docking; Request for Scheduling of," from commander, Submarine Squadron 6, to commander, Submarine Force, U.S. Atlantic Fleet, April 23, 1968.

"USS *Scorpion* (SSN589) Deficiency List; Report on," from commander, Norfolk Naval Shipyard, to commanding officer, USS *Scorpion* (SSN589), May 2, 1968.

"USS *Scorpion* (SSN589)—PAC Program, Electronic Recurring Maintenance Items," from J. J. Henry Co., Inc., to Welton G. Barnes, Norfolk Naval Shipyard, May 14, 1968.

"USS *Scorpion* Drydocking," from COMSUBLANT to NAVSHIPYD NORVA, May 15, 1968.

"Material Aspects of USS *Scorpion* (SSN589)," from commander, Naval Ship Systems Command, to chief of naval operations, May 29, 1968.

"*Scorpion* Submiss—Diver/Recovery Support," from NAVSHIPSYSCOMHQ to RUEDNKA/CINCLANTFLT, May 29, 1968.

"USS *Scorpion* (SSN589)—Material History of USS *Scorpion*," from commander, Naval Ship Systems Command, to chief of naval operations, May 30, 1968.

"*Scorpion* SAR Status," from Vice Adm. Arnold F. Schade, COMSUBLANT, to ALSUBLANT, May 30, 1968.

"USS *Scorpion* (SSN589)," from N402 to N40, May 31, 1968.

"USS *Scorpion* (SSN589) Presumed Lost," from chief of naval operations, to NAVOP, June 6, 1968.

"Report of Casualty," from Casualty Branch by direction of chief of naval personnel to interested persons (family), June 6, 1968. Sent to families of *Scorpion* crewmen notifying them that crew member was "Missing to Determined Dead."

"USS *Scorpion* (SSN589) Freon," from N402 to N40, June 17, 1968.

"USS *Scorpion* (SSN589) Overhaul Planning," from DEPCOMSUBLANT to RUECD/NAVSHIPSYSCOMHQ, June 17, 1968.

"Temporary Additional Duty," from commanding officer, Naval Inactive Ship Maintenance Facility, Philadelphia, to TM2 Eugene A. Jaskiewicz, USN, 697 84 99, June 28, 1968.

1969

"Personal Comments Concerning Problems in the Nuclear Power Program," from Lt. Frederick P. Wales (USN), to commander, Submarine Squadron 2, January 11, 1969.

"An Analysis of the Search for the USS *Scorpion* (SSN589)," from chairman, Technical Advisory Group, *Scorpion* Search, to chief of naval operations, November 5, 1969.

1973

"Request for determination of eligibility for award of the Navy Expeditionary Medal," from TM2(SS) Eugene A. Jaskiewicz, USN, to commander, Submarine Force, U.S. Atlantic Fleet, August 25, 1973.

1974

"Report of Separation from Active Duty: Jaskiewicz, Eugene A.," March 11, 1974.

1986

"Submarine Engineered Operating Cycle (SEOC) Program," OPNAV Instruction 3120.33B, from chief of naval operations, June 5, 1986.

1987

"Subsafe Program—History and Application," memorandum for Vice Adm. Rowden; Department of the Navy, March 16, 1987.

"Subsafe Program—Origins and Application," memorandum for counsel, Department of the Navy, March 10, 1987.

1992

"SSN Overhaul Cost/Manday Summary for *Skate*, *Swordfish*, *Skipjack*, *Triton*, *Sargo*, *Scorpion*, and *Seadragon*," NAVSEA 393, June 25, 1992.

Correspondence

Bohne, Arliss M., widow of Senior Chief Yeoman Leo W. Weinbeck, a *Scorpion* crew member. Collection of personal correspondence with her husband.

Duncan, Vice Adm. C. K. (chief of naval personnel). Telegram to Mrs. Donald R. Powell, wife of Interior Communications Electrician Third Class Donald R. Powell, advising that personnel on board the overdue USS *Scorpion* are in "missing status," May 30, 1968. Example of telegram sent to families of *Scorpion* crew members.

————— . Telegram to Mrs. Donald R. Powell confirming death of her husband, June 6, 1968. Example of telegram sent to families of *Scorpion* crew members.

Hogeland, Mrs. Richard C., widow of Electronics Technician First Class Richard C. Hogeland, a *Scorpion* crew member. Collection of personal correspondence.

Johnson, Mrs. Robert, widow of Senior Chief Radioman Robert Johnson, a *Scorpion* crew member. Collection of personal correspondence.

Johnson, President Lyndon B. Letter of condolence to Mrs. James F. Tindol III, widow of Communications Electronics Technician Second Class James F. Tindol III, June 22, 1968. Example of letter sent to families of *Scorpion* crew members.

Livingston, Mr. and Mrs. John R., parents of Electronics Technician First Class John W. Livingston, a *Scorpion* crew member. Collection of personal correspondence.

Moorer, Adm. T. H. (USN). Letter to Mrs. Donald R. Powell advising of status of Court of Inquiry investigation, November 6, 1968.

Naval Ordnance Laboratory official correspondence regarding developmental issues of the Mk-37 torpedo and Mk-46 silver-zinc primary battery, 1956–1981. Archives of Frederick Bowers.

Price, Robert S. Letter to author, May 12, 2003.

Rickover, H. G. Letter of condolence to Vernon and Sybil Stone, parents of Machinist's Mate Second Class David B. Stone, a *Scorpion* crew member, June 7, 1968.

Robertson, Ingrid B., widow of Communications Electronics Technician Second Class James F. Tindol III, a *Scorpion* crew member. Collection of personal correspondence with her husband.

Rogers, Daniel L. Personal collection of documents.

Schade, Vice Adm. A. F. (USN). Announcement of *Scorpion* memorial, June 20, 1968. Example of transmittal letter sent to families of *Scorpion* crew members.

————— . Letter transmitting *Scorpion Memorial Book* to Mrs. Donald R. Powell, June 5, 1968.

Seifert, Mr. and Mrs. Robert, parents of Fireman Phillip A. Seifert, a *Scorpion* crew member. Collection of personal correspondence with their son and various naval officers.

Stone, Vernon and Sybil, parents of Machinist's Mate Second Class David B. Stone, *Scorpion* crew member. Collection of personal correspondence with their son.

Sturgill, Ruby, mother of Electrician's Mate Second Class John P. Sturgill, *Scorpion* crew member. Collection of personal correspondence with her son.

Thorne, Charles. Letter to Dr. John Craven, January 10, 1994. Author's collection.

Williams, Mr. and Mrs. Richard F., parents of Seaman Ronald R. Williams, a *Scorpion* crew member. Collection of personal correspondence.

Incomplete documents.
No ascertainable authors, dates, and/or subjects.

"Account of *Pomodon* Disaster," enclosure of SUBPAC Notice 3040, July 18, 1955.

"Attached LTR [NAVSHIPS says this letter has become the most important document in *Scorpion* case]," from deputy chief of staff, Logistics/Managements (N4), to unknown, June 13, 1967.

"Attached MSG Re *Scorpion* Hull Inspection," from 402 to 40, October 26, [mid-1960s?].

"Equipment and Material," enclosure relating to USS *Scorpion* (SSN 589), pre-1968.

"Equivalent Full Power Hours (EFPH) Remaining on USS *Scorpion* (SSN 589); Request Schedule Change due to [redacted]," from commander, Submarine Squadron 6, to commander, Submarine Force, U.S. Atlantic Fleet, n.d.

Handwritten document; proposed overhaul schedule for submarines.

Handwritten document; USS *Scorpion* (SSN 589) maintenance history.

Handwritten document; "Scheduled Availabilities."

"Pertinent Correspondence/Action Steps Relative to 2/1/67 Start Date & Sub-safe Deferral for USS *Scorpion* (SSN589) Overhaul"; list.

"Problem Areas Encountered during USS *Scorpion* Refueling Availability 2/1/67–10/6/67."

"Section 536-4, Garbage Disposal; Trash Disposal United Operating Instructions," USN Manual, n.d.

"*Skipjack* Hull Crack," C-SS585/9110, Ser 525-0354, from W. A. Brockett, n.d.

"Submarine Piping System Surveillance Program Conference of July 27–29, 1966, at NAVSHIP—Report on."

"Sub-Safe on *Scorpion*—Deferral Chronology," June 1963 through November 15, 1966.

"Your Note on 589 EMBT Blow MSG," from 402 to 401, October 26, [1965?].

Miscellaneous

General Dynamics Corporation v. United States, 585 F.2d 457 (U.S. Court of Claims, 1978).

"*Mizar* Photographic Coverage Width Chart." Archives of Chester L. Buchanan.

"*Trieste II (III)* Phase II Operations Personnel Roster." Archives of Cmdr. Robert F. Nevin (USN).

Video Recording

Buckner, Joel, and Rob Whittlesey. "Submarines, Secrets, and Spies," *NOVA* Production by the Documentary Guild for WGBH/Boston in association with Sveriges Television, 1998; PBS airdate January 19, 1999.

Interviews

Oral History

Hamilton, Gordon. "Oceanography: The Making of a Science; People, Institutions, and Discovery." Transcript of videotaped-recorded interview produced by the Oral History Project of the H. John Heinz III Center for Science, Economics, and the Environment in conjunction with the Colloquia Series. Conducted at Naval Historical Center, Washington, D.C., March 10, 2000.

Williams, Vice Adm. Joe Jr. Transcript of interview recorded for CNN series *Cold War*, August 31, 1996. National Security Archives, George Washington University.

Personal

Adams, Anthony P. Manhattan, Mont. Telephone interview by author, March 9, 2002.

Alger, Richard J. Alexandria, Va. Telephone interview by author, January 19, 2002.

Allen, Alvah David. Bethesda, Md. Telephone interview by author, June 13, 2002.

Amtower, Mrs. Maurice L. Keyser, W. Va. Telephone interview by author, May 20, 2002.

Anderson, Erwin W. Burtonsville, Md. Telephone interview by author, May 7, 2002.

Anderson, Lois Saville. South Glens Falls, N.Y. Telephone interview by author, May 19, 2002.

Anderson, Raymond O. Warren, Pa. Telephone interview by author, January 20, 2003.

Ayers, James Bodine. Playa Del Rey, Calif. Telephone interview by author, September 5, 2002.

Barash, Robert. Silver Spring, Md. Telephone interview by author, January 16, 2003.

Barnaba, Mike. New Freedom, Pa. Telephone interview by author, November 13, 2002.

Barnes, Welton G. Virginia Beach, Va. Telephone interview by author, February 27, 2002.

Baxa, Jane. Las Vegas, Nev. Telephone interview by author, March 24, 2002.

Bellah, James. Norfolk, Va. Telephone interview by author, May 21, 2002.

Bellah, Phyllis. Norfolk, Va. Telephone interview by author, May 21, 2002.

Berg, Robert. Oakville, Wash. Telephone interview by author, January 20, 2002.

Berman, Dr. Alan. Santa Fe, N.M. Telephone interview by author, October 7, 2002.

Bessac, Norman. Georgetown, Tex. Personal interview by author, June 19, 2002.

Bigaj, Dolores. New Smyrna Beach, Fla. Telephone interview by author, May 23, 2002.

Blair, Marvin S. Omaha, Neb. Telephone interview by author, January 13, 2003.

Blalock, Willard D. Vienna, Va. Telephone interview by author, December 23, 2002.

Bode, Robert. North Hampton, N.H. Telephone interview by author, January 23, 2003.

Bogen, John A. Bremerton, Wash. Telephone interview by author, April 5, 2002.

Bond, Tom. San Diego, Calif. Telephone interview by author, April 8, 2002.

Bowers, Frederick M. Silver Spring, Md. Telephone interview by author, December 3, 2002.

Broderson, Mary. Babylon, N.Y. Telephone interview by author, November 19, 2002.

Brown, Christopher H. Beaverton, Ore. Telephone interview by author, December 13, 2002.

Brueggeman, Kenneth. Oak Creek, Wis. Telephone interview by author, May 21, 2002.

Bryan, Betty Jo. Virginia Beach, Va. Telephone interview by author, March 26, 2002.

Bryan, Samuel Steve. Moycock, N.C. Telephone interview by author, March 23, 2002.

Buchanan, Chester L. ("Buck"). Hugo, Minn. Telephone interview by author, March 5, 2002.

Burciaga, Manny. El Cajon, Calif. Telephone interview by author, January 16, 2002.

Burke, Jolene. San Bernardino, Calif. Telephone interview by author, June 13, 1992.

Burke, Tom. Mesa, Ariz. Telephone interview by author, March 6, 2002.

Byrnes, David T. Leonardtown, Md. Telephone interview by author, October 23, 2002.

Calveard, Sam. Kennewick, Wash. Telephone interview by author, November 10, 2002.

Carey, Bayard. Santa Fe, N.M. Telephone interview by author, February 19, 2003.

Carey, Earl. Washington, D.C. Telephone interview by author, June 1, 2003.

Carey, William Polk. New York, N.Y. Telephone interview by author, March 2, 2003.

Carr, Douglas. Fort Wayne, Ind. Telephone interview by author, February 25, 2002.

Christian, Curtis T. III. Eutawville, S.C. Telephone interview by author, April 1, 2002.

Clancy, George. Fairbanks, Alaska. Telephone interview by author, November 11, 2002.

Clark, Bill. Duluth, Minn. Telephone interview by author, January 17, 2002.

Crane, Mark F. Annapolis, Md. Telephone interview by author, January 2, 2003.

Craven, John P. Honolulu, Hawaii. Telephone interview by author, October 10, 2002.

Crowley, Ruthann. Danville, Pa. Telephone interview by author, April 26, 2002.

Curtze, Charles A. Erie, Pa. Telephone interview by author, August 5, 2002.

Cutler, Lee M. Carmel, Calif. Telephone interview by author, August 1, 2002.

Czul, Ernie. Port Orange, Fla. Telephone interview by author, May 31, 2003.

Davis, Bob. Brooksville, Fla. Telephone interview by author, April 7, 2002.

Decker, Clyde A. Portsmouth, Va. Telephone interview by author, February 28, 2002.

DeGrasse, Albert. Tequesta, Fla. Telephone interview by author, November 18, 2002.

Deichert, Edmund. Bremerton, Wash. Telephone interview by author, April 7, 2002.

Delonga, David. Pensacola, Fla. Telephone interview by author, November 22, 2002.

Dempsey, Bobby G. Marietta, Ga. Telephone interview by author, March 7, 2002.

Deuel, Jamieson K. Albuquerque, N.M. Telephone interview by author, September 9, 2002.

Dockendorf, Donald O. Van Nuys, Calif. Telephone interview by author, November 15, 2002.

Draper, Harry. Bronx, N.Y. Telephone interview by author, November 13, 2002.

Duke, Beth Houge. Suffolk, Va. Telephone interview by author, May 11, 2002.

Dunn, Anthony Thomas. San Diego, Calif. Telephone interview by author, October 17, 2002.

Elnicki, Andrew. Jewett City, Conn. Telephone interview by author, June 10, 1992.

Elrod, William G. Oakdale, Conn. Telephone interview by author, June 8, 1992.

Evans, Roger. Idaho Falls, Idaho. Telephone interview by author, December 12, 2002.

Evans, Thomas W. Arlington, Va. Telephone interview by author, May 22, 2002.

Feury, Edward A. Hartford, Mich. Telephone interview by author, January 17, 2002.

Fiske, Dr. Richard S. Bethesda, Md. Telephone interview by author, September 5, 2002.

Flor, Robert. Staten Island, N.Y. Telephone interview by author, June 20, 2003.

Fogarty, Frank C. Idaho Falls, Idaho. Telephone interview by author, August 5, 2002.

Forbes, Donald L. Onancock, Va. Telephone interview by author, October 23, 2002.

Ford, Alfred. Washington, D.C. Telephone interview by author, August 19, 2003.

Fountain, Robert R. Falls Church, Va. Personal interview by author, May 22, 2002.

Franks, Otis. Louisville, Ky. Telephone interview by author, January 25, 2002.

Frost, Barrie. Oakland, Calif. Telephone interview by author, April 9, 2003.

Gaspin, Joel B. Takoma Park, Md. Telephone interview by author, April 19, 2002.

Gautier, Robert Henry. San Diego, Calif. Telephone interview by author, March 7, 2002.

Geherin, Gerard. Virginia Beach, Va. Telephone interview by author, July 12, 2003.

George, William B. Warrensburg, Mo. Telephone interview by author, August 9, 2002.

Geringer, Marilou. Sugar City, Colo. Telephone interview by author, March 5, 2003.

Ghormley, Ralph M. Arlington, Va. Telephone interview by author, July 11, 2002.

Gill, William. North Weymouth, Mass. Telephone interview by author, April 20, 2003.

Glovier, Harold A. Waterford, Va. Telephone interview by author, April 18, 2002.

Gontarz, Ron. Lawrenceville, Pa. Telephone interview by author, April 1, 2002.

Grobler, John. Keyport, Wash. Telephone interview by author, February 20, 2003.

Guglielmo, Richard. Morris Plains, N.J. Telephone interview by author, March 12, 2002.

Guyer, Edwine ("Edie"). Paris, Maine. Telephone interview by author, April 21, 2002.

Hamilton, Gordon R. Rockville, Md. Personal interview by author, May 23, 2002.

Hanson, James E. Middleton, Mass. Telephone interview by author, February 9, 2003.

Hartdegen, Carl Jr. Westfield, Mass. Telephone interview by author, September 28, 2002.

Hartley, Allan. Lenoir, N.C. Telephone interview by author, April 15, 2002.

Hayman, Douglass Jr. Annapolis, Md. Telephone interview by author, August 1, 2002.

Heckman, David C. Phoenix, Ariz. Telephone interview by author, September 12, 2003.

Helt, Richard B. ("Dick"). Aston, Pa. Telephone interview by author, February 26, 2002.

Hofer, Richard L. Painesville, Ohio. Telephone interview by author, February 4, 2003.

Hogeland, Patricia. Birmingham, Ala. Telephone interview by author, April 13, 2002.

Huckelberry, Mary. Jeffersonville, Ind. Telephone interview by author, March 23, 2002.

Hurley, Robert F. Jr. ("Bob"). Baja California, Mex. Telephone interview by author, March 9, 2002.

Jackson, Harry A. Groton, Conn. Telephone interview by author, March 7, 2002.

James, John. Washington, D.C. Telephone interview by author, August 19, 2003.

Jarvis, Laura Hawley. Ridge, Md. Telephone interview by author, October 10, 2002.

Jaskiewicz, Eugene. Lynchburg, Ohio. Telephone interview by author, June 24, 2003.

Jaster, Dennis Gary. Mechanicsburg, Pa. Telephone interview by author, April 24, 2002.

Jones, Ben. Bluffton, Ind. Telephone interview by author, August 6, 2002.

Kahanek, Charles E. San Antonio, Tex. Telephone interview by author, January 23, 2002.

Kane, John ("Jack"). Falls Church, Va. Personal interview by author, May 24, 2002.

Karmasek, Donald. Baltimore, Md. Telephone interview by author, October, 17, 2002.

Kaufman, Robert Y. V. Potomac, Md. Telephone interviews by author, June 25, 1992, and May 22, 2002.

Kellogg, Edward S. III. San Diego, Calif. Telephone interview by author, January 19, 2002.

Kelly, Jim. Los Angeles, Calif. Telephone interview by author, April 5, 2002.

Kern, Donald. Saunderstown, R.I. Telephone interview by author, March 10, 2002.

Kestner, Jack. Saltville, Va. Telephone interview by author, March 15, 2003.

Klemz, Daniel J. Rochester, N.Y. Telephone interview by author, January 14, 2003.

Leach, Allen C. ("Chauncey"). Kalkaska, Mich. Telephone interview by author, April 11, 2002.

Levey, Sanford N. Clifton, Va. Telephone interview by author, March 19, 2003.

Livingston, Erich. West Chester, Ohio. Telephone interview by author, March 4, 2003.

Loucks, Steven J. Rochester, N.Y. Telephone interview by author, April 11, 2003.

Lough, Raymond. Ridgefield, Wash. Telephone interview by author, February 6, 2002.

MacKerrow, Donald. Reno, Nev. Telephone interview by author, April 9, 2003.

Maclaren, John. Mountain City, Tex. Telephone interview by author, November 13, 2002.

MacVean, Charles. San Diego, Calif. Telephone interview by author, June 10, 2002.

Mahoney, Jim. Seneca, S.C. Telephone interview by author, June 17, 2002.

Mahre, Mike. Danville, Calif. Telephone interview by author, July 26, 2002.

Malatesta, Ron. Mercer Island, Wash. Telephone interview by author, August 20, 2003.

Manganello, Sam. Pittsburgh, Pa. Telephone interview by author, April 25, 2002.

Marsh, Larry. Great Falls, Va. Telephone interview by author, April 15, 2002.

Matteo, Donald A. Alexandria, Va. Telephone interview by author, February 28, 2002.

McClain, Robert C. Longwood, Fla. Telephone interview by author, March 6, 2002.

McCune, J. Denver. Carlsbad, Calif. Telephone interview by author, April 4, 2002.

McDonald, Carlton A. Clyde Hill, Wash. Telephone interview by author, March 13, 2002.

McGrew, Dr. C. J. Jr. ("Dan"). Spring Hill, Fla. Telephone interview by author, January 15, 2002.

McKinney, Henry C. Washington, D.C. Telephone interview by author, March 4, 2002.

Middents, Paul W. Silverdale, Wash. Telephone interview by author, April 1, 2002.

Milford, Frederick. Columbus, Ohio. Telephone interview by author, April 3, 2002.

Miller, J. A. L. Jr. Charlotte, N.C. Telephone interview by author, January 23, 2002.

Miller, William Layton. Woodland Park, Colo. Telephone interview by author, September 17, 2002.

Moore, Robert L. Fall River, Mass. Telephone interview by author, December 23, 2002.

Morgan, Dr. William B. Bethesda, Md. Telephone interview by author, August 3, 2003.

Morin, Allan L. Loudon, N.H. Telephone interview by author, July 1, 2002.

Morris, John. Napa, Calif. Telephone interview by author, December 4, 2002.

Moss, Danny R. Arvada, Colo. Telephone interview by author, November 8, 2002.

Murphy, Ruth. Denton, Md. Telephone interview by author, February 6, 2003.

Nevin, Robert F. Saint Marys, Ga. Telephone interview by author, February 11, 2003.

Newman, Barbara. Jacksonville, Fla. Telephone interview by author, November 24, 2002.

Newman, Mike. Jacksonville, Fla. Telephone interview by author, November 24, 2002.

Nicholson, John H. La Jolla, Calif. Telephone interview by author, March 20, 2002.

Odening, Robert. Los Angeles, Calif. Telephone interview by author, January 22, 2002.

O'Quinn, Kathy Karmasek. Baltimore, Md. Telephone interview by author, March 30, 2002.

Owens, William. Seattle, Wash. Telephone interview by author, July 17, 2003.

Palermo, Peter M. Alexandria, Va. Personal interview by author, October 10, 2002.

Parent, Leo. Chula Vista, Calif. Telephone interview by author, September 21, 2003.

Patten, James. Champaign, Ill. Telephone interview by author, January 27, 2003.

Patton, James H. North Stonington, Conn. Telephone interview by author, October 28, 2002.

Pautler, Al. Hilton Head Island, S.C. Telephone interview by author, March 11, 2002.

Peercy, James M. The Villages, Fla. Telephone interview by author, February 28, 2002.

Perham, Joseph. West Paris, Maine. Telephone interview by author, February 20, 2002.

Perkins, Robert Jr. Papillion, Neb. Telephone interview by author, August 20, 2002.

Perry, Robert M. McCall, Idaho. Telephone interview by author, February 21, 2002.

Peters, John. Aiea, Hawaii. Telephone interview by author, April 1, 2002.

Pettey, Daniel Kent. Pensacola, Fla. Telephone interview by author, April 1, 2003.

Pirie, Robert B. Jr. ("Robin"). Bethesda, Md. Telephone interview by author, May 23, 2002.

Pratt, Jerry. Osceola, Iowa. Telephone interview by author, March 20, 2002.

Price, Robert S. Burtonsville, Md. Telephone interview by author, May 1, 2002.

Reaves, Rufus. San Diego, Calif. Telephone interview by author, October 22, 2002.

Reese, Dorothy Watson. Tyrone, Pa. Telephone interview by author, January 11, 2003.

Rehm, Judy. Wilber, Neb. Telephone interview by author, March 25, 2002.

Reid, Clarence. West Paris, Maine. Telephone interview by author, December 20, 1992.

Rich, Harold G. Brunswick, Maine. Telephone interview by author, August 23, 2002.

Riel, Nelda. Pittsfield, N.H. Telephone interview by author, July 1, 2002.

Ring, Bill. Wauchula, Fla. Telephone interview by author, February 17, 2002.

Roberts, Rebecca Ann. Oak Ridge, Tenn. Telephone interview by author, February 22, 2004.

Robertson, Ingrid B. Shreveport, La. Telephone interview by author, March 10, 2002.

Roe, Ronny. Columbia, S.C. Telephone interview by author, June 25, 2003.

Rogers, Daniel L. Houston, Tex. Personal interviews by author, 1987–1994.

Roth, Bob. Clifton Springs, N.Y. Telephone interview by author, September 11, 2002.

Ruble, Byron C. ("Barney"). Palm Harbor, Fla. Telephone interview by author, May 21, 2002.

Runkle, Thomas. Raleigh, N.C. Telephone interview by author, March 31, 2002.

Sablo, Barbara. Raleigh, N.C. Telephone interview by author, January 20, 2003.

Salive, M. L. Rockville, Md. Telephone interview by author, August 19, 2002.

Satloff, Dr. Aaron R. Pittsford, N.Y. Telephone interview by author, February 23, 2003.

Saville, Lois Anderson. South Glenn Falls, N.Y. Telephone interview by author, March 17, 2004.

Saxon, Ross E. Spring, Tex. Personal interview by author, May 30, 2002.

Schmidt, Kenneth. Wood Lake, Minn. Telephone interview by author, March 15, 2002.

Schwartz, Doyle W. Crane, Tex. Telephone interview by author, February 24, 2002.

Scorza, Lou. Brooklyn, N.Y. Telephone interview by author, June 25, 2003.

Searle, Willard Bill. Alexandria, Va. Telephone interview by author, September 30, 2002.

Sessoms, Faison T. Chapel Hill, N.C. Telephone interview by author, May 10, 2003.

Shearer, Ollie. Vienna, Va. Telephone interview by author, September 9, 2002.

Shelton, Donald K. Naples, Fla. Telephone interview by author, September 18, 2002.

Siefried, Hilda. Sugar City, Colo. Telephone interview by author, February 19, 2003.

Simms, William E. Sr. Alexandria, Va. Telephone interview by author, April 15, 2004.

Skoog, Joseph L. Issaquah, Wash. Telephone interview by author, September 5, 2002.

Smith, Tom. Williamsburg, Va. Telephone interview by author, April 4, 2002.

Soliozy, Charles S. Newport, R.I. Telephone interview by author, December 23, 2002.

Sonosky, Robert ("Bob"). Virginia Beach, Va. Telephone interview by author, June 25, 2003.

Spelbring, Daryl. Vienna, Va. Telephone interview by author, April 18, 2002.

Staehle, Charles M. Palm Beach Gardens, Fla. Telephone interview by author, July 9, 2002.

Stank, Edward. Saint Marys, Ga. Telephone interview by author, December 12, 2002.

Stevens, Rebecca. Wauchula, Fla. Telephone interview by author, February 17, 2002.

Stone, Fred. Fort Myers, Fla. Telephone interview by author, February 25, 2002.

Stone, Sybil. Ames, Iowa. Telephone interview by author, September 12, 2002.

Stone, Vernon. Ames, Iowa. Telephone interview by author, September 12, 2002.

Strickland, Alan Dennis. Fort Worth, Tex. Telephone interview by author, April 3, 2002.

Strickland, Charles L. Encinitas, Calif. Telephone interview by author, July 11, 2002.

Strong, James. Champaign, Ill. Telephone interview by author, April 23, 2002.

Sturgill, Ruby. Oak Ridge, Tenn. Telephone interview by author, April 19, 2002.

Sueflow, Allie. Virginia Beach, Va. Telephone interview by author, June 10, 1992.

Sunahara, Keith. Skokie, Ill. Telephone interview by author, July 13, 2003.

Surprenant, J. Paul. Rockledge, Fla. Telephone interview by author, March 10, 2002.

Synder, Edward J. McLean, Va. Telephone interview by author, February 20, 2003.

Tesorioero, Frank. Washington, D.C. Telephone interview by author, August 19, 2003.

Thompson, Frank. Cabot, Vt. Telephone interview by author, February 26, 2002.

Traser, Dick. Ridgecrest, Calif. Telephone interview by author, February 17, 2002.

Treischel, Robert W. Port Ludlow, Wash. Telephone interview by author, April 5, 2002.

Trost, C. A. H. Annapolis, Md. Telephone interview by author, December 12, 2002.

Turner, Byron. Friendswood, Tex. Telephone interview by author, September 15, 2003.

Underwood, Diane. Clinton, Iowa. Telephone interview by author, February 14, 2003.

Victor, Francis Ward. Gales Ferry, Conn. Telephone interview by author, February 25, 2002.

Violetta, Samuel. Media, Pa. Telephone interview by author, January 11, 2003.

Vonalt, Christopher J. East Falmouth, Mass. Telephone interview by author, January 23, 2002.

Wahl, John. Summerville, S.C. Telephone interview by author, June 5, 2002.

Walker, Charles M. Jacksonville, Fla. Telephone interview by author, August 8, 2002.

Wallace, Terry. Tucson, Ariz. Telephone interview by author, September 17, 2002.

Walters, Debra Mazzuchi. Winston-Salem, N.C. Telephone interview by author, July 15, 2002.

Ward, Sibley Logan III. Coronado, Calif. Telephone interview by author, February 28, 2002.

Watson, Forrest J. Goodyear, Ariz. Telephone interview by author, March 4, 2002.

Weber, Gustave. Cedaredge, Colo. Telephone interview by author, August 22, 2002.

Weeks, Robert. Wallingford, Vt. Telephone interview by author, December 2, 2002.

Weinbeck, Kurt. Medicine Lake, Minn. Telephone interview by author, November 17, 2002.

Wells, Bill. Albion, N.Y. Telephone interview by author, July 19, 2004.

Wick, Margaret. Clay, N.Y. Telephone interview by author, February 18, 2003.

Wilhelm, Kelly. Hagerstown, Md. Telephone interview by author, April 29, 2002.

Williams, Joe Jr. Chadds Ford, Pa. Telephone interview by author, May 19, 2002.

Wilson, Alex. Coatesville, Pa. Telephone interview by author, April 23, 2002.

Wilson, Kenneth E. Kennett Square, Pa. Telephone interview by author, December 2, 2002.

Worzel, J. Lamar. Wilmington, N.C. Telephone interview by author, March 1, 2002.

Wyeno, Darla. Olney Springs, Colo. Telephone interview by author, September 3, 2002.

Yeager, John. Fort Lauderdale, Fla. Telephone interview by author, May 17, 2002.

Yencer, Clyde. Hersey, Mich. Telephone interview by author, August 1, 2002.

Yurso, Joseph F. Virginia Beach, Va. Telephone interview by author, July 12, 2002.

Zober, Norman. North Bethesda, Md. Telephone interview by author, October 2, 2002.

Index

Page numbers in *italics* refer to photos and illustrations.